Post-Industrial Society

Julia Kovalchuk
Editor

Post-Industrial Society

The Choice Between Innovation and Tradition

palgrave
macmillan

Editor
Julia Kovalchuk
Moscow State Institute of International Relations (MGIMO University)
Moscow, Russia

Moscow Aviation Institute, Moscow, Russia

ISBN 978-3-030-59738-2 ISBN 978-3-030-59739-9 (eBook)
https://doi.org/10.1007/978-3-030-59739-9

This Palgrave Macmillan imprint is published by the registered company Springer Nature Switzerland AG.
The registered company address is: Gewerbestrasse 11, 6330 Cham, Switzerland

Preface

This book examines the contradictions, advantages, and problems inherent in post-industrial development as an intensive and continuous process. Turbulent times, futuristic innovations and new technologies have not only entered into our lives rapidly and created new opportunities for developing society and the economy, but have also lead to challenges and threats that inevitably cause negative reactions and dilemmas regarding further transformations. The post-industrial society is a diverse series of paradoxical ecosystems; it has predictable and unpredictable manifestations; there are positive and negative aspects; it requires modern values and challenges (to nature, people, and the economy) and relies upon new advanced technologies (for business and society, including megatrends and development), yet requires conservative steps during the period of transformation. To present this complex world as comprehensively as possible, this book—written by a big group of Russian and international researchers—deals with public administration, economy, law, and psychology, and is intended to provide a comprehensive overview of the opportunities and challenges associated with modern developments across society, production, and consumption. Combining the work of recognized scientists and specialists in various scientific fields, this book provides a comprehensive understanding of post-industrial development, highlighting the driving forces and limitations, strategies, funding sources, tools, and technologies for their implementation.

Moscow, Russia | Julia Kovalchuk

Acknowledgments

The authors are grateful to the REGION Group (Moscow, Russia) for financial support in the implementation of research projects and to Moscow State Institute of International Relations (MGIMO University), Moscow, Russia.

Contents

Notes on Contributors

Julia Bogdanova is a leading researcher at the Institute of Economics of the Russian Academy of Sciences and at the Council for the Study of Productive Forces (SOPS), Russian Foreign Trade Academy of the Ministry of Economic Development of the Russian Federation. Research interests include the development of methodology and implementation of strategic planning in the Russian Federation, regional socio-economic development, as well as the study of technological and institutional factors in the formation and development of innovative activities of companies, including high-tech industries. She holds her PhD in Engineering Science.

Lyudmila Chernikova is Doctor in Economics and professor at Financial University under the Government of the Russian Federation and Deputy Head of the Department of Corporate Finance and Corporate Governance. Her research interests cover a wide range of modern aspects of financial management of the companies in emerging economies. She advises leading Russian insurance companies. She is the author and editor of numerous publications on economics, business, and finance. She has more than ten years of experience in conducting research and lecturing about corporate finance development in the digital environment.

Igor Dolzhenko is Deputy General Director of LLC Fashion Group, Moscow, Russia. He has more than 37 years of experience in the textile and garments sector, managing different Russian companies and being one of the leading Russian experts in the field of textile and garments from fiber to ready-made garments as well foreign trade. His research interests are connected with the fashion and consumer sector, digitalization, and global operations of multinational companies. He is the author of different publications on the fashion and textile sector.

Sergey Kamolov is the Chair in Public Governance, School of Governance and Politics, Moscow State Institute of International Relations (MGIMO University) and an associate professor. He holds a PhD in Economics. From 2003 to 2015, he was Public Governance Executive in Regional and Federal Service, responsible of IT and Governance Technological Enforcement. He is also an adjunct professor at Yonsei University, Seoul, Korea. He is a member of the "Smart City" working group of the Russian Ministry of Construction, creator of the Public Governance and Technology co-evolution theory, and author of 80 publications in Russia and abroad.

Yulia Kandalintseva is a senior analyst at the Institute of Smart Cities Comparative Studies (Moscow). He holds a master's in Public Administration (MGIMO University). He is an expert in smart cities management systems and an author and conference speaker.

Antonina Kazelskaya is engaged in research and preparation of a dissertation on Economics and at the same time conducts private practice in accounting and auditing. Her research interests are related to production planning and cost accounting. Her articles are devoted to the application of cognitive modeling in the management of modern industrial enterprises.

Natalia Konina is Doctor in Economics, professor, and since 2016, Head of the Department of Management, Marketing and Foreign Economic Activities at Moscow State Institute of International Relations (MGIMO University). She received her PhD from MGIMO University in Moscow in 1991 and further continued her scientific research, with a doctoral thesis in 2009. She has more than 30 years of experience in researching and business consulting, specializing in different aspects of international management, geoeconomics, competition and competitiveness, and transnational corporations. Her research interests are focused on the dynamics of business environment in digital era, globalization and digitalization, modern strategies of big multinational corporations, global value chains, digital transformation of companies, and evolution of management in post-industrial society. Her many contributions to the literature include *Management: Theory, Practice and International Aspect* (ed.), *Management of International Firms: How to Win in Competition*, *Competitiveness of the*

Firms in the Global World, chapters and articles in professional journals. She is Vice-Head of the joint Dissertation Council MGIMO University–RUDN University, Moscow.

Julia Kovalchuk is Dr.Sc. (Econ) Chief Researcher of Asset Management Department at Moscow State Institute of International Relations (MGIMO University), and a professor at the Department of Energy Service and Energy Saving Management at Moscow Aviation Institute (National Research University). Choosing strategic aspects of industrial development as a scientific priority, she has long specialized in industrial modernization, including reindustrialization. She has accumulated a wealth of experience in strategic research of the high-tech industry, including competition and cooperation factors. Her research interests include digital transformation of companies and value creation in the digital arena.

Maria Kozlova is an associate professor at the Department of Economic Theory, MGIMO University. She holds a PhD in Economics from the same university. She is also Deputy Head of the Department of Economic Theory for Educational and Methodological Work. Her research interests include the analysis of the national innovation system of Russia, the theoretic aspects of scientific development, the instrumental cultural policy, the relations between culture and economics, and global public goods.

Tatyana Kreydenko is an associate professor at the Department of Regional Economics and Geography, Faculty of Economics, RUDN University. She is also an associate professor at the Department of Industrial Markets, Financial University under the Government of the Russian Federation. In 2015–2017 she was a leading researcher at the Council for the Study of the Productive Forces (SOPS), Russian Foreign Trade Academy of the Ministry of Economic Development of the Russian Federation. She is the author of more than 50 scientific and educational works related to the study of issues of spatial analysis of socio-economic, technological, and innovative development of territory of the world's countries. She holds her PhD in Economic, Social and Political Geography.

Irina Larionova is Doctor in Economics, professor at Financial University under the Government of the Russian Federation and professor at MGIMO University. Her research interests include economic issues in banks and banking, international standards of Basel II and III, financial stability in emerging markets, and quantitative methods for assessing confidence in financial intermediaries in the face of digital transformation. She is the author of numerous monographs and scientific articles in national and international journals. She has been the leader and responsible executor of more than 15 research papers on those issues. She has more than 20 years of experience in giving lectures for master's students, specialists of the Central Bank of Russian Federation, and top management of commercial banks.

Anastasia Makarenko is an associate professor at the Department of French Language of MGIMO University. She is also a teaching specialist at European Studies Institute, MGIMO University. She is working on her PhD thesis related to legal aspects of free trade agreements of the European Union with Third World countries'.

Alekxey Medkov is a candidate of Economic Sciences, a leading researcher, and Head of Transit Economy Research Center of the Laboratory of integration of the Russian economy into the world economy at Market Economy Institute of the Russian Academy of Sciences (MEI RAS). He is a specialist in the economics and finance of the public sector of economy and branches of production infrastructure, processes, financial-industrial integration, corporatization, and development of public-private relations in the fields of industrial infrastructure, primarily in the rail transportation market and in the road sector. His special research interest lies in the methodology of macroeconomic analysis of the national economy and the development of evolutionary and institutional research and historical analysis in relation to the formation of a model of transport and transit economy.

Elena Meshkova is an associate professor at the Department of Banks and Finance Markets, Financial University under the Government of the Russian Federation, where she teaches courses on finance, money turnover and credit. She has more than 15 years of experience in research and lecturing on banking and risk management. She has worked as Head of Risk Management Department, Russian Agricultural Bank. Her professional and research interests include banks' risk management and banking regulation. She has published books and articles in national and international journals on the problems of stress testing, regulation of financial intermediaries, and macro- and micro-analysis of financial regulation.

Yuri Monastyrsky holds a PhD in Private International Law from the Institute of State and Law of the Russian Federation, and is the founder of "Monastyrsky, Zyuba, Stepanov and Partners" law firm, ranked third in the Forbes' rating for Russia in 2020. He is the author of more than 40 articles on civil law liability. He is a member of the International Law Association from 1990 onward, awarded with MGIMO distinctions for achievements in 2005 and 2011.

Elena Nebolsina is an associate professor at MGIMO University, School of International Economic Relations. She previously worked for a well-established reinsurance company, Kapital Re, as a specialist, senior specialist, and acting Head of Outward Reinsurance Department. Elena researches and publishes on international insurance and reinsurance, financial ecosystems as well as economic integration. She is an active participant in courses for continuing professional development, including, but not limited to, those arranged by global insurance market players and the Chartered Insurance Institute, UK. She holds a PhD in International Economics.

Vladimir Osipov is Doctor in Economics and professor at Asset Management Department at MGIMO University (Russia) and guest professor at the School of Economics and Management, Beijing Jiaotong University (China). He is a member of the American Law and Economics Association and Editorial Board member of several scientific journals. He has published over 160 articles in professional journals and 16 books as author, co-author, editor, and co-editor. His primary research expertise embraces institutional policy and public administration. He is Vice-Head of the Dissertation Council of Lomonosov Moscow State University.

Galina Panova is Doctor in Economics and professor at International Finance Department and former Head of "Banks, Monetary Circulation and Credit" Department at MGIMO University and former Vice-Rector of the Finance Academy under the Russian Federation government. She is a consultant, author, and editor of numerous publications on monetary policy and banking in Russia and abroad. Her primary research expertise embraces modern finance, global and national finance markets and financial intermediaries in the face of digital transformation, and banks and banks' management. She has been the leader and responsible executor of more than 20 international research and development projects on those issues. She has more than 30 years of consultancy experience for top management bankers of the Central Bank of Russia and commercial banks.

Alexander Pavlov is Deputy Head of the Department for the Development of the Arctic, Ministry for the Development of the Russian

Far East and Arctic Region. His research interests include the study of tax preferences in Russia. His activities are related to the development of mechanisms for state support of business activities in the Russian Arctic zone.

Tamara Petrovic is Director of Innovation Project Management Center (IPM Center Ltd.), Pancevo, Serbia. She holds a PhD in Economics from MGIMO University. Her research interests focus on project management, innovative ecosystems, public-private partnerships, and international cooperation.

Zhanna Pisarenko is Doctor in World Economy and Finances and is an associate professor at Risk Management and Insurance Department, St. Petersburg State University. Her research interests are closely connected with institutional investors, green finance, financial convergence and financial conglomerates, and financial ecosystems. She is the author of numerous research papers published in leading scientific journals.

Vladimir Podolskiy is a Bauman Moscow State Technical University graduate and a post-graduate fellow at the Chair of Computer Architecture and Parallel Systems of the Technical University of Munich (TUM), Germany. He is a lecturer of a practical course on the Internet of Things for master's students at TUM. Since 2014, he has been a practitioner in IT consulting industry. He has also published 12 research papers on cloud applications autoscaling and resource management aspects of cloud computing. he has served as a co-organizer of the International Workshop on Computing Continuum (IWCoCo) at the HiPEAC'20 and as a program committee member of leading conferences and workshops (EuroSys'20, AIOPS'20, SOCA'19, SOCA'18, DASC'18, and I-SPAN'18). He has also been a reviewer for journals: *Transactions on Network and Service Management* (IEEE), *Transactions on Services Computing* (IEEE), and *Software: Practice and Experience* (Wiley).

Evgeny Popov is an associate professor at the School of Governance and Politics, MGIMO University. He has more than 20 years of experience in research and lecturing on investment law, dispute resolution, and governance. He is the Editor-in-Chief of the *WTO Law Journal* and is on the editorial board of a number of leading Russian law journals. He has acted as an arbitrator under London Court of International Arbitration (LCIA) International Chamber of Commerce (ICC), Moscow Court of International Arbitration (MCIA) and (United Nations Commission on International Trade and Law (UNCITRAL) Arbitration Rules.

Dmitry Prozorov is an associate professor at the Department of Management and Marketing of High-tech Industries, Moscow Aviation Institute (National Research University). He is one of the leading lecturers on innovation management and project management. His more than 40-year research work focuses on the management of innovative projects in the aviation industry and innovation in international relations.

Zhaklin Sarkisyan is Head of the Department of Economics and Finance at Moscow State Institute of International Relations (MGIMO University) and has graduated from the Faculty of International Economic Relations, MGIMO University. She holds her PhD in Law from MGIMO University. Her research interests include anti-crisis risk management in Russian companies.

Anna Shashkova is Professor of Constitutional Law Chair, Moscow State Institute of International Relations. She is Doctor of Science (Politics) & Candidate of Science (Law). She is the author of 23 books on entrepreneurial law and has numerous publications in Russian and foreign periodicals on legal, anti-money laundering, and anti-corruption issues. She holds a diplomatic position as Honorary Consul for St. Vincent and the Grenadines in the Russian Federation. She is mentioned in "Who is Who" 2015.

Monika Siennicka graduated from Emlyon Business School with a master's degree in Luxury Management and Marketing. She pursued a bachelor's degree in Management at University of Warsaw. Following her strong passion and will to work in the luxury sector she joined the L'Oreal Luxe Division in Warsaw in February 2019. Since that time she has been developing her professional skills, being responsible for Giorgio Armani's strong growth in the Polish market as well as the Valentino launch—new brand installation. Her research interest focuses on luxury product management and marketing.

Igor Stepnov is Dr.Sc. (Econ) Head of Asset Management Department at Moscow State Institute of International Relations (MGIMO University) and Professor of Corporate Finance and Corporate Governance at Financial University under the Government of the Russian Federation. With more than 30 years of experience in researching the dynamics of production and economic systems and businesses consulting, he formed the theory of organizational platform of interaction, which includes an original model of strategic development of companies. His research interests are focused on the dynamics of digital ecosystems and their elements, such as pricing and profit control in business models, investment attractiveness of digital business and digital asset management, and digital business models' design.

Kirill Teteryatnikov is Doctor in Economics and Management and in Law, and a full member of the International Academy of Management, an advisor and member of the Management Board at VEB.RF Institute of Research and Expertise, and the CEO of Independent Consulting Group. Kirill is also a member and leading expert of the Management Board at the Free Economic Society of Russia. He also holds the distinction of being a twice national public award winner—Manager of the Year in banking and strategy consulting, and winner of the Golden Pen national award for scientific and practical publications on banking management and international business development. His main research interests include public and corporate governance, economics of growth and development, international and Russian business development, smart cities, green economy, and BRICS and EAEU(Eurasian Economic Union).

Maya Tikhonova is the CEO of Soglasie Insurance Company, has graduated from the Department of International Economic Relations, Moscow State Institute of International Relations (MGIMO University), and holds the FRM (Financial Risk Manager) GARP (Global Association of Risk Professionals) certificate. Her research interests are concentrated on anti-crisis risk management, and anticipation and adaptation to critical risk issues in financial institutions.

Michel Verlaine hold a PhD in Economics and Management. He is an associate professor at ICN Business School and is specialized in topics relating to the financial industry and decision theory as well as political economy of finance and the interaction between law and finance. He manages the "banks, funds, and markets" specialization, which trains specialists who understand the value chain and business models of the finance industry. Before academia, he has worked for the Ministry of Economics in Luxembourg and was notably involved in preparing and attending the Finance Ministers' Eco/Fin meetings. He has also worked at Risk Advisory department at Ernst & Young.

Kobilzhon Zoidov is an associate professor, a candidate of Physical and Mathematical Sciences, and Head of the Laboratory of integration of the Russian economy into the world economy at Market Economy Institute of the Russian Academy of Sciences (MEI RAS). He is a specialist in the field of economic and mathematical modeling, modeling of cyclical processes in the national economy, macroeconomic and sectoral problems of forming an innovative economy, modeling of business processes of industrial enterprises, and methodology of non-equilibrium analysis of the economic system in conditions of integration and global instability. His special research place lies in the methodology of econometric analysis of the national economy development, the problems of forming an evolutionary model of the economic system, the problems of ensuring economic security of the macroeconomic system, and the problems of modeling cyclical processes.

List of Figures

List of Tables

CHAPTER 1

Post-industrial Modernization: Problems and Prospects

Julia Kovalchuk

In current, turbulent times, futuristic innovations and new technologies have not only entered into our lives rapidly and created new opportunities for developing society and the economy, but also lead to challenges and threats that inevitably cause negative reactions and dilemmas regarding further transformations. In this book, we look at the contradictions, advantages, and problems inherent in post-industrial development as an intensive and continuous process, primarily in the economy, affecting all areas of life.

The modern economy is complex and diverse, and the prolonged recession, touching both developing and developed countries, makes it necessary to adapt economic policy instruments and search for a new model of socio-economic development that will ensure economic growth in the post-crisis period of economic development.

The theoretical foundations for new industrialization as an independent type of social transformation were laid down by the works of Galbraith (1967) and then developed in the ideas from Bell about the

J. Kovalchuk (✉)
Moscow State Institute of International Relations (MGIMO University), Moscow, Russia

Moscow Aviation Institute, Moscow, Russia

J. Kovalchuk (ed.), *Post-Industrial Society*,
https://doi.org/10.1007/978-3-030-59739-9_1

"post-industrial society" (Bell 1973). Toffler expanded these ideas into "the third wave", which (he argues) will incomparably change the world as did the agricultural and industrial revolutions and many other stages of international development (Toffler 1980).

Bell argues that the post-industrial society inevitably updates itself, as classical production fades into the background and service production predominates, practical knowledge is replaced by theoretical knowledge, and technology is a priority for universal development; at the same time, though, the values and norms of society are similarly changing under the influence of ongoing transformations. The same thing is also happening now, as digitalization provides many technologies for economic and social transformations, ultimately changing not only society but also its mentality (Ayhan 2017).

The time of post-industrial development was the evolutionary result of society's awareness of the consequences of deindustrialization, when developed countries actively transferred production to developing countries and refused to modernize their national industry. On the one hand, this helped to increase the economic growth rates of developing countries and increased employment; it did, on the other hand, not contribute either to producing top-quality products or dealing with unemployment in developed countries. It should be noted that modern scientists consider not only the economic consequences of losses resulting from deindustrialization, but also the social, cultural, and ideological consequences of the mass shutdown of factories in some countries (Nettleingham 2019), and also call deindustrialization a historically disruptive force (Pula 2017).

Furthermore, the active growth of the service sector ("service production") in developed countries did not provide a stable rate of economic growth, which became especially apparent after the global financial crisis of 2008, which revealed the value of industrial development and the opportunities that innovative technologies bring. From a historical point of view, industrialization made the United States, the Soviet Union, Canada, Britain, Germany, France, Italy, and Japan the leaders of the global economy. The most economically developed among developing countries are Brazil, China, and India, where industry has been a major factor in their rapid rise over the last 20 years, and which will allow economists to maintain economic growth; conversely the countries of Africa, South America, the Middle East, and East Asia will develop new forms of production, which will provide the impetus for economic recovery due to the corresponding changes in the structure and technology of industrial production.

We concur with the position of González from the University of Santiago de Compostela that the term "post-industrial economy" (González 2019) has become synonymous with reformatting the economic structure of countries with a predominance in the tertiary sector, meaning they produce services for a new economy with a predominance of innovation and high-tech enterprises. At the same time, we must also understand that the explanation of the nature and manifestations of processes associated with economic development inevitably lies in the channel of conjugation between economics and sociology. For example, economists view deindustrialization as a natural stage of economic development caused by strong productivity growth in manufacturing (which reduces demand for labour) and rising consumer welfare (which disproportionately increases the demand for services) (Kollmeyer 2020). According to sociologists, deindustrialization involves many social problems, such as growing income inequality, persistently high unemployment, and a serious decay in society.

The most relevant trends concerning the economic dynamics of the development of developed, developing, and transition economies include re-industrialization, new industrialization or "innovative industrialization", neo-industrialization, and super-industrialization. Despite the similarity of possible meanings, these concepts still have significant differences.

Reindustrialization is the restoration, modernization, and innovative renewal of traditional industries based on new industrial technologies, accompanied by the creation of new economic sectors and industries. It should be noted that reindustrialization in no way implies restoring an industry to its former formats—it is industrialization with new principles and technologies, reconstructing the material and technical base for economic development. Reindustrialization focuses on overcoming the consequences of deindustrialization in the changing business environment when it is necessary to restore either production links within technological chains (production cooperation or combination), or even to restore entire industries that have fallen into decline due to lack of competitiveness in the international market, and provides the ability to acquire a finished product on favourable terms in international markets.

Post-industrialization developments through the innovative economic sector—not because of crowding out traditional industries, but because of initial technical and technological renewal—should give the country's historically specialized industries a high-tech and knowledge-intensive appearance.

Neo-industrialization is the development of fundamentally new industries of the sixth long cycle, following Kondratiev's theory (Kondratiev 2002). To some extent, it is also impacted by the Fourth Industrial Revolution, in accordance with Schwab's concept, when robotics, the Internet of Things, virtual reality, 3D printing, biotechnology, artificial intelligence, and other modernistic concepts become the components of a new economic reality (Schwab 2017) and universities create new science (Torkunov 2019).

Super-industrialization is neo-industrialization from the position of focusing on accelerated development in terms of technological development. Here, great emphasis is placed on significant breakthrough technologies, which are partly the further development of technologies of the fifth long economic cycle: biotechnologies (molecular biology and genetic engineering), nanotechnologies, artificial intelligence systems with the active development of space technologies, global information networks, nuclear energy, and so on.

New industrialization is a radical technological re-equipment of material production (traditional industrial sectors) based on Nano-, Bio-, IT- and Cognitive (NBIC) technologies. It is an integrating concept, including both re-industrialization and neo-industrialization. It is also new industrialization that, in addition to the fundamentally technological renewal of industry, implies significant changes in the institutional environment.

Thus, conceptually, each of these terms has a certain specificity, just as each country has its own unique socio-economic state and its potential for involvement in the world's post-industrial development. For some countries, a reindustrialization strategy based on the growth of industrial production (tradition) is appropriate; others must use a fundamentally innovative strategy, for example, new industrialization (innovation) or a combination of these strategies.

In the essence of the processes and changes occurring in the industry, the new industrialization of the United States, Canada, and Western Europe implies returning production facilities (previously withdrawn to Southeast Asia) to a new robotic base, closer to research centres and consumer markets. US reindustrialization is based both on traditional competitive advantages (leading positions in scientific and innovative spheres) and on new ones (cheaper energy resources, new energy-intensive industries using cheap gas and electricity), which will ultimately help reduce dependence on industrial imports. Despite the obvious advantages of reindustrialization, some experts note that returning production to the United States is likely to increase labour productivity, but guarantees neither a reduction in the costs of large companies nor the growth of quotations of their valuable securities—it seems it is still companies in either the high-tech or the banking sector that have the highest capitalization rate.

Chinese industrialization was based on the mass copying of foreign technologies and the use of cheap labour; the new Chinese industrialization (in fact, during the third wave after the Second World War) has been focused on building a complete innovation cycle from applied R&D to the development of new industries (environmental and energy-saving equipment, computer science, biotechnology, new materials).

Taking Russia, Latin America, and Africa under consideration, the issues of whether to fundamentally modernize or to traditionally restore potentially competitive economic sectors, the gradual creation of high-tech industries, and the inclusion in global networks as producers of goods and services with high added value are more relevant there.

The concept of new industrialization, based on the list of tasks to be solved within its framework, essentially corresponds to the development paradigm; this, however, is still catching up to the standards of modernity. In Russia, for example, it therefore can only be successfully implemented if it is progressive and accelerated. As international experience shows, at the initial stage of a new long economic cycle, countries lagging behind have a unique opportunity to jerk, get ahead, and become leaders, especially when the corresponding potential is accumulated.

Nevertheless, despite the development of terminology, as well as the state of the economy and industry in specific countries, both theorists and practitioners agree that reindustrialization, as the restoration of traditional industries, should be accompanied not merely by promising technologies, but fundamentally by neo-industrialization: the technological renewal of traditional industry and the development of new industrial production sectors in accordance with new technologies. The introduction of this is already happening. At the same time, we note that economic growth is not based on new technologies, but is creating the potential for technological leadership and the corresponding specialization of production, which will make it possible to implement the classical postulates of the comparative advantages theory by Ricardo: if a country has failed to provide technological development, then it borrows modern technologies from abroad and further improves them without expecting significant added value. At the same time, those countries involved in creating new products and mastering new technologies at the final stage of their life cycle may already have a larger output volume with a significantly smaller contribution to GDP.

The study of Hausmann and Hidalgo, who monitored the development of countries over the past 60 years, proved that as soon as a nation begins to expand the knowledge and capabilities necessary for producing goods and providing them to global markets, this nation paves its way to prosperity. Besides, the study determined that the availability of knowledge allows for the production of more complex products, and the development and implementation of more advanced production processes leads to even greater economic prosperity. The authors' study also argues that a combination of knowledge (competencies) and opportunities for the commercialization of new technologies is a major factor in differences in national incomes (Hausmann et al. 2013). Consequently, advanced production is a key factor in creating high added value through job creation and economic prosperity.

Innovation is the engine of development. Any innovative economy should be interested in Schumpeter's theory of "creative destruction" (or "creative destruction"), which, he argued, can renew the economy and society, but this requires destroying the existing order of things to create a new one (Schumpeter 1983). In various classifications, there are various types of innovations that are essential for the identification and implementation of new industrialization, such as:

- Nascent innovations–intensively developing technological areas with a high potential for generating inventions, innovations, and associated significant economic and social consequences (Gokhberg et al. 2013).
- Destructive innovations—technologies with fundamentally new consumer properties that can completely change the structure of markets (Christensen 1997). Such innovations can be defined as innovations that change the "rules of the game".
- Technological applications—technologies in interdisciplinary technological fields that can significantly affect socio-economic development and change people's lives (Silberglitt et al. 2006).

The first type of innovation is identified at the stage of research and development, and the second and third when products based on these technologies can already be partially introduced into the market.

The current situation for reversing economic downturn, implemented across the global economy, requires new theories of economic development. We instead conclude that this structural crisis can be overcome by the introduction of new technologies that open up new production capabilities which provide a breakthrough in improving economic efficiency and instigate the transition to a new stage of height.

It is obvious that each country chooses its own "window of opportunity", and the strategies chosen by world leaders do not apply for the most part to the conditions of the Russian economy. For example, the "transfer" strategy, characteristic of Japan, is based not just on the use of foreign scientific and technological experience, but also on the creation and development of its own scientific, technological, and production potential with full provision of the innovation cycle; however, not only does it require significant financial costs (for acquiring licenses), but it also forms a direct relationship with technologically advanced countries, thereby creating a threat to the country's national security. The strategy of "catching-up development", which is characteristic of China, is based on the creation of its own scientific and technological potential, supported by a combination of state and market forms of innovation. However, the implementation of such a strategy requires attracting foreign capital whilst investing more than a third of GDP; in addition, this strategy cannot create institutions that protect the economy and focus on modernizing all sectors of the economy at once. The "build-up" strategy, which is characteristic of the United States, is based on the use of internal scientific and technical potential with the involvement of foreign scientists and designers, and the integration of the fundamental science of universities and the applied science of firms. Despite the obvious positive results of the implementation of this strategy (the creation of new products, high technologies that are being implemented both in production and in the social sphere, ensuring a constant build-up of innovations), this strategy requires a reasonable choice between a limited number of highly effective areas of scientific and technological development, then providing them with state funding with the obligatory involvement of a private investor.

Moreover, for every evolutionary change—or revolutionary transformation—in the industry, society and people must be the focus. Indeed, new technologies of post-industrialism are changing the business models of companies, so they should develop strategies to support the employment of workers in conjunction with the development of robotics and artificial intelligence, or organize training on high-tech equipment and employee involvement. This must be done promptly and speedily; whereas the first, second, and third industrial revolutions took a relatively long period of time, the dynamics and speed of the spread of digital technologies make these tasks extremely timely, and public control is necessary.

Therefore, our book is based on an analysis of three main areas of the development of the post-industrial society, alongside the dilemmas associated with its transformation:

(a) the impact of new (including digital) technologies on economic relations, as well as the prospects for the introduction and impact of various innovative technologies on the development of industry and services, business, consumer behaviour, market behaviour, and so on;
(b) the transformation of existing "traditional" institutions in connection with the penetration of new technologies of the post-industrial economy into practice; and
(c) a study of the contradictions between modern productive forces and getting out of date production relations.

The post-industrial society is a diverse series of paradoxical ecosystems; it has predictable and unpredictable manifestations; there are positive and negative aspects; it requires modern values and challenges (to nature, people, and the economy) and relies upon new advanced technologies (for business and society, including megatrends and development), yet requires conservative steps during the period of transformation. To present this complex world as comprehensively as possible, we present our book as a collection of the following chapters.

Chapter 2, "Development Institutions and Sovereign Wealth Funds as a Tool for Implementing Transformation Processes in the Economy", contains an original approach to researching the role of special organizations created by governments for investing in the implementation of economic development projects (development institutions and foundations) and for solving tasks of conservation and financial stability in times of crisis (sovereign wealth funds). This creates the basis for public administration at a new stage of post-industrial development, when the financial resources accumulated during periods of industrialization or favourable economic conditions should be used to increase the potential for future development projects, creating opportunities to increase the competitiveness of countries, companies, and their products, and increase welfare citizens.

Chapter 3, "Managing for the Future: Crisis Management Under Post-industrial Modernization", includes an assessment of the factors that influence post-industrial modernization processes and lead to crises. The authors emphasize the adoption of measures to prevent the risks of post-industrial transformations for companies at different stages of their life cycle based on current management tools and a combination of scenario and matrix approaches ("management for the future"), which will reduce the likelihood of bankruptcy and increase sustainability.

Chapter 4, "High Technologies for Smart City Development", will lead the reader into an exclusive manifestation of post-industrialism and digital technologies—smart cities. We are used to the fact that the municipal management system is quite traditional, but a modern city is a special environment for introducing innovations and high-tech solutions aimed at achieving the highest possible quality of resource and infrastructure management, ensuring optimal level of service and security for the population, and maintaining a sustainable environment for living and business activity.

Chapter 5, "Digital State: Creation Through Project-Functional Structure of Public Administration", analyses the public administration system and assesses barriers to innovation, especially in digital technology. The digital state apparatus is already a real future, but for the transition from the existing bureaucracy to the state apparatus of the digital platform, it is important to develop the skill of projective problem solving, where the design and functional structure of the state apparatus will solve conflicts of management systems.

Chapter 6, "Innovative Ecosystems for Attracting Investment in a Post-industrial Society", contains specific tools for taking advantage of international cooperation and public-private partnerships, including attracting foreign capital for joint innovation programmes. The authors assess the potential for interaction between countries (using the example of Serbia and Russia) and cooperation in industry and services, which creates conditions for access to the latest technologies.

Chapter 7, "Transformation of a Traditional Financial Conglomerate into a Financial Ecosystem", considers the evolution of financial convergence in the global financial market and the development of technology as essential prerequisites for creating a new type of financial conglomerate, called the ecosystem financial conglomerate (EFC), and a specific business model. This contributes to a paradigm shift in the global financial market, highlights the need to take changing customer needs and various risks into account, notes the emergence of new global players operating through the EFC, and requires reviewing prudential measures and crisis management tools.

Chapter 8, "International Investment Law: A Journey from the Past to the Future", analyses the legal aspects of international investments and dispute resolution regimes in the future, taking into account the geographic expansion of interactions in the post-industrial economy. Due to the rapidly changing forms and content of investments across modern international political, economic, and social landscapes, the authors turn to the study of the intermediate evolutionary process from a rich past to a multiverse future.

Chapter 9, "'Who Will Rule?': Institution of State in the Transformation Process of the Twentieth and Twenty-First Centuries", contains a deep multidisciplinary study of transformation processes in public administration and its institutionalization, when, in a post-industrial society, a service state as a new model for solving the vetocracy problem cannot be recognized as the right way for society regardless of its socio-economic development.

Chapter 10, "'New Generation' EU Free Trade Agreements: A Combination of Traditional and Innovative Mechanisms", examines the current provisions and new approaches to the legal regulation of trade relations in various areas: electronic commerce, the resolution of investment disputes, and the relationship between trade, labour, and environmental protection. The development of the post-industrial economy and international cooperation makes it possible to recognize electronic contracts, which itself could completely abolish customs duties in electronic commerce, suggest a new system of investment courts, and require the active participation of civil society in implementing trade agreements.

Chapter 11, "Value Creation by the Sharing Economy in the Post-industrial Society", explores a new form of economic exchange, which, while developing, has always been a source of societal development. The author carries out a value measurement of a shared economy through the prism of certain components (social approval, economic choice [based on benefits], and digital coordination), identifies types of new ways to create and redistribute income, and takes into account the contradictions between saving and consumption. An important conclusion is that the sharing economy has a key advantage: it relies on real rather than formed demand, which substantially eliminates marketing errors.

Chapter 12, "Change of Tax Policy Model as a Base for Innovation Development While Transferring from the Pre-industrial to the Industrial Society", discusses the inevitable changes in taxation as a stage of development for the modern economic system. An analysis of Vietnam's experience is chosen for historical review, and comparison is conducted of its taxation model at the turn of the nineteenth and twentieth centuries, as well as the transition from pre-industrial to industrial taxation in the twenty-first century, which led to the innovative development of the country.

Chapter 13, "Civil Liability Concept Transition in Post-industrial Countries", is devoted to the evolution of an important legal institution that takes into account the possibility of monetary compensation for negative property consequences and liability for non-fulfilment of contractual or non-contractual property obligations. It is also important that in the post-industrial economy, in connection with the development of new technologies, the importance of accounting for lost profits as an important component of damage is increasing.

Chapter 14, "Global Competitiveness of High-Tech Companies: Factors, Barriers, Government Support", allows readers to familiarize themselves with what it means to be a high-tech company in the post-industrial economy, the criteria for classifying industries as high-tech industries, and what government support preferences are available. The authors also emphasize the importance of knowledge-intensive and technology-intensive industries in the global economy, as well as the factors and barriers to their international competitiveness.

Chapter 15, "Intellectual Evaluation of the Economic Systems' Performance in Post-industrial Society", is focused on finding solutions to the problems of forecasting the development of companies that are affected by rapid and unforeseeable environmental changes. It is proposed to use a risk analysis and management algorithms using cognitive modelling technologies and neuro-fuzzy networks to provide decision support.

Chapter 16, "Transit Economy in Global Post-industrial Eurasia", assesses innovative development of all types of transport, based on the formation of a single digital transport and logistics environment. The authors note the importance of developing and implementing mechanisms for generating, distributing, and redistributing income from the transit economy on the territory of Global Eurasia in the context of automation, robotics, digital transformation, the introduction of artificial intelligence, and the transition to paperless and uninhabited technologies.

Chapter 17, "Defining the Readiness for Smart City Concept: Russian Municipalities Study", analyses the practices of Russian municipalities in implementing the concept of "smart cities" as projects supporting the post-industrial economy. The authors applied the expert assessment method and assessed their readiness to implement digital technologies, the availability of budgetary resources, and the coordination of the goals and objectives of the digital agenda.

Chapter 18, "The Evolution of Fashion Consumer Perception in the Post-industrial Era", is atypical on the stated topic, as the authors discuss the influence on the creation and marketing of fashionable clothes of the changed behaviour of new consumer groups—in particular the issues of eco-friendly fashion and sustainable development—as well as the active use of digital technologies. The post-industrial economy not only is focused on marketing achievements, but also takes into account and shapes consumers' perception of fashion.

Chapter 19, "National Innovation System: Formation and Development in the Post-industrial Economy", considers how to modernize the national innovation system in developing and post-Socialist countries through creating a virtual investment community, forming priority development areas, reforming the regional financial system and structural policy, and optimizing budgets.

Chapter 20, "Does a Solution Exist to the Paradox of Trust in Financial Institutions?", considers issues of creating a trusting environment, using the example of financial market institutions, assessing trust, and developing strategies to increase the trust level across various scenarios of economic development. The authors identified the factors that have a positive and a negative impact on the level of trust, and created a set of recommendations for practical use.

In general, this book—written by professors and scientists from Russia, Serbia, Germany, France, Poland, and Tajikistan—deals with public administration, economy, law, and psychology, and is intended to provide a comprehensive overview of the opportunities and challenges associated with modern developments across society, production, and consumption. Combining the work of recognized scientists and specialists in various scientific fields, this book provides a comprehensive understanding of post-industrial development, highlighting the driving forces and limitations, strategies, funding sources, tools, and technologies for their implementation.

The book includes the practice of countries such as Russia, which is moving from large-scale new industrialization to an undecided but informed choice of its industries' future, including the restoration of traditional industries and the creation of promising new ones. The book is based on specific attitudes to the state management of development finance, the feasibility of interaction between the state and business in the management of scientific and technical breakthroughs with maximum application for viable industries' potential, and the best positioning of newly created industries as part of a new technological cycle.

We sincerely hope that this book will be an informative source of knowledge about the development of the post-industrial society, and also will be useful to scientists, economists, sociologists, and politicians; however, we also hope that it allows each reader to understand a lot of real dilemmas that are inherent in the modern stage of economic modernization, and draw their own conclusions about its values. We are only at the beginning of a revolution (some will call it post-industrial, some will call it digital) that will fundamentally change the way we live, work, and communicate.

The authors are grateful to the REGION Group (Moscow, Russia) for financial support in the implementation of research projects.

References

Ayhan, B. (Ed.). (2017). *Digitalization and Society*. Bern: Peter Lang D.

Bell, D. (1973). *The Coming of Post-Industrial Society: A Venture of Social Forecasting*. New York: Basic Books.

Christensen, C. M. (1997). *The Innovator's Dilemma: When New Technologies Cause Great Firms to Fail*. Boston: Harvard Business School Press.

Galbraith, J. K. (1967). *The New Industrial State*. Princeton: Princeton University Press.

Gokhberg, L., Fursov, K., Miles, I., & Perani, G. (2013). Developing and Using Indicators of Emerging and Enabling Technologies. In F. Gault (Ed.), *Handbook of Innovation Indicators and Measurement* (pp. 349–380). Cheltenham: Edward Elgar.

González, R. C. L. (2019). Postindustrial Economy. In A. M. Orum (Ed.), *The Wiley Blackwell Encyclopedia of Urban and Regional Studies*. Hoboken: Wiley.

Hausmann, R., et al. (2013). *The Atlas of Economic Complexity: Mapping Paths to Prosperity*. Cambridge, MA: MIT Press.

Kollmeyer, C. (2020). Deindustrialization. In G. Ritzer (Ed.), *The Blackwell Encyclopedia of Sociology*. Malden: Blackwell.

Kondratiev, N. D. (2002). *Big Cycles of Conjuncture and the Theory of Foresight*. Moscow: Ekonomika. (In Russian).

Nettleingham, D. (2019). Beyond the Heartlands: Deindustrialization, Naturalization and the Meaning of an "Industrial" Tradition. *The British Journal of Sociology, 70*(2), 610–626.

Pula, B. (2017). Industrialization and Deindustrialization. In B. Turner (Ed.), *The Wiley Blackwell Encyclopedia of Urban and Regional Studies*. Hoboken: Wiley.

Schumpeter, J. A. (1983) [1934] The Theory of Economic Development: An Inquiry into Profits, Capital, Credit, Interest, and the Business Cycle. New Brunswick: Transaction Books.

Schwab, K. (2017). *The Fourth Industrial Revolution*. New York: Crown Business.

Silberglitt, R., Antón, P. S., Howell, D. R., & Wong, A. (2006). *The Global Technology Revolution 2020, In-Depth Analysis: Bio/Nano/Materials/Information Trends, Drivers, Barriers and Social Applications*. Santa Monica: RAND Corporation.

Toffler, A. (1980). *The Third Wave*. New York: Morrow.

Torkunov, A. V. (2019). University as a Part of National Economy. *Voprosy Ekonomiki*, (12), 111–122. https://doi.org/10.32609/0042-8736-2019-12-111-122.

CHAPTER 2

Development Institutions and Sovereign Wealth Fund as a Tool for Implementing Transformation Processes in the Economy

Julia Kovalchuk

Introduction

For more than half a century, the global economic policy has been to consider development institutions and sovereign wealth funds as one of the most pressing issues. This is due to the fact that it is those development institutions that, somehow, work across many countries with extremely different levels of socio-economic development to realize their intentions of developing faster than the "invisible hand of the market" allows. The very idea of such institutions came from the notion that the economy is divided into segments, some of which deserve to be developed better than others, either because these segments play a key role, or because they are underdeveloped and are in need of support, which will, in the end, lead to accelerated economic growth, growth of GDP, and a better quality of life.

J. Kovalchuk (✉)
Moscow State Institute of International Relations (MGIMO University), Moscow, Russia

Moscow Aviation Institute, Moscow, Russia

J. Kovalchuk (ed.), *Post-Industrial Society*,
https://doi.org/10.1007/978-3-030-59739-9_2

Currently, based on the concepts of classical and the neoclassical economic theories, two main opposing approaches to describing the functionality of economic systems have been developed:

- The market approach: the economy is considered a market system, where individuals are free to exchange goods while restricted only by common provisions of the law extending to every individual involved on an equal basis.
- The directive approach: the economic system exists and functions under a special mechanism of state governance.

The market is generally viewed as a self-regulating economic system designed to best satisfy the needs of society without conscious regulation. In the quest for profit a person satisfies the needs of other members of society through the "invisible hand of the market" (as Adam Smith famously coined). This interpretation is links to the "free market theory" (Friedman 1982) of the 1970s, based on the idea the market distributes resources and risks independently and that the state's intervention into the economy should remain minimal. Fundamental economy theory defends the main thesis that the market strives for balance and that market players pursuing their own goals fully reflect the interests of society as a whole. However, in the conditions of the ongoing financial crisis it is state intervention that has come to the markets' rescue.

In reality, modern economic systems, functioning in the new post-industrial economy, may be classified as "mixed economies" with both the "invisible hand of the market" and fair state regulation equally present. The development of economics (in particular, the institutional economic theory) has shown that the "invisible hand of the market" also contains certain rules of the game: namely institutions, directing the individual on their way to make society better.

Institutions fulfilling their special functions in society and the economy are the driving force behind economic actors gaining not just economic profit exclusively from business activity, but also additional economic profit directly linked to conducting activity, under the direct influence of these institutions.

In this regard, an issue arises, of creating a mechanism aimed at stimulating the free market and the self-development of the economic system under the new economic conditions of post-industrial development, based on the functioning of development institutions. Such institutions are, namely, special institutions (including those created in the form of sovereign wealth funds) driving the creation of the additional free flow of capital for the purposes of modernizing the economy and implementing national socio-economic and innovation development strategies, as well scientific and technological breakthroughs in some countries, ensuring a significant improvement of the macroeconomic position of the country and the quality of life for its citizens. Moreover, such institutions include sovereign wealth funds specifically established by governments and secured by hydrocarbon income (Schena and Ali 2017), allowing financial stability to be preserved in times of crisis and to serve as a tool of global investment.

Methodology

The issue of economic development as a whole, and of raising the competitiveness of national economies in particular, is extremely pressing, which is evidenced by the annual country competitiveness rating drafted by the World Economic Forum. Despite 70% of the rating being survey data, the Forum includes the assessment of such important factors of economic growth as increasing the efficiency of commodity markets, the economy integrating into global value chains, improvement to conditions of business activity, widespread use of IT, and such. With that said, the level of development of global value chains—determining the competitiveness of the economy—depends above all on the quality of institutions and infrastructure, the efficiency of commodity markets, and innovational activity. The rating data show that even with a developed infrastructure, institutions (i.e. the "rules of the game" on the domestic market) remain the weakest link in the sequence of development factors of global value chains. Corruption, taxation, and access to financing slow down the growth of competitiveness in an institutional sense, considering that the remedies for property and minority shareholders remain insufficient and state policy remains onerous.

The data from private indexes makes construct an integral indicator possible, showcasing the movement of the national economy in the right direction and its modernization (Table 2.1). Moreover, despite different levels of institutional development in different countries, it is worth noting that the largest sovereign funds function in those countries ranking relatively low in the global competitiveness rating drafted by the World Economic Forum (World Economic Forum 2019).

Table 2.1 Competitiveness indicators per country according to the World Economic Forum (2019)

	Global Competitiveness Index	*Institutions*	*Infrastructure*	*Innovation capability*	*Macroeconomic stability*	*ICT adoption*	*GDP per capita, US$*	*GDP (PPP) % world GDP*	*Presence of the largest sovereign funds*
Singapore	1	2	1	13	38	5	64,041	0.42	*
United States	2	20	13	2	37	27	62,605	15.16	
Hong Kong	3	5	3	26	1	3	48,517	0.36	*
Netherlands	4	4	2	10	1	24	53,106	0.72	
Switzerland	5	6	4	3	1	17	82,950	0.41	
Japan	6	19	5	7	42	6	39,305	4.14	
Germany	7	18	8	1	1	36	48,264	3.22	
Sweden	8	10	19	5	1	4	53,873	0.4	
United Kingdom	9	11	11	8	1	31	42,558	2.25	
Norway	17	8	44	20	1	10	81,694	0.29	*
United Arab Emirates	25	15	12	33	1	2	40,711	0.54	*
China	28	58	36	24	39	18	9608	18.69	*
Qatar	29	35	24	38	40	8	70,779	0.26	*
Saudi Arabia	36	37	34	36	1	38	23,566	0.8	*
Russia	43	74	50	32	43	22	11,326	3.12	*
Kuwait	46	65	66	108	1	37	30,839	0.23	*
Turkey	68	71	49	49	129	69	9346	1.7	*

Source: Drafted by the author based on: World Economic Forum (2019), Sovereign Wealth Fund Institute (2020)

Generally, taking into account the overall positive macroeconomic stability and infrastructure improvements, the existing risks and issues of institutional development in Russia should be noted, as they do not bring about any significantly increased efficiency or quality of the country's economic development. As a result, research into the appearance and functioning of development institutions in Russia, and evaluation of their efficiency, remains relevant and necessary.

Results

In the broadest sense, institutions are understood as both formal and informal interaction means between economic agents. There is both no generally accepted terminology pertaining to institutions, and the institutions themselves are perceived from a minimum of three angles:

- As organizational aspects of the functioning of an institution. A development institution is a special organization facilitating the distribution of resources for the purposes of furthering the new potential of economic growth in the industry, region, and country as a whole.
- As internal organization of an institution. A development institution is a conventional interaction norm between economic agents, resulting in changes in the system and a decrease in uncertainty.
- As an economic regulatory body. A development institution is a tool of state policy aimed at making up for "market failures" and securing investment resources inflows into segments with lower private commercial capital influxes.

As such, development institutions are considered both an environment (conditions) ensuring the development of the economic system of any class (business [organization], industry, region, country) and a tool of state policy.

An important distinctive feature of development institutions is the regulating role of the state in their functioning, which is why development institutions are primarily viewed as state-established organizations designed to secure priority financing and complex support of certain projects and key segments of the economy: either because they affect modernization levels of the economy as a whole, or because institutions, despite their value for society, are considered slow in development. Due to low profit margins, risks, and their large scale, they fail to attract private investors and therefore require special means of support. Financing with the help of development institutions sits at the crossroads of commercial financing of profitable projects and budget allocations. With that in mind, development institutions drive the distribution of resources benefitting projects of economic growth potential.

The need for development institutions emerges upon the slowdown of economic growth caused by traditional economic structures and increases in international competition. Development institutions are a catalyst for innovational activity. They serve as a key element of the innovational scenario of economic development. Improvement of infrastructure and investment in human resources are the basis of development. Conditions for the creation of development institutions include:

- A need for concentration of resources in key areas of economic modernization.
- The insufficiency of exclusively governmental resources for effecting of large-scale projects.
- Lack efficiency of direct expenditures by the state.
- Lack of interest of investors toward large projects.

Notable defining features of development institutions compared to other formats of state support include:

- The re-distribution of resources for the benefit of development projects aimed at creating economic growth potential in infrastructure, human potential, new technologies, and support for new, thus far non-dominant, sectors of the economy in need of initial support for their development.
- A constant organizational structure and certain rules allowing development institutions to conduct systematic activity; they have a clear-cut system of liability and control.
- Development institutions are not-for-profit organizations and not a means for the state to increase its share in the economy; their activity is aimed at development of private businesses in new sectors of the economy.

The need for development institutions emerges upon the slowdown of economic growth caused by traditional economic structures and increases in international competition. It should be noted that they function in the form a particular inherent element of the economic development scenario, based on improvements to infrastructure and investment in human resources.

Development institutions emerge at the crossroads of interests of economic agents in the form of the government, businesses, financial institutions, scientific and educational institutions, and the expert community, thanks to which a coalition in support of development institutions is formed. As such, development institutions open new possibilities for more productive use thereof.

Development institutions are thought to be structures designed for accumulating finances and directing them toward the development of promising economic sectors, innovations, and the implementation of significant infrastructural and social projects. From this point of view, development institutions are designed for leveling out and stimulating regional policies, allowing territories lacking in development to gradually narrow the gap between them and more developed regions.

International experience allows a large number of different types of development institutions to be identified. They generally specialize in support of individual sectors of the economy (industrial development institutions), certain regions (regional development institutions), or conducting particular operations (specialized development institutions). However, multifunctional development institutions may also exist.

One of the results of our research is the author's *development institutions classification*. The following types may be identified:

1. State development institutions. Aim: effecting investment policy driving the development of the national economy. Formats: sovereign (state) investment funds, state investment corporations (companies). Tasks: (a) solving managerial issues, stabilizing the state budget in times of decreases in state revenues and/or a long-term reserve fund for public needs; financing of the creation of other development institutions and the provision of additional funds thereto; (b) financial tasks—a more profitable management of state assets (active direct and indirect investment).
2. Financial development institutions. Aim: provision of additional financing upon insufficient levels of development of the financial market (generally, regional markets). Formats: international financial organizations, financial and banking institutions, venture

funds, direct investment funds, guarantee funds, and public-private partnership (PPP). They provide financial services, namely: attracting investments in the form of public-private partnership, soft-term financing of priority sectors of the economy, investments in direct investment funds, and loan guarantees (PPP).

3. Industrial (innovational) development institutions. Aim: supporting industrialization and reindustrialization of manufacturing in different areas. Formats: industrial development corporations. They provide financial, coordinating, expert services by developing clusters of small business support, and stimulation of innovations.
4. Science and technology (innovational) development institutions. Aim: uniting members of government, business, and academic and education communities around the general notion of scientific and technological development and general approaches to developing appropriate technologies. They are implemented in the form of technological platforms aimed at the technological modernization of the economy, raising the competitiveness of individual industries, expansion of new technologies, and development of "breakthrough" technologies for new high-tech products markets.
5. Regional development institutions. Aim: creating new manufacturing plants and/or other types of economic activity in the region. They are implemented in the form of development corporations for individual regions, special economic zones, and regional clusters. They provide financial services by attracting investments in the form of public-private partnership, giving out loan guarantees.
6. Infrastructural development institutions. Aim: attracting various forms of financing including public-private partnership in infrastructural projects (transportation and logistical projects, techno-park projects, industrial parks, etc.). They are implemented in the form of business incubators, techno-parks, and industrial parks. They provide business services, access to unique industrial equipment and the ability to products produce in cooperation.
7. Coordinating development institutions. Aim: coordination of business and state development strategies. They are implemented in the form of councils, associations, and unions. They provide coordination services: development and maintenance of communication platforms for exchange of opinions between main agents in the economy.

8. Development institutions for raising businesses' investment appeal. Aim: support of regional internationalization aimed at attracting foreign investments and export support. Thy are effected in the form of export agencies providing marketing, informational, legal, and technological support for the promotion of goods in new markets and for businesses entering global markets.
9. Specialized social funds. Aim: joint financing of advanced training programs, re-training, and so on. They take on the form of educational institutions providing informational and educational services: provision of legal, market, and financial information concerning activity in new sectors of the economy, and training in new business areas.
10. Expert assessment development institutions. Aim: attracting the expert community to solve real economic issues. They take on the form of expert research centers providing expert and analytical services: analytical verification and expert assessment of development strategies.

Based on priority of establishment state development institutions may be categorized into the following two formats:

- State investment funds (sovereign funds).
- Special organizations established and funded by the state for the purposes of jointly financing (including the use of loans and guarantees) commercial projects of a high economic and social significance. Sovereign funds may be analyzed from two points of view:
- A specialized monetary fund designed to stabilize the state budget in times of decreases of state revenues and/or for long-term public needs.
- A specialized state investment fund consisting of shares, bonds, real estate, and/or other financial instruments denominated in a foreign currency. A portion of funds may be invested domestically.

Sovereign wealth funds are generally established in states with highly market situation-dependent budgets (Cumming et al. 2017), namely those dependent on global commodity prices (Table 2.2). Some countries accumulate capital in these funds in case of a deficit of mineral resources—the fund's reserves may be used to make budget deficiency payments in times of unfavorable situations in the market (Braunstein 2017). Currently

Table 2.2 Largest state investment companies—sovereign wealth funds

Rank	*Profile*	*Foundation year*	*Region*	*Country*	*Total assets, billion USD*
1.	Norway Government Pension Fund Global	1990	Europe	Norway	1186
2.	China Investment Corporation	2007	Asia	China	940
3.	Abu Dhabi Investment Authority	1976	Middle East	United Arab Emirates	579
4.	Kuwait Investment Authority	1953	Middle East	Kuwait	533
5.	Hong Kong Monetary Authority Investment Portfolio	1935	Asia	Hong Kong Special Administrative Region	528
6.	GIC Private Limited	1981	Asia	Singapore	440
7.	SAFE Investment Company	1997	Asia	China	417
8.	Temasek Holdings	1974	Asia	Singapore	375
9.	National Council for Social Security Fund	2000	Asia	China	324
10.	Public Investment Fund	1971	Middle East	Saudi Arabia	320
11.	Qatar Investment Authority (QIA)	2005	Middle East	Qatar	295
12.	Investment Corporation of Dubai	2006	Middle East	United Arab Emirates	239
13.	Mubadala Investment Company	2017	Middle East	United Arab Emirates	232
14.	Türkiye Varlık Fonu Yönetimi A.Ş. (Turkey Wealth Fund)	2016	Middle East	Turkey	222
15.	National Welfare Fund	2008	Europe	Russia	165

Source: Drafted based on data from: Sovereign Wealth Fund Institute (2020)

the total value of assets of the 82 largest sovereign funds in the world amounts to approximately US$1 trillion (Sovereign Wealth Fund Institute 2020).

However, sovereign funds accumulated in state investment corporations are able to create a large source of financing for national economy development projects. Despite sovereign funds having been previously associated with oil-producing countries (e.g. Norway, the UAE, Qatar, Kuwait, etc.), the modern agenda includes non-oil-producing Sovereign wealth funds as well (e.g. South Korea, Singapore, China, etc.). More and more countries without large amounts of oil and a significant exports surplus establish sovereign wealth funds by utilizing non-conventional sources of finance and become more and more driven by domestic development priorities, including infrastructural development (Braunstein and Ali 2019). The number and the size of new sovereign funds also remain uncertain, mainly because the conventional growth factors—in particular oil prices and current account surpluses—have slowed down (Smith and Cannan 2003). For example, sovereign funds are changing their investment strategies to include investment in shares with high profit margins and alternative assets (e.g. real estate). For instance, the Norway Government Pension Fund Global invests in high-tech companies (Apple, Alphabet, Microsoft) and non-oil and gas fields (e.g. into Nestle); Public Investment Fund (Saudi Arabia) has invested US$3.5 billion in Uber; the Qatar government is planning to establish an office in Silicon Valley (the United States) in order to invest in technological start-ups. The new toolset of funds also includes utilizing immigrant-investors attraction programs, borrowing from international financial institutions, and making use of revenue from specialized taxes.

Generally, taking into account international strategies, all sovereign funds around the world should be divided into four categories:

- stabilization funds (for protection against volatility on commodity markets and external shocks),
- provident funds (for future generations, e.g., pension funds),
- development funds and institutions (investments in large projects), and
- reserve pension funds and reserve investment corporations (investments in highly profitable and comparatively risky assets).

The types of funds and institutions described above are fundamentally different in terms of their economic natures. Some function based on the notion of return on investments (Murtinua and Scalerab 2016), while others expend resources to achieve social goals. That is exactly why combining various types into one fund or development institution presents a risk. Based on experience, a system of institutions is required, each of which should be designed to solve its own tasks.

In particular, such an approach was selected in Russia upon forming the institutional environment with almost the whole spectrum of globally accepted development institutions available. The modern history of Russia has basically experienced two waves of establishment of development institutions en masse in a space of approximately 12 years:

- The first wave transpired between 1992 and 1994 and failed to produce meaningful results apart from an inefficient, no-purpose expenditure from the state budget (the Reconstruction and Development Bank of Russia, the Export-Import Bank of Russia). To be perfectly fair, the only fund still active nowadays is the Scientific and Technical Field Small Businesses Support Fund established in 1994.
- The second wave took place in 2006–2007, resulting in a number of new organizations, many of which remain active to this day.

The 2000s featured a course for more active innovational activity; however, significant infrastructural limits have obviously come to light hindering the appearance of new innovational projects and the successful development of the ones already in place. For example, it became evident that a lack of service companies conducting toxicological and molecular biology research on a high methodical level in accordance with international standards may significantly hinder the appearance of biological start-ups in the country. Also, the lack of quality patent and foreign market promotion services may nullify the export potential of Russian high-tech companies (or any companies, regardless of the industry). These services, by themselves, are non-innovational, but they nevertheless remain an important element in the high-tech company support system. In the meantime, private business was not quick to fill this empty "service" niche, as solvent demand for such services on the Russian market is yet to form. Henceforth, it is in this direction that development institutions should be working.

The second wave of institutional reforms came to be in the scenario of the Russian government changing its political course, as a transition occurred from monetarist policies (and a refusal of the state to finance commercial projects) to applying dirigiste measures to stimulate the economy. This situation was also accompanied by a strong feeling of the need for new "distribution outlets" for state allocations in the circumstances of the prevailing growth of budget expenditures relative to GDP growth. Meanwhile, the implementation of "priority national projects" also started taking place, with the projects specifically having been declared economic development projects.

In January 2006, the Eurasian Development Bank was established as per the intergovernmental agreement between Russia and Kazakhstan. In 2006 the Russian venture company "Special Economic Zones" Plc. was established.

In 2007 the Russian Corporation of nanotechnology was established; the Bank for Foreign Economic Activity was reorganized into the "Bank of Development and Foreign Economic Activity" state corporation. This was followed by the Skolkovo Foundation in 2010 and others.

The period 2011–2013 became one of reorganization for Russian development institutions, a time when new players appeared and some tactical corrections were made. The development strategies of the majority of development institutions include development of infrastructure as one of the priorities and, therefore, support is provided precisely in this area.

The decision to establish the Russian Science Foundation (2013), Industrial Development Fund (2014), and Corporation for the Development of Small and Medium-sized Businesses (2015) was basically driven by the current economic situation and the need for active measures in individual areas of state support: science and innovations, industrial policy during import phase-out, and support for the development of small businesses as the most flexible economic agents while under geopolitical pressure, confirmed by falling economic growth rates.

According to experts, there are currently more than 200 development institutions of all known types in Russia. Generally, the necessary conditions hindering the establishment of development institutions are a lack of necessary tools for solving issues of economy modernization and the achievement of long-term socio-economic development goals in Russia, with the scientific and technological development strategy and priority projects in mind.

Conclusions/Recommendations

The conducted study showed that a strategy for achieving target goals is to be developed for all developed and developing economies, simultaneously standing at the start of a new technological breakthrough at a new a stage of postindustrial development. The economic term "development" has many meanings; however, as a process, "development" undoubtedly puts certain additional restrictions on economic mechanisms designed to promote said progress.

The main task of financing through funds and development institutions is the allocation of risks between the state and businesses, and the use of market stimuli in order to efficiently affect important strategic economic development projects. The state generally takes political and administrative risks, as it can manage them much more efficiently than private business. The state also takes some risks concerning the novelty of the proposed projects, which stands in the way of the private sector, effecting them by itself. Private businesses take investment and marketing risks, but only risks they can manage efficiently. Private investments in the project stimulate its effective implementation.

Exclusively state investments are obviously not enough to achieve innovation development, as only private capital is able to stimulate competition in the economy. As such, funds and development institutions have to serve as a tool for implementing state policy of economic modernization at the post-industrial state of development, and have to include:

- Implementation of an anti-crisis policy.
- Activity in the priority areas of modernization.
- Provision of long-term and cheap resources for effecting projects.
- Development of priority sectors.
- Attracting private capital within the framework of public-private partnerships.
- Development of the intermediary sector in capital markets.

References

Braunstein, J. (2017). The Domestic Drivers of State Finance Institutions: Evidence from Sovereign Wealth Funds. *Review of International Political Economy, 24*(6), 980–1003. https://doi.org/10.1080/09692290.2017.1382383.

Braunstein, J., & Ali, A. (2019). New Frontiers in Sovereign Wealth Fund Capitalization. In P. Dobrescu (Ed.), *Development in Turbulent Times. The Many Faces of Inequality Within Europe* (pp. 119–132). Cham: Springer. https://doi.org/10.1007/978-3-030-11361-2.

Cumming, D., Wood, G. E., Filatotchev, I., & Reinecke, J. (2017). *The Oxford Handbook of Sovereign Wealth Funds*. Oxford: Oxford University Press.

Friedman, M. (1982). *Capitalism and Freedom*. Chicago: The University of Chicago Press.

Murtinua, S., & Scalerab, V. G. (2016). Sovereign Wealth Funds' Internationalization Strategies: The Use of Investment Vehicles. *Journal of International Management, 22*(3), 249–264. https://doi.org/10.1016/j.intman.2016.03.003.

Schena, P., & Ali, A. (2017, January–March). Sovereign Wealth Fund Investment in Economic Transformation: Toward an Institutional Framework. *World Economics Journal, 18*(1). https://ssrn.com/abstract=2979528

Smith, A., & Cannan, E. (2003). *The Wealth of Nations*. New York: Bantam Classic.

Sovereign Wealth Fund Institute. (2020). Top 91 Largest Sovereign Wealth Fund Rankings by Total Assets. https://www.swfinstitute.org/fund-rankings/sovereign-wealth-fund

World Economic Forum. (2019). The Global Competitiveness Report 2019. http://www3.weforum.org/docs/WEF_TheGlobalCompetitivenessReport2019.pdf

CHAPTER 3

Managing for the Future: Crisis Management Under Post-industrial Modernization

Zhaklin Sarkisyan and Maya Tikhonova

Introduction

Changes in models of social development have undergone several stages, moving from the initial agricultural (pre-industrial) stage to the industrial stage, and then the post-industrial stage (otherwise known as the "third wave" (Toffler 1980)). The concept of "post-industrialism" (Bell 1999) is currently interpreted as (a) an informational society (which, in reality, is already not the case); (b) as a society founded upon a knowledge economy (which is not in fact a defining feature, since knowledge has always been the driving force behind economic development to some extent); (c) as an economy of innovation (implying that innovations are the main source of economic growth) or as a society of sustainable development (the aim of which is to balance out the many relevant interests); or (d) as a digital economy (implying that a large chunk of data has already been digitalized).

Z. Sarkisyan (✉)
Moscow State Institute of International Relations (MGIMO University), Moscow, Russia
e-mail: g.sarkisyan@odin.mgimo.ru

M. Tikhonova
SOGLASIE Insurance Co. Ltd, Moscow, Russia

J. Kovalchuk (ed.), *Post-Industrial Society*,
https://doi.org/10.1007/978-3-030-59739-9_3

Popular, albeit unexpected, interpretations also include the use of the term "post-economy" (Inozemtsev 1998; Kahn et al. 1976). Real application, however, has already raced ahead of theoretical constructs, and has given rise to new phenomena of changing social structures, which are sufficiently defined as separate economic models but do not as of yet fall into a single economic or social construct. Such phenomena include share economy, which has served to significantly reduce individual consumption (and, thus, the need for it) and conversely to increase the amount of services taking up a big part of the market. However, the key feature of model changes is manufacturing: the demand for its end results is steadily declining, as this is no longer the main source of gross domestic product. A generally accepted criterion for classifying national economies as post-industrial economies is the share of innovations in their GDP. Should the share exceed 50%, this will serve as proof of the economy deserving the classification post-industrial. In general, the number of countries following this GDP structure is increasing, with Bloomberg publishing its Countries' Innovation Index rating annually (Jamrisko et al. 2019). However, concerning the relevance of this study, the growth in innovations of businesses and goods—leading to the number of losers in the innovation race increasing, and with a large number of local crises rising on a microeconomic level—must be taken into account.

The development of "post-industrialism" is intrinsically linked to the concept of "post-modernism", which appeared later as a new ideology for the information society (Lyotard 1984) and which has occurred mainly in the social sphere through its unification of many varied transformations across society. Post-modernism allows controversial economic, political and social phenomena to be viewed as an interconnected, and potentially as a single, object of study. Post-modernism has expanded the possibilities for the coherent study of the many aspects of social activity, as this theory includes such elements in its study process as fragmentation, simulation, ambiguity, and variability; by stressing the destructive influence of "post-industrialism" and the increasing threat of crises on services and manufacturing, those markets arising from instability exist as a normal function.

Many researchers believe post-modernism not to have simply become the basis for certain philosophies, but to have also signified the end of the era of modernization, which occurred over many centuries across the entire world (Inglehart and Welzel 2011).

However, as post-modernism has mostly occurred in the non-material field, we find the rejection of the theory of modernization to be incorrect;

it has not, at the current stage, become an exclusive feature of the new manufacturing and services era. Modernization theory as a whole—not unlike the theories of changing social models (Oleinikov 2016)—must not be equated with the complete domination of manufacturing over consumption; it is wrong to link it with ideas of the market's saturation of manufactured goods, or a decline in demand. Although manufacturers attempt to increasing demand by, for example, quickly updating and reducing the possession period of their goods (when goods become morally obsolete faster than physical wear and tear), consumer behavior is starting to showcase the ineffectiveness of such measures. As a result, the very idea of consumerism is turning into a non-stop update, which brings no satisfaction to the consumer. The reduction of consumption is tightening competition between manufacturers, which could allow the consumer to dominate the markets and to decide upon purchases irrespective of the manufacturing companies' pressure (not including the already limited choice and the existing deficit). The paradigm of the socialization of consumption is also increasing the probability of crisis situations arising for certain manufacturers.

Importantly, putting the concept of post-industrial society into effect in individual national economies, while preserving the need for consumption, is only possible on the condition that several national economies engage in this process while simultaneously changing the structure of the trade balance. Thus, post-industrialist ideas are unlikely to come to fruition without the use of one more concept—the concept of globalism (the global world). It is globalization, after all, that ensures that national economies function properly while reducing production volumes (both in manufacturing and in agriculture). Meanwhile, the construction industry remains "relatively stable"—albeit not due to direct consumption, but rather thanks to the industry having a big share of infrastructure projects. Globalization is making the threat of crisis phenomena even more real for certain businesses, as competition is potentially reaching international levels—something businesses in many countries are simply not ready for.

The combination of post-industrialist factors, the digital transformation, and globalism gives rise to a number of seemingly futuristic issues. What exactly does the future hold for many businesses and organizations? Do the means to influence this future outcome exist at present alongside the prevention of those risks caused by the aforementioned concepts? The modern economic mainstream dictates that it is such ideas for the future that affect decision-making the most.

That being said, a significant number of risks arise from the modernization process itself; the process generates various processes which have already, to some extent, manifested themselves in current affairs. For example, the growth of the service trade may lead to certain production volumes being reduced; the need to search for new digital solutions for monetization models may lead to the appearance of other, non-conventional income sources. A decrease in consumption automatically leads to a decline in a business' economic sustainability despite it maintaining expenses; this may force businesses to reduce the number of workers; this, in turn, leads to crises not just on a micro level, but on a national level as well. Moreover, the instability of the new economic model leads to the making of new organizational and financial decisions that are flawed, which may, in turn, lead to bankruptcy. The process of cutting expenses due to technological updates is especially important, since it might lead to a risk of bankruptcy due to additional personnel issues. This concerns not just staff cuts, but also the consumers pressuring businesses to cut costs or to make additional expenses previously imposed on the consumer (e.g. in e-commerce), which also leads to significant risks.

Traditionally, crisis management (anti-crisis management in Russia) was the tool used to solve those business problems that would otherwise lead to worse indicators and a threat of bankruptcy, with two courses of action available: (1) either a number of procedures would be conducted, aimed at getting the business out of the negative situation, (2) or a number of preventive measures would be initiated, aimed at not letting businesses fall into turbulent times in the first place. The appearance of crisis management allows speculation that it might be possible to devise methods, models, and tools for the purposes of compensating future risks in management. These specific features of crisis management, being in the most demand, have become the basis for this chapter.

Methodology

The futuristic value of current management solutions, and the degree to which they prevent future risks, depends on the set of tools used to achieve their strategic purposes (Pnevmatikoudi and Stavrinoudis 2016). It is possible to attribute the need and the possibility of utilizing next-generation tools to the appearance of new anti-crisis management technology at every level of the economy, as well as to economic processes being accompanied by informational and analytical solutions based on predictive analytics.

Providing the results of these analytics for the purposes of preparing a decision on including all the tools in the base portfolio is most convenient for strategic decisions based on a matrix approach which allows anti-crisis management tools to be compared in pairs while still taking into account the dynamics (or the force) of the influences.

Whether modelling or prognosis is more preferable is, as of yet, an unresolved issue around modern trends (concerning the competition between modeling and prognosis in the digital decision-making platforms of the future); this demonstrates that the methods utilized in this area are in dire need of improvement.

The use of the matrix method for formulating scenarios allows the problem of including situational modeling into the crisis management toolkit to be solved; this in turn allows integral evaluations to be formed around the efficiency of the decisions across the various functional areas of the organization's activity—from financial management to consumers' loyalty, from procurement management to designing new products and services. Such evaluations can determine what has a higher risk of crisis situations occurring due to the modernization processes.

One necessary component of study methods applied to crisis management is the organizations' life cycle theory, according to which the consecutive stages of development may occur in a similar manner for different companies, which allows of the similarities in problems arising during these stages to be seen. For such models, the sustainability of an organization's development is characterized by the number of tools available in the portfolio, which helps in the transition from one stage to another.

Even now, anti-crisis management tools have already developed beyond traditional concepts (Booth 2015; Coombs 2006; Lachlana et al. 2016). Looking at progressive management tactics from creating sustainable development values (Hart and Milstein 2003; Simanis and Milstein 2012) to reverse innovations (Govindarajan and Ramamurti 2016); from open innovations (Chesbrough 2003) to the colors of change theory (Vermaak and De Caluwe 2018); from social transformation (Li and Solis 2013) to Return of Investment (ROI) pyramids in social networks (Owyang 2010); from "blue economy" (Pauli 2010) to Game Design MDA (Mechanics, Dynamics and Aesthetics (Hunicke et al. 2004))—especially pertaining to sustainable development—a pattern can be seen, in which the aims of the tactics correlate to the reduced probability of future crisis situations. The use of comparative analysis, tool selection, and future solutions synthesis is a logical follow-up to the systematization of various approaches.

In order to identify the specific features of "management for future" the following sequence was utilized as a logical construct:

Basic concepts recognized at the current stage of social development → factors affecting basic concepts in terms of development efficiency → an assessment of potential negative elements of the factors occurring in the economy → negative consequences risk assessment → crisis situations forecast on a micro level (businesses and organizations) → comparative analysis of the toolkit → the toolkit application potential assessment to various stages of organizations' development cycle → the inclusion of the tools into the toolkit and crisis management strategies → implementation of the toolkit into organizations' current management structures → prediction of consequences both on the micro and on the macro level of the economy → assessment of the system's sustainability as a whole.

Results

The main result of the study could help to expand an organization's opportunities, to the level of being able to deflect crisis situations; our results identify the required sequence of actions—including both criteria and recommendations—for forming an appropriate toolkit portfolio for managing an organization and identifying such opportunities. Creating a preventive crisis management tool is an appealing idea; however, it has not yet been realized. This is why our hypothesis on forming a toolkit portfolio which corresponds to certain crisis manifestations (not aimed at addressing the crisis itself) remains highly relevant.

In the course of the study, we had to ignore some of the famous classifications of crisis management tools and methods (e.g. application time and sequence classification—anticipative, preventive, reactive, and rehabilitative management; functionality classification—personnel, resources, and costs; state regulation classification—oversight, rehabilitation, provisional management, and bankruptcy proceedings), due to the development of such methods being linked to processing a specific situation for arising at an enterprise. However, within our hypothesis, we speculate that in post-industrial modernization, the effects of which will be felt by most enterprises, the methods of counteracting business sustainability threats must be included into every manager's arsenal in order to minimize the consequences of potential crisis situations, including market exits in certain segments, such as the removal of parts of operational activity. Such an approach does not mean that we are ignoring the classic anti-crisis management procedures in Russia or crisis management procedures adopted in several other countries; we are, however, limiting the study only to the tool applicable at the current management stage.

Systematization of Basic Development Concepts Available at the Current Stage of Social Development

Basing our conclusions on the logical assumption that crisis management is oriented at creating a balance of interactions alongside external factors, the effect of currently available doctrines on the development of social relations, above all economic relations, must firstly be determined.

Apart from the aforementioned theories on post-industrial society, post-modernism, and socio-economic systems modernization, it is also crucial to analyze the knowledge and information digitalization phenomenon, as this leads to the rise of various digital strategies, as well as to platform capitalism (Stepnov and Kovalchuk 2018). Alongside these theories, many variants of crises' cyclical nature concepts, which state that avoiding crises entirely in the modern economic model is impossible, must also be studied. Thus, the main tasks must be viewed in the context of (at least) minimizing the effects of crises on the decreasing fragments of cyclical waves and in the context of solidifying the organization's competitiveness after recovery (on the increasing wave of the cycle).

Although the possibility remains that a crisis can arise from mismanagement and/or from miscalculations by social group choices (which is very common at the current stage of social development), the personal criterion of a crisis is, regardless, much less prevalent than the objective criterion, which is linked to a replacement of the functional model being necessary.

No less important (in terms of potential threats to businesses) is the concept of modern development called "technological leadership doctrine". This is based not only on determining development priorities, but also on identifying selective research and development support, which is then brought to life in development programs, institutions, and mechanism updates (OECD 2018). The Organization for Economic Co-operation and Development (OECD) has identified about 40 future key production technologies, basing its study on the fact that it is these technologies that will allow adequate reactions to global challenges and technological leadership to be secured.

The sustainable development doctrine is also becoming more and more relevant. For example, it has been statistically confirmed (with China's food industry as an example) that leading enterprises in the field of corporate social responsibility are less likely to end up in a crisis situation if their management is more efficient (Qijun and Cong 2010).

In general, taking the "self-fulfilling prophecies" theory into account, management structures aiming for future success should adopt the projected consequences systematization and proposed concepts monitoring and the integration tools for the purpose of forming a single knowledge base.

Identifying Future Factors Affecting the Adoption of Basic Concepts (as Well as Determining the Potential Negative Effects)

One of modern society's defining features, which has served as a basis for objective conclusions on the need to study social development doctrines, is the fact that Bell's predictions on the future post-industrial social format have come true, and the current socio-economic relations model actively seeks to turn this format into reality rather than to counteract it. In terms of crisis management, a conclusion can be made that if the consequences of post-industrialization are known, then there is (and has been) a possibility (not a hypothetical one by any means) to identify the main features of this economic system's social transformation and to speculate on influence factors. Such factors include, for example, the conclusion that "servicization" is the basis for a share economy, and that the car industry will be greatly affected by a decrease in purchases and an increase in concurrent use. In this case, car holdings have to take this factor into account while preparing their strategies and to create new opportunities (in particular, retaining ownership of produced cars and leasing them to new business forms) instead. Real estate markets are experiencing a similar problem with developers going back to leasing real estate instead of selling it. Outsourcing has also become much more significant in new concepts (or, broadly speaking, sourcing (Stapran 2018)), which leads to changes in added value chains. Transactional cost cuts are also growing in relevance, which leads to changes in expense structures on production and providing services.

Determining said factors as new doctrines appear is a heuristic task; it has a lower forecast lag rate than the doctrines' effect assessment, and may be based on already established facts, which can either be accepted by society or not.

Negative effects assessment cannot be performed without situational (more often scenario) analysis and crisis situations forecast on a micro level. It should be noted that, based on the definition of a crisis as a set of unforeseen and unpredictable circumstances which threaten an organization's priorities (Hermann 1963), it is either time for decision-making or making resources available that are the key limits.

Comparative Analysis of the Toolkit and Assessment of Its Application to Various Stages of an Organization's Development Cycle

A number of researchers and practitioners in the field of anti-crisis management (Ryakhovskaya and Kovan 2015) believe that crisis management methods are a special set of knowledge, and that a special place is reserved for anti-crisis management as an established approach among management sciences in Russia. In terms of our hypothesis we allow for the existence of special crisis management methods, but in studying management for a future concept we have to acknowledge the validity of the theory that traditional management methods also have to be included alongside special crisis management methods without separating these methods into different areas of knowledge. First and foremost, this is linked to the unity of corporate governance as exercised by management structures currently in use, like specially appointed or selected by the proprietors. Even in the case of a crisis manager being appointed, he or she will not be able to perform his or her tasks while utilizing exclusively crisis management methods; he or she must also be able to combine and master traditional management methods.

Besides, a change in management priorities—from raising functionality efficiency to ensuring sustainable development—also serves as a decent basis for combining the tools and methods of both traditional and crisis management. Meanwhile, even researchers (Ryakhovskaya and Kovan 2015) who defend the right of anti-crisis management to independence agree that different crisis situation prevention methods may be utilized by regular management as well, going so far as to reach the stage of negative factors taking over.

In a comparative analysis, not only must the possibility of counteracting future negative affects be taken into account, but also the stages of an organization's life cycle. This is why one necessary step in forming a toolkit portfolio is the correlation of the aforementioned tools to current and future life cycle stages. This recommendation also requires correctly structuring an organization's life cycle. The life cycle development model has not experienced changes for a long time.

In order to make an argumentative choice of tools, two approaches may be used: one must either form comparison matrixes for each life cycle stage or include the life cycle stages directly into the matrixes. Each of the approaches poses certain disadvantages, and a choice in favor of either of them must be made with the required degree of detail in mind. If the second approach provides sufficient detail (being more useful for small- and medium-sized businesses), then this approach should take precedence.

Including Tools and Strategies into a Crisis Management Portfolio and Implementing the Toolkit into Organizations' Current Management Structures

The adoption of the selected tools must be based not only on their usage potential but also on their usage possibility. It is at this stage that the organization's staff must accept and ensure the selected toolkits. For example, implementing Agile methodology at early development stages means it will be widely accepted; however, there are no known examples of such a methodology being implemented in crisis situations. We can, however, claim that the implemented Agile methodology will be useful for lowering crisis consequences.

Conclusions/Recommendations

Management for the future, possessing a toolkit portfolio with elements of crisis management, is, undeniably, a highly promising model for future business activities. The uncertainties of the future, due to many social relations having undergone transformation (including digital interaction), require mastering the new toolkit which evaluates not just the possibility of organizations getting out of crises but crisis prevention as well. One feature of our hypothesis is the comparison of contradicting phenomena based on a contextual approach, allowing different spheres of post-industrial influence on business activity to be compared in simpler terms. The supposed formation of a toolkit portfolio with the ability to overcome the consequences of crises would allow management to expand opportunities about future consequence management.

References

Bell, D. (1999). *The Coming Post-Industrial Society*. Moscow: Academia.

Booth, S. A. (2015). *Crisis Management Strategy: Competition and Change in Modern Enterprises*. Abingdon: Routledge.

Chesbrough, H. W. (2003). *Open Innovation: The New Imperative for Creating and Profiting from Technology*. Boston: Harvard Business Press.

Coombs, T. W. (2006). The Protective Powers of Crisis Response Strategies: Managing Reputational Assets During a Crisis. *Journal of Promotion Management, 12*(3–4), 241–260. https://doi.org/10.1300/J057v12n03_13.

Govindarajan, V., & Ramamurti, R. (2016). Reverse Innovation in Emerging Markets. In J. Haar & R. Ernst (Eds.), *Innovation in Emerging Markets* (pp. 140–157). Hampshire: Springer. https://doi.org/10.1057/9781137480293_8.

Hart, S. L., & Milstein, M. (2003). Creating Sustainable Value. *Academy of Management Executive, 17*(2), 56–69. https://doi.org/10.5465/AME.2003.10025194.

Hermann, C. F. (1963). Some Consequences of Crisis Which Limit the Viability of Organizations. *Administrative Science, 8*, 61–82.

Hunicke, R., LeBlanc, M., & Zubek, R. (2004). MDA: A Formal Approach to Game Design and Research. *Proceedings of the Nineteenth National Conference on Artificial Intelligence*.

Inglehart, R., & Welzel, K. (2011). Modernization, Cultural Change and Democracy. In *The Sequence of Human Development*. Moscow: New Publishing House.

Inozemtsev, V. L. (1998). *The Constitution of the Post-Economic State. Post-Industrial Theories and Post-Economic Trends in the Contemporary World*. New York: Ashgate Publishing.

Jamrisko, M., Miller, L. J., & Lu, W. (2019). These Are the World's Most Innovative Countries. Available at: https://www.bloomberg.com/news/articles/2019-01-22/germany-nearly-catches-korea-as-innovation-champ-u-s-rebounds?fbclid=IwAR35I5FBXBWIZB5lIwO7E9qWNJ%2D%2DoUDw09bO1pZaXw4gOu9CD3R_NPca6w0. Accessed 6 Jan 2020.

Kahn, H., Brown, W., & Martel, L. (1976). *The Next 200 Years: A Scenario for America and the World*. New York: Morrow.

Lachlana, K. A., Spence, P. R., Lin, X., Najarian, K., & Del Greco, V. (2016). Social Media and Crisis Management: CERC, Search Strategies, and Twitter Content. *Computers in Human Behavior, 54*, 647–652. https://doi.org/10.1016/j.chb.2015.05.027.

Li, C., & Solis, B. (2013). *The Seven Success Factors of Social Business Strategy*. San Francisco: Jossey-Bass.

Lyotard, J.-F. (1984). *The Postmodern Condition*. Manchester: Manchester University Press.

OECD. (2018). Main Science and Technology Indicators., *2018*(1). https://doi.org/10.1787/msti-v2018-1-en. OECD Publishing, Paris.

Oleinikov, Y. V. (2016). The Main Trends of Post-Industrial Modernizing. *History and Modernity, 1*, 133–153.

Owyang, J. (2010, December 13). Framework: The Social Media ROI Pyramid. *Web Strategist*. Available at: https://web-strategist.com/blog/2010/12/13/framework-the-social-media-roi-pyramid/. Accessed 6 Jan 2020.

Pauli, G. (2010). *Blue Economy -10 Years, 100 Innovations, 100 Million Jobs*. Idaho: Paradigm Pubns.

Pnevmatikoudi, K., & Stavrinoudis, T. (2016). Classification of Hotel Performance Measurement Indicators Presented in International Scientific Research. *European Journal of Tourism Research, 12*, 82–98.

Qijun, J., & Cong, Z. (2010). An Empirical Study on the Crisis Management about Food Enterprises Based on Corporate Social Responsibility. *Proceedings of International Conference on Management and Service Science, IEEE, Wuhan, China*. https://doi.org/10.1109/ICMSS.2010.5576484.

Ryakhovskaya, A. N., & Kovan, S. E. (2015). Crisis Management: Modern Concept and Basic Tools. *Management Science, 3*, 45–55.

Simanis, E., & Milstein, M. (2012). Back to Business Fundamentals: Making "Bottom of the Pyramid" Relevant to Core Business. *Field Actions Science Report, 4*, 82–88.

Stapran, D. A. (2018). On the Role and Prospects of Outsourcing in the Russian Economy. *Bulletin of the Moscow State University*, Series 6, Economy, *5*, 21–32.

Stepnov, I. M., & Kovalchuk, J. A. (2018). Platform Capitalism as the Source of Digital Rentier's Superprofit. *MGIMO Review of International Relations, 4*(61), 107–124. https://doi.org/10.24833/2071-8160-2018-4-61-107-124.

Toffler, A. (1980). *The Third Wave*. New York: Morrow.

Vermaak, H., & De Caluwe, L. (2018). The Colors of Change Revisited: Situating and Describing the Theory and its Practical Applications. *Research in Organizational Change and Development, 26*, 167–216. https://doi.org/10.1108/S0897-301620180000026005.

CHAPTER 4

High Technologies for Smart City Development

Sergey Kamolov, Kirill Teteryatnikov, and Vladimir Podolskiy

Introduction

Urbanization has become major trend of the twenty-first century both for Russia and globally. Megacities across the world accumulate enormous human and technical resources. Currently, the world's population is close to 7.7 billion people, 55% of which (4.2 billion) already are urban residents. According to UN forecasts, up to 2050, the world population will continue to grow. The population of India will count a surplus of 416 million people, China will register a surplus of 255 million, and in Nigeria 189 million people more (The UN 2018).

S. Kamolov (✉)
Moscow State Institute of International Relations (MGIMO University), Moscow, Russia

K. Teteryatnikov
ANO Research and Expert Analysis Institute of Vnesheconombank, The Bank for Development and Foreign Economic Affairs, Moscow, Russia

V. Podolskiy
Technical University of Munich, Munich, Germany

J. Kovalchuk (ed.), *Post-Industrial Society*,
https://doi.org/10.1007/978-3-030-59739-9_4

Today, the most urbanized regions are North America (in 2018, 82% of its population lived in cities), Latin America and the Caribbean (81%), Europe (74%), and Oceania (68%). The level of urbanization in Asia is now approaching 50%. In contrast, Africa remains mostly rural, with only 43% of its population living in urban areas. In the future, by 2050, according to various estimates, urban population will constitute between 66% and 70% of the world's population (6.7 billion people, according to UN forecasts).

Most of the residential and utilities services are consumed by urban people, which leads to multiple problems with the environment. That's why large European cities today try to integrate into the EU project AI4Cities using artificial intelligence (AI) as a solution for cutting down greenhouse gas emissions in the cities. Only in February 2020, six cities—Helsinki, Amsterdam, Copenhagen, Paris Region, Stavanger, and Tallinn—became participants of this three-year EU-funded project, bringing together leading European cities looking for high-technology (HiTech) solutions to reduce their greenhouse gas emissions and meet their climate commitments (Six European cities join project to use AI in move towards carbon neutrality, Feb. 2020).

In 2020, three-quarters of the Russia's population live in cities, generating not only a large share of the country's GDP, but also new models of interaction between the population and the government. However, it is obvious that the growth of urban population entails multiple problems associated with the need to provide citizens with a high standard of living, implying well-paid jobs. Cities play a key role in the Russian economy, which comes along with challenges that impede their effective development: accelerated deterioration of urban infrastructure (more than 60% on average in the country), insufficient budgetary spending, and urban environmental problems. Those challenges call for establishment of sound relationships among municipal authorities, business community, and citizens to ensure sustainable development of society, and eventually eliminate widespread corruption.

These problems may be fixed substantially by introducing a new model for the development of Russian cities—smart cities based on human capital, innovation, and high technologies (Smart Cities – Beyond the Hype 2019). The model implies gradual transformation of cities' governance into an intelligent system embracing all major areas of municipal life: jobs, health, education, energy, transport, resource management, and urban space. Increased workloads and new requirements for the efficiency of urban infrastructure make it vital to intellectualize it. Therefore, a smart city today is not a luxury, but an indispensable condition for boosting economic growth. In this regard, HiTech or smart technologies will play an increasingly vital role for developing local economies (Smart cities to generate 20 trillion USD in economic benefits by 2026, April 2019).

Methodology

Academic research is supposed to effectively support evolution of smart public governance from smart cities to smart regions and then to smart nation, accelerating the national economy growth on various levels. Sharing the best experience of national development of smart cities will predictably lead to sounder and more elaborated models of smart governance as opposed to initiatives utilizing a trial-and-error approach alone. Thus, our research objective was to find new HiTech solutions to various sectors of municipal economy which will contribute to accelerating economic development of the country, offering a bottom-up model of strategic growth based on international and Russian experience (Smart Cities: Digital Solutions for a More Livable Future, June 2018).

A multidisciplinary approach in the qualitative data analysis embracing strategic management, public governance, international and national law, and economics was used to cover all areas of scientific interest and draw necessary conclusions. We also used the experience of organizing cluster associations in the industrial sector of the economy, including high-tech industries (Stepnov et al. 2019), to identify the connecting elements of digital interactions and apply them to form the concept of urban development. To achieve the objectives of the study, that is, making substantiated recommendations of the subject, we have used such methods as comparison, statistics, and content analysis.

Results

Significant investments are made into smart technologies development across the world. The impact of smart city technologies on economic development and gross domestic product (GDP) growth is supposed to affect three dimensions or phases: open data policies: incremental GDP of close to US$1 trillion over the next decade; public investments multiplier effect: incremental GDP of US$10 trillion over the next decade; structural smart urban economy growth: recurring, sustainable growth of 2.8% by

2026; US$10 trillion incremental GDP generated in the next ten years (Role of Smart Cities for Economic Development ABI Research 2018).

Large investments in smart technologies have been made in Russia. The key objectives of smart technologies in Russia are to improve public services to citizens, reduce costs, save energy and increase energy efficiency, and integrate and develop renewable energy sources in the urban environment. We have identified the most important areas where the smart technologies have proved to lead to considerable improvements.

Energy Supply

Smart power supply networks (smart grids) were the first to be used for the intellectualization of energy supply aimed at intelligent generation, transmission, and distribution of electricity. Smart networks are saturated with modern diagnostic tools, electronic control systems, algorithms, and technical devices (e.g., short-circuit current limiters for superconducting lines). The introduction of this technology in the city reduces losses in the transmission of electricity from the generator to the consumer, increases the reliability of power supply, provides additional opportunities for optimal redistribution of energy flows, and reduces peak loads.

New opportunities for the development of smart networks will appear with the development and implementation of cost-effective energy storage devices and the development of electric transport and the corresponding charging infrastructure. Investment programs of Russian network companies include the introduction of intelligent accounting systems in networks. The amount of funding for such projects is now up to 2% of the total amount of the program.

The introduction of smart electricity meters with remote reading will improve the quality of service and reduce commercial losses for network companies. Legislative initiatives are already being prepared to encourage the installation of such metering devices. In the future, technologies for individual automatic weather control will become popular. Thermal energy savings during their implementation are 20–30%.

Urban Lighting

Smart city lighting systems provide light on the streets of the city in the right quality and quantity, at the right time, and for a minimum of investment. That is why smart cities choose energy-saving incandescent lamps.

The potential for energy saving when replacing incandescent lamps with energy-saving ones is up to 90%. Additional savings are achieved through the introduction of automation (motion sensors) and timely switching-off and -on of lighting, reducing the load.

The use of Light-emitting diodes (LEDs) in urban lighting results in energy savings of up to 60%. The main problem of making the new lighting system operational is its high initial cost. The system pays off only after a certain period of time by saving energy. This is not always beneficial for city authorities due to insufficient local budgets and legal regulations. Preferential loans to municipalities for these socially important projects can be one of the ways to attract investment in lighting modernization.

Transportation

To improve the energy efficiency of cities, it is also important to introduce intelligent transport systems. Optimal road traffic may reduce the city's energy consumption by 5–15%. One of the leaders is Moscow, where the corresponding program has already been adopted (Moscow as a Smart City 2019). It includes switching to intelligent traffic light management, giving priority to public transport, dynamic traffic speed control, and routing to prevent traffic jams. Today, every traffic light in Moscow is equipped with an optical channel, allowing to process huge amounts of data. Big data accumulated via traffic sensors serves as a basis for strategic municipal planning of transport system development. Sensors also detect various traffic violations.

The sensors are part of a modernization program of Moscow's current road network systems and have the potential to link up to the city's traffic and control center systems to provide data in real time, which would enable the Moscow city government to better balance demand and improve the process of air and water congestion management. The sensors are also able to detect people walking and other types of traffic, including cars, trucks, motorcyclists, and buses. The same system has been successfully implemented in London (Transport for London Expands Use of Traffic Sensors Using AI, Feb. 2020).

The electronic payment system for public transport is also one of smart city technologies. This system calculates the discount if a person often travels by public transport and constantly uses the same card for payment. The technology has already been implemented in many major Russian cities—Moscow, Yekaterinburg, and Tyumen.

Information Systems

A modern city consists of many subsystems—transport, telecommunications, electricity and water supply systems, and so on—that interact with each other. A comprehensive information system is necessary to control all city systems' functioning, ensure the safety of each resident, receive and archive information about important events, and promptly provide it to the interested entities. It must be able to accumulate, combine, analyze, and group data from multiple sources. This system is the "Safe City" complex, which has been successfully implemented by many local administrations. This is a system of software, hardware and organizational measures to ensure video supervision and technical security in public places (schools, medical institutions, etc.) and management of housing and communal services and other facilities in the modern city.

Internet of Things (IoT)

According to McKinsey Global Institute, the IoT could have a potential economic value of between US$3.9 trillion and US$11.1 trillion annually by 2025, while in the Gulf Cooperation Council (GCC) region, a report by A.T. Kearney found that the value of the IoT solutions market in 2025 would amount to US$11 billion, with a potential economic value of almost US$160 billion.

The Internet of Things (IoT) is becoming part of our day-to-day lives. But still many Russian cities do not have the technology required to run even the most basic of these devices, let alone those that require state-of-the-art, 5G technology (IoT in a 4G/5G World: A Survey of How CSPS Are Preparing to Transition to this New World 2018). Primarily, they lack the funding necessary to implement technological upgrades and lay essential infrastructure. With budgetary cuts in all areas of government, finding a solution to this smart technology deficit is critical for the future of infrastructure in cities. Connecting authorities, public organizations, and businesses to the Internet should be the first objective to be resolved in the smart city, as it will allow to

- make an appointment with a doctor via the Internet;
- vote for city projects on the Active Citizen website;
- submit a request about a problem in the house or yard and monitor its implementation through the "Your City" portal;

- send documents for passport registration, pay for electricity or phone, pay taxes via the Internet, pay for parking via phone; and
- report incorrect parking or other public violations via a special app on a smartphone.

Free Wi-Fi in the city will make all municipal services available for the residents at any time and place. The new 5G broadband Internet will further improve the municipal governance and services.

It is important for municipal authorities to understand that smart technologies are not a fashionable novelty, but necessary a tool for solving problems. Many of the technologies will eventually soon become not only more sophisticated but also more affordable. For example, over the past three years, the price of LEDs in Russia has decreased three times, and of solar panels, seven times. Therefore, today the authorities of many Russian cities are ready to start mass implementation of smart technologies that have until recently been considered a pipe dream.

Advanced results can be achieved by using HiTech, which have already proved their efficiency internationally. For example, the 2020 Smart 50 Awards honor projects in five categories: community engagement, digital transformation, smart mobility, urban infrastructure, and urban operations. Applicants must have achieved results at a municipal scale or equivalent to qualify. These projects exemplify innovation and concrete influence in their communities as a result of HiTech implementation (Smart 50 Awards 2020).

We would also welcome Russia's more active participation (along with other Brazil, Russia, India, China and South Africa (BRICS) states) in the G20 Global Smart Cities Alliance on Technology Governance. Founded in 2019—in conjunction with the G20 Summit in Osaka, Japan—the organization has the goal of creating global norms and policy standards for the use of connected devices in public spaces. Partners include Japan, the Kingdom of Saudi Arabia, the Smart City Mission of India, Cities for All, Cities Today Institute, the Commonwealth Local Government Forum, the Commonwealth Sustainable Cities Network, Connected Places Catapult, Digital Future Society, ICLEI—Local Governments for Sustainability, the International Telecommunication Union, Open and Agile Smart Cities, the Smart City Expo World Congress, United Cities and Local Governments, What Works Cities, the World Economic Forum, and World Enabled (India Joins G20 Global Smart Cities Alliance on Technology Governance, Oct. 2019).

Conclusions

We understand that Russian megacities (there are 16 of them with a population at least 1 million or more) have more access to the entire range of smart technologies, while small residential communities have limited individual solutions. Today, there are about 100,000 settlements across the country with a population of less than 200 people. These citizens have no access to high-quality infrastructure—education services, energy, telecommunications, healthcare, and banking.

A small city model implies that standard modular smart tech solutions may be implemented: autonomous power supply, distant education, telemedicine, and postal and banking services using modern information technologies. Standards of service level have to be established for small communities. Then, if federal, regional, and municipal authorities actively work together with infrastructure ITC companies, these communities will be able to enjoy similar service level as megacities in terms of smart technology.

Surveys of Russian cities' officials, telecom executives, and systems have demonstrated that the key challenges in creating a comprehensive smart city strategy are: funding, partner search, and data management. These challenges will critically affect the success of smart technology implementation. Funding is the most difficult issue due to the significant amount of investment required and the need to develop a unique funding structure for each individual smart city project. Upgrading urban infrastructure through integrated implementation of smart technologies not only is a high-cost project from a financial point of view, but also requires a creative approach in developing short-and long-term goals. To solve this problem, cities need to implement reliable business models that allow them to attract private funds.

The specifics of financing smart city HiTech development projects are determined by the presence of technology risks deterring potential investors generally focused on long-term projects. As a result, financing of smart city development projects is tightly concerned with the development of a comprehensive strategic plan that allows all involved parties to maximize the benefits of the project and ensure that investors are willing to participate in its development. Smart city development projects should be implemented by municipal authorities in a step-by-step approach, starting with the assessment of existing assets, selecting optimal business model, choosing timeline and methods of gaining financial benefits from the project, and planning financial public and private financing.

Nevertheless, "half of the initial investment made by the public sector could generate a positive return, whether in direct savings or opportunities to produce revenue" (McKinsey Global Institute Report 2018). That is why we believe that special focus should be made on helping city authorities build partnerships in order to understand, prioritize, and address their risks and potentials in four ways:

- Design roadmaps enabling private businesses to participate in city development planning processes.
- Establish HiTech project incubators to develop projects maximizing the resilience impact and ensuring cities and business communities have access to technical, financial, and project preparation expertise.
- Create regulatory sand boxes allowing city authorities to test new smart technologies before taking decisions about their implementation in the city's economy.
- Develop end-to-end technologies offering cross-functional and cross-industry solutions. Competent use of end-to-end technologies will ultimately stimulate improvement in the quality of life, comfort of the urban environment, and management of various sectors of the urban economy while reducing resource consumption. For example, geo-information technologies and ultra-precise navigation, together with 5G, are the basis for the emergence of unmanned public transport. Digital technologies for supporting decision-making and processing unstructured data, as well as machine learning, are needed to create smart road infrastructure management systems that include traffic forecasting, smart traffic lights, and even fatigue control for bus drivers.

To sum it up, a smart city is an innovative city that implements complex high-technology solutions aimed at achieving the highest possible quality of resource management and providing services in order to create a sustainable environment for life and business activity of now and future generations. In the nearest future, smart cities will become the basis for smart governments (Dupont Jonathan. The Smart State 2018), bringing along new challenges of global income disparity.

References

Dupont, J. (2018, May 29). *The Smart State*. Redesigning Government in the Era of Intelligent Services. https://policyexchange.org.uk/publication/the-smart-state/

India Joins G20 Global Smart Cities Alliance on Technology Governance. (2019). https://smartcitiesconnect.org/india-joins-g20-global-smart-cities-alliance-on-technology-governance/

IoT in a 4G/5G World: A Survey of How CSPS Are Preparing to Transition to This New World. (2018). https://www.chordant.io/white_papers/iot-in-a-4g%2D%2D5g-world-a-survey-of-how-csps-are-preparing-to-transition-to-this-new-world

Moscow as a Smart City Development Programme Till 2030. (2019). https://www.mos.ru/2030/. [in Rus.].

Role of Smart Cities for Economic Development. ABI Research. (2018). https://www.chordant.io/white_papers/abi-research-role-of-smart-cities-for-economic-development

Six European Cities Join Project to Use AI in Move Towards Carbon Neutrality. (2020). https://www.intelligenttransport.com/transport-news/95084/six-european-cities-join-project-to-use-ai-in-move-towards-carbon-neutrality/

Smart 50 Awards. (2020). https://spring.smartcitiesconnect.org/Smart50Awards/

Smart Cities – Beyond the Hype. Whitepaper. (2019). https://www.smartcities-world.net/whitepapers/whitepapers/smart-cities%2D%2D-beyond-the-hype

Smart Cities to Generate 20 Trillion USD in Economic Benefits by 2026. (2019). https://channels.theinnovationenterprise.com/articles/smart-cities-to-generate-20-trillion-in-economic-benefits-by-2026

Smart Cities: Digital Solutions for a More Livable Future. McKinsey Report. (2018). https://www.mckinsey.com/~/media/McKinsey/Industries/Capital%20Projects%20and%20Infrastructure/Our%20Insights/Smart%20cities%20Digital%20solutions%20for%20a%20more%20livable%20future/MGI-Smart-Cities-Full-Report.ashx

Stepnov, I. M., Kovalchuk, J. A., & Gorchakova, E. A. (2019). On Assessing the Efficiency of Intracluster Interaction for Industrial Enterprises. *Studies on Russian Economic Development, 30*(3), 346–354. https://doi.org/10.1134/S107570071903016X.

The 2018 United Nations Revision of World Urbanization Prospects. (2018). https://www.un.org/development/desa/en/news/population/2018-revision-of-world-urbanization-prospects.html

Transport for London Expands Use of Traffic Sensors Using AI. (2020). https://smartcitiesconnect.org/transport-for-london-expands-use-of-traffic-sensors-using-ai/

CHAPTER 5

Digital State: Creation Through Project-Functional Structure of Public Administration

Vladimir Osipov

Introduction

Strengthening the executive branch entails a change in the democratic regime to an autocratic one. A good example here is the French experience of changing the balance of power between the branches of power since 1958 due to a restriction on the parliamentary initiative. So, gradually the French parliament was limited in its legislative activity, since its initiatives were blocked by the executive branch, and the initiatives of the executive branch, on the contrary, substantially prevailed in the legislative process. So, in 1970, out of 118 bills introduced by the government, 87 (about 75%) were adopted, and out of 709 legislative proposals initiated by the parliament, 18 (2.4%)[1] were adopted. The reasons for this

[1] Demichel, A., Demichel, F., Piquemal M. (1975). Institutions et pouvoir en France. Une traduction institutionelle du capitalism monopoliste d'etat. Paris, Editions Sociales.

V. Osipov (✉)
Moscow State Institute of International Relations (MGIMO University), Moscow, Russia
e-mail: vs.ossipov@inno.mgimo.ru

J. Kovalchuk (ed.), *Post-Industrial Society*,
https://doi.org/10.1007/978-3-030-59739-9_5

weakening of the institution of legislative power were: the majority of Gaullists and Republicans in the parliament, a restriction on the rights of parliamentarians to introduce legislative initiatives that could lead to a reduction in government revenues or an increase in government spending, a restriction on parliamentary debates (the government determined the agenda of the parliamentary meetings) and the organization of parliamentary debates at the request of the government, and other restrictions. The strengthening of presidential power in France in the middle of the last century has corresponding consequences today. The strengthening of executive power at the turn of the century has become widespread (China, Russia, Turkey, the United States, India, ex-USSR countries, Hungary, Poland, etc.). The quality of a policy and its effectiveness depend on the real head of the state.

From the point of view of enhancing economic development, "state efficiency" consists in the formation of effective mechanisms of public administration, that is, those mechanisms that contribute to the formation of a favorable institutional environment for business.

Methodology

The methodology of institutional analysis and the general theory of systems were used in the chapter to identify and justify the connections of elements of systems. An interdisciplinary approach was also used in this research because institutional theory is dualistic due to legal and economic sciences. Legal science laid the theoretical foundations of institutionalism, and economic science contributed to the implementation of the ideas of institutionalism in the practice of state formation and regulation of public relations.

The transition to a service state based on the principles of new public management (Hood 1991) cannot be carried out stepwise. A gradual progressive regime of reforming the public administration system is necessary so that the digital state can take form as an entrenched institution.

For nowadays, the efficiency of the state is synonymous to institutional efficiency. It means that institutions of the state must be useful for business development. At the same time, business development is based on freedom and human rights, as history has shown.

Anyway, the old bureaucratic state with a linear-functional structure has to be changed under the pressure of globalization.

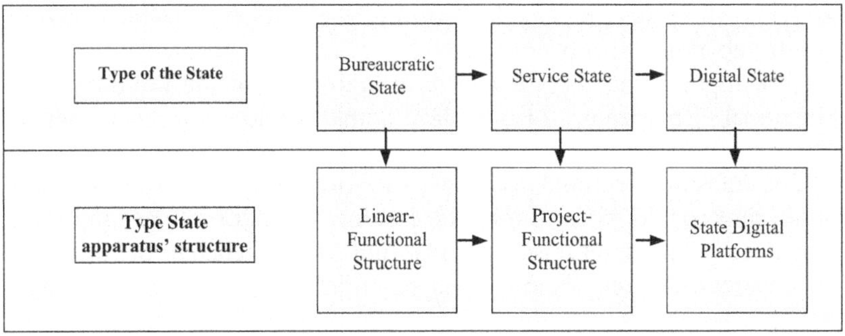

Fig. 5.1 Evolution of the types of state and the structure of the state apparatus

Globalization not only supports global market harmonization, but also strengthens competition between states for investment, human capital, innovations, and so on. This competition between states plays the role of a billiard cue for institutional reforms to make national jurisdiction more competitive than others (Osipov 2019). And in this way the most effective instrument becomes simplification of public administration and transition from process management to a problem-solving system. Problem solving requires a clear identification of the input data, a mechanism for developing and making decisions, and its implementation in reality (implementation). This approach is possible using the project-functional structure of the state apparatus, which was created by the author (Osipov 2016).

If the state apparatus is reformed in this way, we can create a possibility to move to the digital state. Why? Because the state apparatus learns to solve problems and present the results of its activities; it is trained to a certain behavior and a certain order of solving problems. Without these skills, the digital state as the end point of the paradigm is impossible.

The logic of reform fits into Fig. 5.1.

Result

The transition to the project structure of public administration is designed to ensure such a transformation of institutions in which formal and informal institutions receive an impetus for synchronous modernization, that is, with minimal gaps between themselves. The synchronization of formal and informal institutions in the public administration system contributes to the creation of a predictable institutional environment, which is favorable for economic turnover.

This important effect is achieved through the formation of design and functional structures of public administration in departments (Osipov 2016).

The transition to the project structure of public administration, obviously, aims to add dynamism to the existing system of public administration due to the establishment of institutions. The change of the public administration system from a linear-functional organization to a design-functional organization is carried out using appropriate institutions.

The transition to the design and functional management structure of public authorities requires that civil servants understand the transformation of the product of labor. If there were a managerial decision in existing linear-functional structures for managing the product of work of a civil servant, then in the design and functional structure, the product of labor of a civil servant is the result of the project. In the logic of system analysis, we observe here a transition from a process to a result, more precisely, from disparate processes to their systemic set, ending with a specific result. Actually, just such a logic is laid down in the regulatory documents governing the implementation of administrative reform, when numerical indicators become decisive for assessing the performance of employees. Due to such projects and their results, it is possible to change the institutional environment and build relations in it that contribute to economic development in the context of the indicated external constraints.

The outstanding economist F. von Hayek speaks about the need to change the role of the State in his article "Competition as a Discovery Procedure", where he notes that no matter how strange this may seem at first glance, a high growth rate sometimes indicates not so much good politics in the present but bad politics in the past. Consequently, in countries that have already reached a high level of development, there is no reason to expect the same significant growth rates that countries have achieved for some time, where previously the efficient use of resources was long held back by legislative and institutional barriers.

It is important to note that the state as an institution is also significant in economic and theoretical research. Thus, the libertarian economist L. von Mises argued that the state is not only evil, but also represents a necessary and beneficial institution, without which it is impossible to develop and maintain sustainable social cooperation and civilization. At the same time, state bodies should change the forms of interaction with business and society for the benefit of all three of these institutions, since the state can be as strong partner, and also as oppressor of business and society.

It is important to note that the value of such comparative advantages as natural resources, climatic conditions, as well as acquired as a result of its previous historical development, such as the technological level, production experience in modern conditions are significantly reduced. Otherwise the value of such a competitive factor as the institutional structure of the state is growing. That is, the importance of the quality of public administration, and not its strengthening or weakening, is a decisive factor in the competitiveness of the state.

The enlarged or the most important objective elements that make up the institution of the state, as is customary, are the population (nation), a separate territory, and public authority, which has the right to establish the rule of law in this territory and for this nation. It should be ascertained whether the decomposition of one of the constituent objective elements of the institution of the state leads to decomposition of the state. In other words, all three objective elements of the state allow us to assort the existence of the state, or some of them may be lost, while the state retains its significance as an institution. Let us try to analyze what will happen to the state if each of its objective elements is excluded.

A serious omission of Russian reformers was an underestimation of the interests of society and, by and large, unsuccessful attempts to form civil society institutions. The question of taking into account the interests of society, and not just the state, was considered by F.A. von Hayek. He distinguished three representative bodies: one for the occupation exclusively of the Constitution (it will be convened at large intervals only when amendments to the Constitution are required); the other is for the continuous improvement of the code of justice; the third is for the current government, that is, to manage public resources (Hayek 1990).

One representative body establishes the "rules of the game", the other develops priorities and a hierarchy of social attitudes. The main thing is that the executive body should behave exclusively as a non-profit organization whose mission is the realization of public interests. And in this sense, government agencies are market actors. As for the establishment of the "rules of the game", this is the prerogative of the legislative branch, which in principle cannot be a subject of the market.

It should be agreed that the legislative power establishing the rules of the game cannot act as a subject of market relations. But in relation to the fact that the executive branch should position itself exclusively as a non-profit organization, this is quite problematic. Firstly, the subjects of the Russian Federation in times of crisis are forced to engage in commercial activities to maintain infrastructure through the development of various forms of public-private partnerships. Secondly, municipal authorities, empowered, but lacking the necessary budget support, are forced to actively use their potential, developing partnerships with small- and medium-sized businesses, while maintaining social stability.

Separation of powers of authorities is a sign of a civilized state in which the priority of the law is unshakable, where various institutions of civil society control the activities of the state. With this approach, the executive branch acts as an equal subject of market relations with business. The lack of significant civil society institutions, a clear strategy, and tactics for the transition from an administrative-command model to a mixed-economy model have led to a sharp expansion of the state's economic dysfunctions.

Summarizing the above, we have to accent that the digital state as a set of Internet platforms for state services has the same problems as using Internet platforms in business. And first risk here is the extraterritorial regime of operation activity of Internet platforms.

Conclusion

Thus, the Russian Federation began its path to establishing institutions of state regulation of the Internet sphere in the territory of a sovereign state. Of course, this law immediately provoked public debate about the real purpose of its adoption. It should be noted that such attempts by national states do not remove the problem of regulating legal relations on the World Wide Web, and the rules of conduct in it are actively developed and implemented.

On the other hand, governments are actively using the capabilities of the World Wide Web to improve public administration and move to more effective forms of interaction with citizens through platforms such as "open government" and "electronic government".

It is important to note that government actions cannot stop the digital, self-regulatory exchange of services, ideas, and information (Osipov et al. 2018). At the same time, one can observe another trend towards the unification of the rules for the use of resources. Individual managers are forced to harmonize the rules of conduct on their platforms and the methods of access to resources.

The main feature of Internet law will be its extraterritorial nature, as opposed to the territorial nature of national law. The territorial nature of national law was formed on the basis of historical traditions and the characteristics of each national state, and it developed due to its dependence on the former path (path-dependence effect). Even social upheavals and revolutions led to short-term sharp changes in legislation, which subsequently returned to the previous mechanisms and procedures for regulating public relations — the path-dependence effect is so strong. The national state and its authorities intuitively feel uneasy about the spread of the Internet, as they are outside the mechanism of the state's regulation. Any misunderstanding of any person initially causes fear or anxiety; this is normal. Gradual addiction to the unknown, its ongoing research, removes a sense of fear. Fear is replaced by curiosity, and then interest, as the new turns out to be an effective tool for solving a certain group of problems. This behavior is characteristic of the individual, but why is not so characteristic of public authorities? Here it is possible that fear causes a threat to the existence of the state, because one of the most important functions of producing positive law is lost. Obviously, the rejection of rulemaking is unthinkable for the state. However, whether the state is able to withstand the new reality remains a question. In our opinion, even if China is unable to completely isolate the sovereign Internet from the global Web (only a part of the common platforms is blocked), then, probably, attempts to isolate the Internet in a separate segment in a separate territory of a nation-state are all the more utopian. It would be more logical to take advantage of Internet platforms to implement the state's own policies, and without taking into account national borders. Actually, the Russian Federation is trying to realize this idea by promoting its own national values through world platforms, explaining its position on pressing issues of international relations and defending historical memory against attempts to distort it for the sake of the populist momentary needs of individual leaders of nation-states. In our opinion, Internet platforms, through self-organization, strive for a balanced flow of information, even under pressure on the media; however, you can find different versions and points of view on the same issue. Another thing is that bots are algorithmized in such a way that people see only the information they prefer to see. And if the user has repeatedly accessed one source of information that he trusts, the user will receive information in accordance with his preferences and never one that contradicts the selected source. This creates fertile ground for manipulating the consciousness of society. The authorities are tempted to make use of social engineering, which can influence the behavior of citizens in the way necessary for the authorities. The platforms help convince citizens to vote for a single party or candidate. A logical question arises: does the voter make a choice or is the choice made for the voter, but is made out by his hands? On the other hand, are government bodies of national states so wrong in regulating the Internet if there is a real threat of a change in the political order in the country? The color revolution in Egypt could not take place without using the Internet to organize the activities of protesting citizens. This means that the threat to the political order in the country is real, and hence the state's desire to control the network is justified.

If the norm does not contain sanctions, then the likelihood of compliance is not too high, because non-compliance with any adverse consequences will not follow. A completely different situation exists in Internet law, as violation of the rules leads to sanctions (blocking access, deleting content, fines, etc.). There are practically no unauthorized norms, since there is no sense in introducing them, as no one will comply with them. What is the difference in Internet law and, for example, in administrative or criminal law? The difference is that in real life no one can find out about an individual's violation. In this regard, numerous security cameras are installed for the safety of citizens. But also, the presence of security cameras is correcting people's behavior according with formal norms.

The Internet space breaks the correspondence between a legally significant action and the physical location of the subject of the action.

The legitimacy of the national government's actions to implement the rules applicable to global phenomena is also detached from the geographical position of the subject of legal relations, which leads to its opportunistic behavior. It follows that the Internet is changing the system of forming rules based on the boundaries between the physical space and the physical position of the subject of legal relations—the network user. It becomes completely natural for an individual that the national government cannot regulate the behavior of individuals in the network, that the state is weaker in network relations than in the physical world within the borders of the national territory.

The digital state is trying to find the possibility of controlling the material flow, which is managed online.

It is important to understand how the state could control the financial flow in the network. Banks that carry out plastic card transactions can be of great help here. Under pressure from central banks and national governments, banks disclose information about the transactions of their customers, usually when exceeding a certain amount of transfers. Under the guise of combating the financing of terrorism and money laundering, financial flows are monitored through the network. Capital flows can have a much more destructive effect on the political order than material flows, as financing can be directed to support opposition parties or politicians to overthrow a legitimate government, as was done during the color revolution in Egypt and several other countries. However, even here, individuals seem to have found a way to circumvent control by nation-states. Offshore banks located again outside the physical borders of national states where the individual is physically located provide anonymous financial services.

Some states are testing systems of electronic barriers or filtering information flows, because faced with the consequences of an uncontrolled flow of information or finances, and realizing the inability to control electronic flows due to their virtuality and ability to cross physical boundaries, governments are not inactive. It is important to note that the emergence of state-initiated electronic filters is accompanied by the creation of new configurations of information flows, finances, and objects, which reduces government efforts to a minimum of efficiency (Johnson and Post 1996). Creation of a new configuration is carried out in the interests of users in accordance with their request. This is because the network operates on the basis of self-organization with a large number of capable and proactive players, because the network does not have a geographically localized meeting of leaders who would have a stronger right to regulate than other groups or individuals with programming abilities. The right to regulation is actually tied to the ability to program, which makes participants in network relations equally strong in the right of regulation, and again, regardless of their geographical location.

The extraterritorial principle of the functioning of the network also creates certain difficulties with the regulation of legal relations between the participants within the network (Silvestrov et al. 2019). What right is there to apply if, geographically, the participants in the legal relationship are far from each other and have different citizenships?

This situation of virtual entities is attractive for economic and other activities, since the lack of control compared to offline activities offers additional benefits, in addition to the comfort of uncontrolled behavior in the network. This trend was picked up, as it turned out, primarily by financial organizations. In fact, there are no more classical banks; they all have transferred their activities to the virtual space and manage operations through special mobile applications.

Modern cyberspace researchers propose considering cyberspace not only without being tied to the territorial borders of states, but as a whole that needs legal regulation. For example, the many legal and substantive difficulties created by electronic communications that cross borders can be resolved thanks to one simple principle: representing cyberspace as a separate place for legal analysis by recognizing the legally valid border between cyberspace and the real world (Johnson and Post 1996). Hard possibility to determine the boundaries within cyberspace, calls other method of regulation the network as a whole. Any way legal regulation is desirable to prevent fraud and more efficient distribution of resources on the basis of embedded institutions.

References

Demichel, A., Demichel, F., & Piquemal, M. (1975). *Institutions et pouvoir en France. Une traduction institutionelle du capitalism monopoliste d'etat*. Paris: Editions Sociales.

Hayek, F. A. (1978). *New Studies in Philosophy, Politics and the History of Ideas*. Chicago: University of Chicago Press.

Hayek, F. A. (1990). *The Political Order of a Free People*. London: Overseas Publications Interchange Ltd.

Hood, C. (1991). A Public Management for all Seasons? *Public Administration, 69*(Spring), 3–19.

Johnson, D. R., & Post, D. (1996). Law and Borders – The Rise of Law in Cyberspace. *Stanford Law Review, 48*, 1367.

Osipov, V. S. (2016). Project-Functional Structure of Management for Public Administration. *Public Administration Issue, 3*, 219–230.

Osipov, V. S. (2019). The Rise of Unemployment in the Cyber Economy. *The Cyber Economy. Contributions to Economics, Part F2*, 105–116.

Osipov, V., Zeldner, A., & Skryl, T. (2018). *Making the Smart City: Technologies, Experiences, and Future Perspectives*. MATEC Web of Conferences/Volume 212, ICRE.

Silverstrov, S. N., Osipov, V. S., & Zeldner, A. G. (2019). The Role of State Corporations in Redesign of Sectoral Supply Chain Management. *International Journal of Supply Chain Management, 8*(5), 314–324.

von Mises, L. (1978). *The Ultimate Foundations of Economic Science: An Essay on Method* (p. 98). Princeton: Van Nostrand.

CHAPTER 6

Innovative Ecosystems for Attracting Investment in a Post-industrial Society

Tamara Petrovic and Igor Stepnov

Introduction

The ecosystem concept, which includes the concepts of "business ecosystems" and "innovative ecosystems", has long been used in the scientific literature.

Certainly, the concept of the ecosystem—taking into account its initial systemic character—correlates with interaction; this interaction is considered outside the existing organizational structures (which is how the entrepreneurship ecosystem is clarified in the works by J. Moore 1993).

Adner considers the ecosystem as a form of coordination between partners in exchange networks, which are characterized by both cooperative and competitive relations at the same time (Adner and Kapoor 2010). He

T. Petrovic
Innovation Project Management Center (IPM Center Ltd.), Pancevo, Serbia

I. Stepnov (✉)
Moscow State Institute of International Relations (MGIMO University), Moscow, Russia

Financial University under the Government of the Russian Federation, Moscow, Russia

J. Kovalchuk (ed.), *Post-Industrial Society*,
https://doi.org/10.1007/978-3-030-59739-9_6

clarifies that the innovative ecosystem "is a cooperation mechanism by means of which firms combine their individual offerings into a single consumer-oriented product" (Adner 2006).

More attention to innovation issues is paid in the work of Gomez et al., who unpacked the innovative ecosystem through its evolution, gaps, and trends (Gomes et al. 2016); this work is a more theoretical than practical matter, however.

The term "innovative ecosystem" has become widespread after the publications of Wessner calling it "a set of interconnected participants whose aim of functioning is to ensure technological and innovative development" (Wessner and Jackson 2007). In doing so, Wessner considered the presence of financial institutions in ecosystems to be an integral component.

The development of the notion of an "innovative ecosystem" also included an expansion of the list of participants, without indicating the possibility of creating an open ecosystem (e.g. between the state and society (Rinkinen 2016)). In some publications there have been proposals that contradicted Moore's initial notion of the ecosystem; for example, the division of the innovative ecosystem into constituent parts (into the business ecosystem and the knowledge ecosystem) is possible (Papaioannou et al. 2007).

Other definitions exclude the explicit role of the state becoming a participant of the system "as a system of actors (participants), interacting, exchanging resources and transforming some of their types into other types" (Belousov and Penukhina 2018). This gap allows us to form a clarified notion of "the innovative ecosystem of joint investments" in which key accents are made on interaction within the framework of financial decisions, platform issues, the openness of the system, and accounting for its operating activity.

Consequently, for the purposes of the present study, the authors view the innovative ecosystem as an open, evolving, institutional environment for interaction between key actors, across regional, national, and international levels. An innovative ecosystem ensures the implementation by economically engaged participants of jointly funded innovative programmes and projects within a single-platform solution. The evolution of the interaction being formed provides the possibility of more multivariable achievement of the goals set.

It should also be noted that the comparative analysis of approaches shows that most authors lay stress on the declaration of joint interaction (Collins and Lazier 1992), leaving out consideration of the aspects of a particular activity. These omitted activities include, first of all, funding ecosystem projects (as a rule, funding is "hidden" under the term "resources"), managing or organizing structures are mentioned without sufficient detail (their functioning is hidden under the concept of "network interaction"), openness (often, locking the activity of such ecosystems with the national character of interaction or extending without restrictions to the entire world economic system), and the operational activities of individual participants (the results of their activities are usually related to the resource transformation processes).

The aim of the study is to justify the fundamental possibilities and advantages of the ecosystem approach in creating an institutional environment for attracting private and foreign investment to joint projects, and for supporting the development of countries undergoing their post-industrial development.

The transition of the former republics of the Socialist Federalist Republic of Yugoslavia (SFRY) to the market economy, after almost 50 years of the planned industrial economy, created the need for numerous reforms amongst some sectors and systems, in order to achieve macroeconomic stability and market liberalization. These countries were still encountering the difficult circumstances of inherited hyperinflation, significant external debt, the loss of the Yugoslav market, and shortages of foreign exchange reserves necessary to stabilize and maintain the national currency.

The reasons for Serbia's disadvantaged position should be seen in the economic isolation that led to the loss of all foreign markets, complete deindustrialization and inadequate privatization (which led to the closure of factories and the destruction of industries that were once the main exporters), insufficient inflows of foreign direct investment, and the non-competitiveness of domestic goods and services.

State regulation of the economy—by means of indirect participation in supporting and increasing the country's pace of socio-economic development, supporting scientific and technological development, promoting innovative company development, and implementing balanced budgets and social policies—creates opportunities for strengthening its economic potential. However, due to limited financial resources, both economically and historically (Sokolov 2019), foreign investment is considered an additional source of financing for socio-economic development projects.

Methodology

In their research, the authors rely on the possibilities of modelling the systemic interaction of economic players at various levels (countries, industries, government, enterprises, organizations of various forms) on the basis of the formation of the innovative ecosystem; this involves project initiation being self-organized by the participants of international cooperation, reducing the costs of the state in order to save its budget funds. In the process of the study, macroeconomic data were used, the statistical analysis of which revealed the current problems of the Serbian economy and helped to establish that it is impossible to find a solution unless competitiveness is stimulated, efficiency and innovation are developed, and institutional support is strengthened for the promotion of export activities of Serbian enterprises.

Results

In the current context, countries seek to improve their global competitiveness, but each country is at its own level of development, which either provides maximum benefits in global markets or forces it to look for ways of economic recovery, building up innovative capacities or active mutually beneficial interactions with partner countries. The project approach demonstrated greater decision effectiveness regarding the future of those countries in the post-industrial economy. That allowed their target development trajectory to be determined based on consistent implementation of interconnected projects, which ensure the sustainable development of the priority business segments and territories as a basis for solving the socio-economic problems of the country.

As a rule, it is possible to draw a conclusion on the status of the national economy based on macroeconomic data analysis. The main economic indicators—such as real GDP and GDP per capita growth, external debt, foreign trade deficits, unemployment, and foreign direct investment (FDI) inflows—clearly indicate that the transition from the planned to the market model of the economy in most former Yugoslav countries was unsuccessful. Unfortunately, their economy is still at the same level—or even below—as it was before the collapse. Explanations for this have their roots in the consequences of the war on the territory of the former SFRY, the dissolution of economic relationships, the unstable political situation, sanctions, and NATO bombing in the Federalist Republic of Yugoslavia

(FRY)—mostly on the territory of today's Serbia, and in the models of the transitional processes and economic policy implemented by these republics.

GDP is an indicator of the dynamics of economic development, and being expressed per capita, it reflects the true measure of the economic progress of one country. This is why, on the basis of the data presented in Table 6.1, it can be safely concluded that the economic growth in the republics of the former Yugoslavia has been unsustainable since 2000. With the exception of Slovenia, all the other former Yugoslav republics are far behind the average rates in the EU.

By fixing the place of the SFRY countries by 2018, the following conclusions can be drawn (the authors used the World Development Indicators data to formulate their conclusions):

- Serbia's GDP amounted to $50.6 billion, ranked 85th in the world, and was at the levels of Slovenia ($54.0 billion), Lithuania ($53.5 billion), Sudan ($50.5 billion), Uzbekistan ($50.5 billion), and Congo ($47.1 billion); Serbia's share of GDP in the world was 0.059%.
- Bosnia and Herzegovina's GDP amounted to $19.8 billion, ranked 115th in the world, and was at the level of Afghanistan ($20.5 billion) and Botswana ($18.6 billion); the share of Bosnia and Herzegovina's GDP in the world was 0.023%.
- Macedonia's GDP amounted to $10.7 billion and ranked 138th in the world; the share of Macedonia's GDP in the world was 0.14%.
- Slovenia's GDP amounted to $54.0 billion, ranked 83rd in the world, and was at the level of Lebanon ($56.4 billion), Lithuania ($53.5 billion), Serbia ($50.6 billion), Sudan ($50.5 billion), and

Table 6.1 The share of export in the country's GDP (%)

	2000	*2004*	*2008*	*2012*	*2016*	*2017*	*2018*
Bosnia and Herzegovina	28.7	27.8	26.8	32.4	35.6	40.1	41.4
Montenegro	36.8	42.0	39.5	43.7	40.5	41.1	43.2
Serbia	9.9	24.2	28.4	35.8	48.6	50.5	50.9
Slovenia	50.0	55.0	66.1	73.1	77.8	82.9	85.2
Macedonia	32.9	30.7	43.2	45.4	50.7	55.4	60.3
Croatia	36.5	39.5	38.5	41.5	48.7	51.1	51.2

Source: Compiled by the authors based on the data of World Development Indicators

Access mode: https://databank.worldbank.org/source/world-development-indicators#

Uzbekistan ($50.5 billion); Slovenia's GDP share in the world was 0.063%.
- Croatia's GDP amounted to $61.0 billion, ranked 76th in the world, and was at the level of Panama ($65.1 billion), Costa Rica ($60.1 billion), Belarus ($59.7 billion), Uruguay ($59.6 billion), and Tanzania ($58.8 billion); Croatia's GDP share in the world was 0.071%.
- Montenegro's GDP amounted to $5.5 billion, ranked 159th in the world, and was at the level of Fiji ($5.5 billion), Cayman Islands ($5.5 billion), and the Maldives ($5.3 billion); Montenegro's GDP share in the world was 0.0064%.

Bearing in mind that export stimulation is one of the main prerequisites of sustainable economic growth—and that export growth is in a direct positive correlation with GDP, trade liberalization has become one of the key pillars of the transition to the new economy of the former Yugoslav republics. Despite the positive results achieved by all the former Yugoslav republics in the area of trade liberalization, they continue to import more goods and services than they export.

Analysing the structure of the gross value added, it becomes clear that the candidate countries have a much larger share of agriculture and, as a rule, a smaller share of services in generating GDP than the EU (Eurostat 2019).

Choosing Serbia as the subject of the research in the post-industrial economy has been justified by the authors by the fact that this country has the largest share of industry in GDP, both in the region and in relation to the EU. Thus, industry accounts for 26.5% of Serbia's GDP, while in the EU it is below 20%. This can serve as a good argument for those who claim that Serbia needs industrialization in order to achieve the European economy level. On the other hand, services dominate in the EU with 73%, while in Serbia they account for just over 60% of GDP. It is also interesting to note that agriculture contributes only 1.7% to GDP of the EU, while in Serbia it is about 10%, and in the structure of employment it is more than 20%.

The manufacturing industry in Serbia is characterized by a high level of production concentration and the importance of supporting export-oriented enterprises that depend on the demands of external markets (especially European). Such enterprises include the Fiat automobile assembly plant, the Hesteel Serbia iron and steel plant (formerly Železara

Smederevo), the Michelin tire factory, the Naftna Industrija Srbije (NIS) refineries, the Philip Morris cigarette factory, the Gorenje household electrical engineering factories, the Stada pharmaceutical plant, and more. Traditionally, oil refining and petrochemical industries have played a prominent role in the industrial production of the country. In the field of oil refining, a monopoly is held by the largest company of the country in terms of turnover, Naftna Industrija Srbije (NIS); this has been owned by the Russian company Gazpromneft since 2008.

EU countries account for about 65% of Serbia's foreign trade. Serbia specializes in the export of mechanical engineering products (mainly cars and their components, household electrical equipment, and high-voltage equipment), food products (fruit, vegetables, cereals), beverages and tobacco products, petrochemical and chemical products (drugs, and plastic and rubber products), ferrous and non-ferrous metallurgy products, and clothes and shoes. At the same time, the volume of export in the structure of GDP occupies about 50%, which is optimal compared to the other countries of the region, and reflects the active role of the state and business in the development of the economy. At the beginning of 2000, Serbia had a minimum share of export in GDP among the other countries (Table 6.1).

Consequently, of all the countries analysed, Serbia increased its export-to-GDP ratio as an important indicator of its economic openness between 2000 and 2018, which indicates its more active participation in international trade.

At the same time, Serbia is certainly the most significant recipient of investment in the region: in 2017, net foreign direct investment amounted to 2.4 billion euros. The rest of the Western Balkans raised about 2.1 billion euros that year.

However, this is 100 million euros less than the net investment inflow in 2007. Excluding outflows, gross FDI inflows in 2007 were 650 million euros higher than in 2017.

The volume of inflows of foreign direct investment (FDI) largely determines labour and capital market opportunities. In order to create new jobs and reduce unemployment, countries with transition economies should focus on attracting FDI by removing existing barriers in the form of underdeveloped infrastructure, administrative barriers, corruption, political risk, low liquidity and profitability, limited domestic consumption, draining of professional staff, and so on.

The volume of FDI attracted does not yet allow the economy of Serbia to be characterized as dependent on foreign capital. Record levels of FDI inflows to GDP were recorded in 2006–2007 (14% and 9%) and in 2011 (10%). As a rule, in the first half of the 2010s the country's level did not exceed 4–5% (in 2017—about 6.5%). At the same time, the share of FDI in the structure of gross investments in fixed assets is high—it varies between 30% and 35%, which indicates a shortage of internal sources of investment (Lobanov 2019). Serbia has shown a steady growth in foreign direct investment over the past three years. It should be noted that the volatility of FDI flows to the economy is characteristic of developing countries, and depends on the implementation of certain projects aimed either at intergovernmental support or secured by corporate investment.

When it comes to FDI, biggest net investments to Serbia in period 2010–2018 came from Austria, the Netherlands, and Cyprus; they were followed by Greece, Slovenia, Italy, and Russia. In 2015–2017 the Netherlands and Austria strengthened their leadership in the list of countries exporting capital to Serbia, while Italy, France, Germany, Luxembourg, and the UAE are among the countries most actively expanding their investments. In the industrial structure of FDI, the share of the real sector has been increasing: the share of the manufacturing industry increased from 15–20% in the late 2000s to 35–40% in 2013–2015 (25% in 2017), though the share of the mining industry remained low (about 2–3%). Besides, the investment attractiveness of the construction sphere and real estate operations has increased: its share rose from 6–10% in the late 2000s to 23% in 2017.

The analysis of the aforementioned economic indicators suggests that the situation in the Serbian economy is worse than in other former Yugoslavian republics; it lags behind Slovenia and Croatia and, on the whole, it is at about the same level of development as Macedonia, Montenegro, and Bosnia and Herzegovina, which were much less developed during the former Yugoslav Federation than Serbia. The recovery and growth of the Serbian economy will not be possible without a purposeful approach to solving the problem of the low level of economic activity, increasing the competitiveness of domestic goods and services in international markets within the overall global trend of development in the post-industrial economies, and creating more favourable conditions for FDI inflows.

Today, the existing legislation of the Republic of Serbia allows joint projects to be implemented, and provides them with the necessary regulation. However, the implementation of large-scale infrastructure projects requires some additional rulemaking and government regulation as part of strategies of the territorial socio-economic development and the development of Serbia's innovative ecosystem.

Taking into account the need for active economic development and increased global competitiveness on the part of developing countries with similar conditions, the authors suggest considering the possibilities of adapting the ecosystem approach to the mechanisms for attracting investment when implementing innovative projects. At the same time, the active use of the opportunities of international cooperation should be used to their maximum extent, without contradicting the principles of mutual and beneficial cooperation.

Prior to a detailed consideration of innovative ecosystem mechanisms, and defining the basic forms of investment in such an environment, it is necessary to conduct a release analysis of the concept proposed with a direct project approach. The quintessence of this is the formation of a project office for the investment programmes being implemented. The authors believe that such a project office can become an excellent and effective solution for organizing interaction in the implementation of international innovative projects.

First of all, we cannot but mention the undeniable fact that if an investment project could be successfully implemented using internal resources, then attracting investors would be an insignificant and irrelevant task. However, historical experience shows that the success of most economic systems during the period under review was achieved by means of external financing, however attractive it is to be reliant on internal resources and attracting foreign investment. Among the most engaging ways to attract money to investment projects, especially of an innovative character, is direct investment, which is also attractive for foreign capital. The comparison of direct and portfolio investments makes it possible to conclude that in solving problems the state faces, project investments—within the framework of the project approach to management being developed—are the most attractive, as they make local interaction with a potential investor possible. At the same time, the combination of the project approach in management with the features of direct investing allows implementing such processes, both in supporting innovative ecosystems and in developing the technology of project offices.

The innovative ecosystem, considered by the authors in this chapter, involves the self-organization of the initiation of projects, which reduces the costs of the state in order to save its budget. An ecosystem that brings together investors, participants, and consumers turns out to be a more authentic environment for investment, especially with the assumption that such a system will be able to design compliance markets, ensuring the equal participation of all actual and potential participants.

The aforementioned features make it possible to state that within international projects, the innovation ecosystem will also gain additional benefits: the role of public authorities is reduced in regulating investment processes, whilst the role of the new non-governmental actor (environment) is strengthened, which builds interaction based primarily on economic interests and benefits, instead of on political or populist decisions.

For example, currently the main efforts of public administration in Serbia are aimed at creating conditions for greenfield investments, although most of the significant projects were possible due to personal agreements. Under the new stage of privatization, the number of mergers and acquisitions has increased: in particular, brownfield investments. The country's authorities continue the policy of external borrowing to support their own investment projects, where targeted loans allocated by strategic partners on preferential terms are becoming more and more important. In addition to the European Union, such partners include Russia, China, and the UAE. It is supposed that the implementation of large investment projects should give an impetus to develop the construction service sector and related sectors of economy. The concession form of attracting foreign investment has become widespread; primarily it is used to create or modernize the transport network.

However, it should be noted that a comparison between "the innovative direct investment ecosystem" and "the direct investment project office" makes it possible to conclude that there are a number of projects for which a more regulated procedure of the project office is more advantageous.

For example, projects with guaranteed financing, limited investors, and high certainty will be more effectively implemented within the framework of stricter monitoring and control procedures from the project office. Such projects, for instance, include toll sections of roads: these do not normally require generating new knowledge but implementing routine competencies. For spheres requiring a proactive approach and searching for significantly different ways of completing tasks, the most favourable environment will be the formation of an innovative ecosystem. For example, while forming large infrastructure development programmes, the project office demonstrates its advantages, and proves its economic practicality using cost criteria as restrictions. At the same time, with the further development of projects (especially at the regional level), there is a need to bring more and more interests into accord, which becomes more significant as the number of participants is increasing. Accordingly, we can conclude that the innovative ecosystem is a freer organizational structure than the project office, which makes it possible to support initiative solutions at all stages of the project.

The development of the ecosystem concept increases the number of project financing options; the openness of the system enhances the economic interest of ecosystem participants. When an innovative ecosystem is developed, it significantly reduces the cost of attracting foreign investors, because it uses actual interactions supported by publicly available institutions rather than local agreements; there are no special agreements, solutions, and approvals. Compared to the intergovernmental project office (intergovernmental commission), decision-making is significantly more flexible in the innovation ecosystem of attracting foreign investment to joint projects, especially with considerable uncertainty.

For the initial stages of the development of the ecosystem, some areas of interaction and innovation should be pointed out. Among the options of ecosystem interaction, the authors suggest the following:

- contracting, including supplies to government agencies;
- concession agreements; and
- cooperation and collaboration.

"Contracting" involves creating a procurement-related environment, which ensures transparency and efficiency. More broadly, contracting is a kind of outsourcing. Barley and Kunda argue in their research that contracting currently represents a revival of a professional organization with a decrease in bureaucracy. The study of contracting provides a strategic viewpoint for viewing, evaluating, and possibly even forming changes taking place in global economies (Barley and Kunda 2006).

"Concession" allows the use of economic funds, natural resources, and other assets by the investor for a limited period. Concession lets relationships be formed without transferring ownership. One of the most common forms of public-private partnership contracts is concession, and one of the most famous types of concessions is the so-called BOT agreement (Build, Operate, Transfer), which is when a private partner is entrusted with building an infrastructure tool, managing it and using it for a predetermined period of time. After the due date the infrastructure object is returned to the state partner (Vlašković and Žarković 2018).

"Cooperation" involves the formation of value chains among businesses not connected by a single ownership right. The practice of the European Union confirms that cooperation is a development-oriented complement to competition, which contributes to the development of relations between people, organizations, nations, and states (Drakulić 2005).

The combination of the three approaches mentioned above will allow the innovation ecosystem to make the most of the opportunities for attracting investors through legislation, covering almost all aspects of economic society: from the purchase of agricultural products to the formation of value chains in processing; from the formation of infrastructure to the efficient use of such infrastructure; from the formation of clusters to the globalization of economic activity.

Our description of the separate fragments of the ecosystem will be incomplete without taking into account industry characteristics; the opportunities for innovative growth will be different in different industries:

- Today, for example, the tourism industry or education should be considered as a niche of the rapid emergence of new products and services in the development of contracting models in new markets.
- Also, the interaction of agricultural manufacturers and processers should be considered as a development of cooperation combining new factors of productive forces.
- The formation of infrastructure demands the most comprehensive solutions, and when implementation is based on concession agreements, it makes it possible to put into practice other combinations of production factors and to provide access to new markets new sources of raw materials or other beneficial resources.

Conclusions/Recommendations

Having conducted a large study of developing economies, on the example of Serbia, and taking into account the trends in post-industrial development, the authors argue that it is advisable to adapt the ecosystem approach to the mechanisms for attracting investment, through implementing innovative projects. Within the process of forming an innovative ecosystem, active and mutually beneficial usage of the opportunities for international cooperation and collaboration will stimulate the development of industry, increase the number of projects in public-private partnerships and the number of concession agreements, and develop cooperation with other countries in the priority sectors of the economy.

The study presented points out the key features of the innovative ecosystem for attracting financing to joint projects:

- regional, national, and international focus;
- institutional stability and legal security;
- the main participants' initiative;
- the system's openness to new participants, both domestic and foreign;
- the universal character of models for different projects;
- rejection of sectoral and territorial divisions;
- the possibility of consolidating actors without suppressing the rights of all participants of the ecosystem, creating interaction based on economic interests, minimizing the possibility of changing of such interaction in other ways than economic ones; and
- finding a compromise between the interest groups of all the participants of the ecosystem.

Having considered the features and properties of the innovation ecosystem, it is possible to conclude that for direct investment (as a method of investment), the most developed form of joint participation in projects so far has been the creation of a public-private partnership that allows the implementation of joint projects with foreign participation, and it is in this direction that the economic development of Serbia needs to be promoted.

References

A New Wave of Economic Growth? Scientific Report. Moscow: Institute of Economics of the Russian Academy of Sciences.

Adner, R. (2006). Match Your Innovation Strategy to Your Innovation Ecosystem. *Harvard Business Review, 84*(4), 98–107.

Adner, R., & Kapoor, R. (2010). Value Creation in Innovation Ecosystems: How the Structure of Technological Interdependence Affects Firm Performance in New Technology Generations. *Strategic Management, 31*(3), 306–333.

Barley, S. R., & Kunda, G. (2006). Contracting: A New Form of Professional Practice. *Academy of Management Perspectives, 20*(1), 45.

Belousov, D. R., & Penukhina, E. A. (2018). On the Construction of a Qualitative Model of the Russian ICT Ecosystem. *Studies on Russian Economic Development, 29*(3), 295–302.

Collins, J., & Lazier, W. (1992). *Beyond Entrepreneurship: Turning Your Business into an Enduring Company*. Prentice: Prentice Hall.

Drakulić, D. (2005). Ograničenja razvoja i stanje kooperacije u Srbiji. *Privredna izgradnja, 48*(1–2), 71–79.

Eurostat. (2019). *Basic Figures for the Enlargement Countries*. https://ec.europa.eu/eurostat/en/web/products-catalogues/-/KS-03-19-048

Gomes, L., Facin, A., Salerno, M., & Ikenami, R. (2016). Unpacking the Innovation Ecosystem Construct: Evolution, Gaps and Trends. *Technological Forecasting and Social Change, 136*, 30–48.

Lobanov, M. M. (2019). *Problems of Serbia's Development: How to "Stay on the Crest"*

Moore, J. F. (1993). Predators and Prey: A New Ecology of Competition. *Harvard Business Review, 71*(3), 75–86.

Papaioannou, T., Wield, D., & Chataway, J. (2007), Knowledge Ecologies and Ecosystems? An Empirically Grounded Reflection on Recent Developments in Innovation Systems Theory. *The 6th International Triple Helix Conference on University-Government-Industry Relations, 16-18 May 2007*, Singapore.

Rinkinen, S. (2016). *Clusters, Innovation Systems and Ecosystems. Studies on Innovation Policy's Concept Evolution and Approaches for Regional Renewal*. https://www.doria.fi/bitstream/handle/10024/129972/Satu%20Rinkinen%20A4.pdf?sequence=2

Sokolov, A. (2019). Some Aspects of the Concession, W. A. Harriman to Russia ("Loan Harriman"). *ISTORIYA, 10*(12), 86. https://doi.org/10.18254/S207987840008233-5.

Vlašković, V., & Žarković, J. (2018). U susret EU integracijama, Unapređenje pravnog i institucionalnog okvira javno-privatnog partnerstva u Srbiji. *Institut za teritorijalni ekonomski razvoj (InTER)*.

Wessner, C., & Jackson, D. J. (2007). What Is an Innovation Ecosystem? *Innovation Policies for the 21st Century: Report of a Symposium*.

World Development Indicators. (2018). https://databank.worldbank.org/source/world-development-indicators#

CHAPTER 7

Transformation of a Traditional Financial Conglomerate into a Financial Ecosystem

Elena Nebolsina and Zhanna Pisarenko

Introduction

If any system expands, it faces new mechanisms which can no longer be subject to the previous regulation regime. The phenomenon of financial ecosystems developed gradually and revealed itself before long. Over the past decades, the global financial landscape has seriously changed and is currently characterized by both increasing interdependence of all participants in the global financial market and speed of transactions, which results from the rapid development and distribution of information and communication technologies, extended functions of financial institutions, structural adjustment of the market, and strengthening competition.

E. Nebolsina (✉)
Moscow State Institute of International Relations (MGIMO University), Moscow, Russia
e-mail: e.nebolsina@inno.mgimo.ru

Z. Pisarenko
St. Petersburg State University, Saint Petersburg, Russia
e-mail: z.pisarenko@spbu.ru

J. Kovalchuk (ed.), *Post-Industrial Society*,
https://doi.org/10.1007/978-3-030-59739-9_7

Since the mid-1980s, financial intermediaries representing different segments of the financial market have demonstrated a higher level of interaction penetrating those segments that are non-typical of them.

Whereas, they apply a mechanism of financial convergence which is specific to the financial market. Digital technologies have only accelerated the process of interpenetration, giving them a fresh impetus and leading to the emergence of financial ecosystems.

The objective of this study is to determine the role of financial ecosystems in the overall evolution of financial institutions. It complements previous literature by developing a theoretical framework and practical issues of building a new business model on the global financial market, namely a financial ecosystem which is most in evidence amid transformation of a traditional financial conglomerate into an ecosystem financial conglomerate.

The study of the phenomenon of convergence of the nature of the financial market and its segments dates back to the 2000s (Van den Berghe and Verweire 2000). Some researchers (Hölzl 2003) consider convergence with regard to convergence in the country development indicators. Dowrick and Bradford DeLong (2003) developed a hypothesis that the least developed countries are unable to reach the level of income of the most developed economies, thus being locked in a "poverty trap". The convergence analysis with regard to general changes in financial institutions in national and regional financial markets was carried out by Di Giacinto and Esposito (2012) and Murinde et al. (2004). Kuznetsova and Chernova (2001) and Belozerov and Pisarenko (2014) made a serious contribution to the development of the theoretical basis of financial convergence as well as development of financial conglomerates and modification of financial markets in a crisis of a welfare state.

The concept of ecosystem, that is, a comprehensive perception of the financial market as a single organism, with all the elements being interconnected and interdependent, was unknown until relatively recently. Doroshenko and Shelomentsev (2017) and Walsh (2019) give a brief overview of building the entrepreneurial ecosystem and its understanding by modern authors. Epstein and Rhodes (2019) tried to explain the changes in the behaviour of banks prior and pursuant to the financial ecosystem crisis.

The ecosystem approach is considered to be a new approach towards the provision of social services (Aksoy et al. 2019). Zorio-Grima and Merello (2020) have revealed the causality links between consumer confidence and other agents within the financial information ecosystem with economic information. Customers are becoming more demanding and search for more personalized services, which results in the emergence of insurtech and fintech giants, whereas traditional players have to adapt to the new reality by developing online platforms (Nebolsina 2018). The ecosystem approach implies the use of the so-called platform type of competition (Konopatov and Salienko 2018). However, in this case, the concept of ecosystem is considered in a narrow sense. By transition to an ecosystem business, we understand not only the use of modern technologies by businesses and transformation of business processes, thanks to these technologies, but also the transformation of the basic foundations of doing business, the erosion of traditional segments of the financial market (banking, insurance, investment, pension funds, etc.), and the formation of an innovative model of the ecosystem financial conglomerate (EFC).

The chapter is arranged as follows. The following section describes data and research methodology. Section "Results and Discussion" reveals and discusses major results. Conclusions and suggestions are provided in the final section.

Data and Methodology

This problem-oriented study is the result of mixed method research (Johnson and Onwuegbuzie 2004), with quantitative and qualitative research techniques and approaches combined.

The study is based on such methods of scientific research as historical analysis, comparative analysis, synthesis, deduction, induction, and a case study.

Based on the purpose of the study, the authors suggest the hypothesis that the process of financial convergence results in the development of financial ecosystems.

The major directions of the research are as follows: (1) revealing factors of developing financial convergence and modification of the traditional model of financial conglomerates (historical analysis, comparative analysis), (2) defining the stages of building financial ecosystems on the global financial market (historical analysis, synthesis, and a case study method), and (3) revealing risks of developing a financial ecosystem (prospective analysis).

The research data was obtained from open sources on the Internet; official websites of international companies (Allianz, PingAn, AIG, etc.); consulting and rating agencies; international organizations (the European Union [EU], the Eurasian Economic Union [EAEU], the World Bank, etc.); financial market regulators: Japan Financial Services Agency, the

European Commission, the Federal Reserve System, the Bank of Russia; and laws and regulations of the EU, the EAEU, Russia, Japan, the United States, and so on. Authors have analyzed more than 40 theoretical research papers and empirical studies on the topic of interest, a part of which is included in references. The whole list cannot be provided due to the chapter size limits.

Results and Discussion

Financial Convergence, Factors of Its Development and Financial Conglomerate

On the basis of theoretical analysis, we define financial convergence as a mechanism of intersectoral competition, implemented either through combining the activities of entities operating in different segments of the financial market or through the interpenetration of the activities of competing entities, namely participants in different segments of the national and/or global financial market (as a system of interconnected national financial markets). That is, the essence of the process of financial convergence is the penetration of institutions of one segment of the financial market into segments which were previously non-typical of them. For example, insurance companies implying long-term saving insurance products that resemble banking products can compete with traditional deposits of the banks.

The rapidly changing environment of financial markets requires rethinking and complementing existing studies on the analysis of the causes of financial convergence. In our opinion, the most important drivers for stimulating financial convergence processes today are as follows:

- financial globalization and regional integration;
- breakthrough development of information technology and widespread digitalization;
- liberalization, deregulation and unification of work standards at national and international levels;
- creating a regulatory framework for financial convergence and financial conglomerates.

Financial Globalization and Regional Integration

According to most researchers, the beginning of full-scale financial globalization is considered to be the robust external expansion of national banks and the emergence of the first multinational banks in the 1990s, which turned into multinational giants by the beginning of the twenty-first century. Such changes happened due to several simultaneous trends: on the one hand, the development of information technology (IT) and a lower strain from supervision authorities; on the other hand, a tougher control and initiatives of international institutions. Quantitative measurement of the speed of financial globalization can be determined, among other things, by changes in foreign direct investment (FDI), the increase of which is especially evident in the 2000s and coincides with the rapid development of IT. Transitive and developing economies are lagging far behind, but capital flows from advanced economies benefit both groups, allowing for increased investment in capital-poor countries (Prasad et al. 2003).

Another process that changes the landscape of the global financial market and promotes financial convergence is regional integration. Regional economic/political associations create their additional incentives for the development of regional financial markets, providing free movement of capital. In the global economy, they are likely to become a new way to defend their interests. The major centers increasing institutionalization at a supranational level are the European Union and the Eurasian Economic Union (EAEU). If the EU, as a unique supranational association, has already existed for more than 30 years, purposefully creating a single financial market with minimal bureaucratic barriers and having an extensive structure of supranational regulation of financial markets, a legislative framework for financial conglomerates, the EAEU is at the early stage of evolution. The EAEU authorities are working on harmonizing legislation of the participating countries, ensuring free movement of capital and money, creating a common financial market which contributes to the process of financial convergence.

Breakthrough IT and Ubiquitous Digitalization

The paradox of financial convergence is that it allows rethinking the current business model. This is especially important for the oversaturated financial markets of developed countries, where more than 90% of the population already use financial services and the prospect of further growth is very vague. Along with digital transformation, financial convergence makes it possible to avoid the "profit gap", creating new flexible and more attractive products and services, backed by an emerging ecosystem of business models that maximize value for the end user.

Today, the market players jockey for clients in the age of economic globalization and easy access to information, thanks to the development of the Internet and mobile applications, when it becomes possible to quickly find the necessary information and compare offers and prices. Such opportunities reduce the transaction time for the client, but imply serious expenses for the IT infrastructure of the service provider. As a result, the life cycle of the product shortens, making it necessary to consistently develop new offers and modify existing ones. Since consumption is now a display of wealth to mark one's social standing and distinguish oneself from the crowd, online round-the-clock financial services expand the options. They provide access to remote territories and encourage socialization through social networks, which changes not only the landscape of service provision, but also the consumer behaviour.

Liberalization, Deregulation, and Unification of Work Standards at National and International Levels

The further spread of financial convergence is fuelled by the gradual liberalization of financial legislation, with regulators of the national financial markets of Europe conducting pioneer research. Basically, new regulatory initiatives covered the interaction of the insurance and banking segments, which resulted in the removal of certain restrictions and led to increased competition within the sectors. Back in 1985, the first steps were taken towards the merger of banking and insurance capital in the United Kingdom and France. Germany and Italy began to follow the same path in 1986 and 1990 respectively, as a result of which banks were able to start investing in insurance companies. In the United States, in 1999, the Gramm-Leach-Bliley Act on Financial Modernization abolished the Glass-Steagall Act of 1933, which barred banks from engaging in investment and insurance activities. The Act revolutionized the US financial market, enabling banks to penetrate the insurance sector of the financial market.

Creating a Regulatory Framework for Financial Convergence and Financial Conglomerates

A rigorous separation of the services-provision-related functions of financial institutions forces owners and interested parties to search for tools to overcome such regulatory restrictions. As a result of the development of financial convergence, it leads to the diverse economic agents joining major global associations, namely financial conglomerates (FC). The classical model of FC is designed as follows: banking, insurance, and investment lines of business. However, these are informal groups of large multinational corporations from different sectors of the global financial market. The form of the conglomerate is blurry, the structure is unstable. As an institutional and organizational form of financial convergence, financial conglomerates have certain particular features. For example, similarity parameters are client, product, and technological and sales communities of different sectors of the financial market; there are different ways of pooling funds within the financial conglomerate.

The European Union and Japan have the most elaborate concepts of financial conglomerate. In the EU, a group qualifies as a FC if, first, more than 50% of group activities is financial and, second, if the shares of the banking and insurance sectors in the total of the financial activities amount to 10–90%. If the minority share has a balance sheet larger than 6 billion euro, the group is regarded as a financial conglomerate (Curi 2016). A list of major financial corporations officially regarded as FC is published annually in the EU. In 2019, the list included 78 FCs.

The FSA, which is a Japanese integrated financial regulator, defines a financial conglomerate as a corporate group that includes the following areas of activity: insurance, banking, securities, trust management, or investment and consulting business. This approach represents the conglomerate as a group of organizations, focusing on the group. In Russia, the concept of FC has not yet been legally fixed. In 2016, the Central Bank (CB) of Russia, which is a mega-regulator of all financial markets of the country, issued a report for public consultation which states the presence of de facto 314 active informal conglomerates in the territory of the Russian Federation (RF; the CB relies on the definition of the FC from EU Directive No. 2002/87/EC). However, in the RF, the work on the development of regulatory initiatives has only just begun.

The foregoing partly proves the hypothesis. The process of financial convergence results in the development on financial markets of entirely new super-powerful multinational financial giants—financial conglomerates.

The primary process of financial convergence, which is basically heterogeneous, fuels rapid development of the necessary infrastructure (both vertical and horizontal) for servicing these products, which begin to form new financial ecosystems amid advancement in digital technologies. Meanwhile, financial services, primarily insurance and banking, naturally integrate into many ecosystems. In the economic literature there is no unambiguous approach to the definition of the term "ecosystem" and its model. The ecosystem is considered as

- a group of participants interacting with the organization, directly or indirectly participating in the creation of the "value chain", as well as its customers;
- an ecosystem as a marketplace for goods and services, which offers a variety of integrated products and services that cover the widest possible range of customer needs of the same job profile;
- an ecosystem as a self-developing organization that uses innovative approaches to management and considers the company as a "living organism".

On analyzing the existing literature, we propose to define the financial ecosystem as a model of complex economic relationships that is formed by transforming a traditional type of financial conglomerate into interdependent business environment thanks to modern technologies and innovations. This model requires in-depth knowledge of consumer needs, ability to analyze a large amount of dynamic data to elaborate an effective pricing policy, as well as processing capabilities for instant offers focused on a particular consumer of the product. In fact, in this model, a new individual financial product is formed with each purchase.

We distinguish four stages in the model formation (Fig. 7.1). At the first stage, globalization and regional integration, modern trends in the development of society and the economy, liberalization, and increased competition on the financial markets make individual financial market institutions using financial convergence mechanisms form associations in related segments of the financial market.

Then this process becomes more complex, with company alliances emerging. The pioneers of financial conglomeration were banks. The liberalization of financial markets caused a continuous series of mergers and

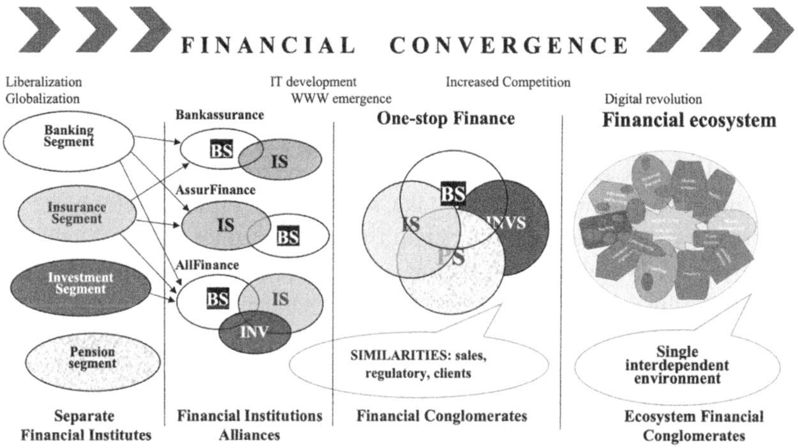

Fig. 7.1 Evolution of the ecosystem approach on financial markets. (*Source*: Compiled by the authors)

acquisitions, which began in the 1980s, and spawned a new type of financial institution, namely bancassurance groups. They laid the foundation for such new concepts as bankassurance/assurfinance/allfinance, denoting the integration of banking and insurance services and the partial transfer by the insurance company of its selling functions to an intermediary represented by a bank, or vice versa. The advantage of this type of organization was its ability to offer its customers a complete package of financial services, including both basic banking and insurance services. Meanwhile, the insurance division of such an organization, having a large amount of "long" money, was able to make short-term investments through a banking division. For example, it provided short-term loans to customers. Bancassurance groups were much more ubiquitous, as banks have a significant network of branches and representative offices. Thus, we moved from the concept of isolated financial services to the concept of a complex converged financial product, the provision of which, due to legal requirements, becomes possible only as part of a group of financial market institutions. In a particular case, great value for an individual client implies lower costs, since the set of business processes remains unchanged, and the price may be higher.

At the next stage, along with the concept of financial conglomerate being integrated into legislation, financial conglomerates emerge.

Penetration into new sectors of the financial market allows FC participants to master the technologies of competitors from other sectors and begin to develop hybrid financial products that have features of both a deposit and an insurance policy.

The concept of ecosystem, that is, a comprehensive perception of the financial market as a single organism, where everything is interconnected and interdependent, begins to take shape amid rapid development of information technologies. Ecosystem thinking becomes the most valuable competency, as it allows combining online and offline "worlds". A financial conglomerate is an institutional and organizational form of integration of its member firms from different sectors of the financial market, aimed at increasing the competitiveness of these firms by combining capital and interpenetration into each other's activities. It has powerful resources and becomes the main beneficiary of the emerging ecosystem approach on the global financial market. Financial conglomerates have already begun the transformation towards financial ecosystems, forming a new type of FC, namely the ecosystem financial conglomerate (EFC).

Financial ecosystems have become a symbol of China's technological vanguard and make a significant contribution to the country economy. The transformation and rapid growth in the number of ecosystem companies is based on powerful incentives for innovation and support for entrepreneurship; competition for traditional sales channels by "Internet insurers", and thereby lower insurance rates; and high-tech "financial ecosystems" designed by insurance corporations to change the concept of insurance services and develop new consumer habits by means of smart phone applications.

An example of a successful merger is the emerging financial ecosystem of the largest Chinese insurance company PingAn, which is transforming its business from purely insurance to a model of an ecosystem financial conglomerate. The company (actually being a FC) is switching to an ecosystem-based business model which includes insurance, banking, investment, and technological business services provided to almost 90 million customers. PingAn became the largest competitor of the Allianz insurance FC, which also initiated a paradigm shift. With the Allianz digital business division, the insurer invests in the development of a digital business model. On the one hand, Allianz takes on the role of organizer, creating, and supporting several ecosystems (data intelligence and cybersecurity, wealth management and retirement benefits, connected solutions in healthcare, property, and mobility, etc.) and providing interfaces for portfolio companies. On the other hand, Allianz takes on the role of a donor, connecting its own digital products to ecosystems outside the Allianz group. Combining these two typologies, Allianz applies a hybrid strategy and actually forms a financial ecosystem. A new technology for the production of a financial product is created, with a single set of services being provided by various legal entities. They are followed by other reputable enterprises in their attempts to catch up with the new financial market reality. HSBC, one of the largest financial conglomerates in the world, has created its own innovative fintech solutions. AXA, Alibaba and Ant Financial Services have signed a global partnership to distribute insurance products via Alibaba's global ecosystem.

Financial innovations have been and remain one of the important sources for improving economic results in the medium term, and their development should be encouraged. To increase their overall effectiveness, it is required to provide carefully prudential measures, financial protection systems, and crisis management mechanisms. The increased complexity of the system and the emergence of new global players in the face of eco-friendly financial conglomerates demand more precise regulation.

The conducted empirical analysis has proved the hypothesis that the process of financial convergence and technology development results in the emergency of financial ecosystems.

Given the circumstances, regulators face the following challenges:

- the contradiction between the international nature of the financial business and the national basis for its regulation;
- lack of uniform standards for supervision and regulation;
- lack of coordination (interaction) of national regulators;
- underestimation of information technology risks;
- availability of regulatory arbitration (using the difference in the regulatory framework of various jurisdictions to one's advantage);
- the risk of excessive influence of transforming financial conglomerates on the decision-making of both individual states and interstate associations, and non-governmental organizations;
- increased systemic risk.

The combination of different financial institutions causes risk concentration, which requires new innovative approaches to the technique of measuring and managing risks in a conglomerate. Firstly, risk management is mainly a problem of individual financial institutions rather than institutions within a group; therefore, there is no understanding of the risk profile for the group. Building a risk management system poses a risk management dilemma: manage by business processes or by homogeneous risks? Secondly, when creating a unified and interconnected reporting and accounting system which is essential for the control and management of a financial conglomerate, it is necessary to link non-matching accounting and reporting systems of banks and insurance companies. Thirdly, at the stage of evaluating the financial results achieved by the group as a whole, additional obstacles arise due to the use different techniques applied by the members of the group.

In addition to the above risks, when combining insurance and banking within a financial conglomerate, endogenous consecutive failures become more likely. If bank deposit insurance is provided by an insurance company that is a member of the conglomerate placing its reserves within this conglomerate, the loss event will cause disruptions to the entire system. The bank will lose money not only due to direct damage from the event, but also due to the withdrawal of reserves by the insurance company.

An increasing number of financial conglomerates are determined by changes in the management structure and the development of a new organizational management mechanism, since the interpenetration of cultures of integrating sectors (banking, insurance, investment, pension funds) within a financial conglomerate has the risk of losing the competitive advantage of the conglomerate due to insufficient staff qualifications.

Conclusions

The conducted research is the first attempt to determine the role of financial ecosystems in the overall evolution of financial institutions. We have revealed that the transition from the traditional model of a financial conglomerate to a model of financial ecosystems has become an obvious and logical response to the development of technologies and changing needs of market consumers of goods and services, as well as in respect to quality and speed of service. The objective of this study has been achieved.

First, it is shown that financial ecosystems are developing not only as a modern business model, but also as a methodological concept.

Second, it is demonstrated that financial ecosystems can give modern customers an opportunity to solve their daily problems via mobile devices and online platforms. This enables financial ecosystems to lie at the heart of the digital market.

Thus, the conducted research has proved our hypothesis. Ecosystem financial conglomerates as new entities of the global financial market receive additional international competitive advantages, including but not limited to the field of insurance, banking, investment and pension, and technologies, which is facilitated by the convergence of relevant interests, the similarity of activities, and communion of client interests.

The ability and willingness of entrepreneurs to take risks and create new innovative converged financial products, as well as participate in new market associations that can successfully sell newly created products (create demand), can become an additional catalyst for economic growth amid the ongoing economic downturn.

The combination of different financial institutions leads to risk concentration, which requires innovative tools to efficiently measure and manage risks in the conglomerate as well as adequate supervision measures.

The directions of further research are connected with an increasing number of ecosystem financial conglomerates, which determines a change in the management structure and the development of a new organizational management mechanism, since the interpenetration of integrating sectors within a financial conglomerate may ruin the competitive advantage of the conglomerate. It would be desirable to conduct risk structure analysis for the whole ecosystem financial conglomerate rather than for its individual components.

References

Aksoy, L., Alkire (née Nasr), L., Choi, S., Kim, P., & Zhang, L. (2019). Social Innovation in Service: A Conceptual Framework and Research Agenda. *Journal of Service Management, 30*(3), 429–448.

Belozyorov, S. A., & Pisarenko, Z. V. (2014). Empirical Analyses for Financial Convergence of Russian Insurance Market. *Economika Regiona*, (3), 198–208.

Curi, C. (2016). *Valuing Financial Conglomerates. Stylised Factors and New Evidence from Financial Crises.* Milano: FrancoAngeli Editore.

Di Giacinto, V., & Esposito, L. (2012). Convergence of Financial Structures in Europe: An Application of Factorial Matrices Analysis. In R. De Bonis & A. Pozzolo (Eds.), *The Financial Systems of Industrial Countries* (pp. 183–215). Berlin, Heidelberg: Springer.

Doroshenko, S. V., & Shelomentsev, A. G. (2017). Entrepreneurial Ecosystem in Modern Socioeconomical Research. *Journal of Economic Theory*, (4), 212–221.

Dowrick, S., & Bradford DeLong, J. (2003). "Globalization and Convergence", NBER Chapters. In *Globalization in Historical Perspective* (pp. 191–226). National Bureau of Economic Research, Inc.

Epstein, R., & Rhodes, M. J. (2019). Good and bad banking on Europe's periphery: pathways to catching up and falling behind. *West European Politics, 42*(5), 965–988.

Hölzl, W. (2003). Convergence of Financial Systems: Towards an Evolutionary Perspective. *Journal of Institutional Economics, 2*(1), 67–90.

Johnson, R. B., & Onwuegbuzie, A. J. (2004). Mixed Methods Research: A Research Paradigm Whose Time Has Come. *Educational Researcher, 33*(7), 14–26.

Konopatov, S. N., & Salienko, N. V. (2018). Platform-Based Business Models. *Scientific Journal NRU ITMO, Series "Economics and Environmental Management", 1*, 21–32.

Kuznetsova, N. P., & Chernova, G. V. (2001). Convergence in the Sphere of Financial Services. *Bulletin of Saint Petersburg State University of Engineering and economics, Series: Economics, 2012*(3), 431–433.

Murinde, V., Agung, J., & Mullineux, A. (2004). Patterns of Corporate Financing and Financial System Convergence in Europe. *Review of International Economics, 12*(4), 693–705.

Nebolsina, E. (2018). Peculiarities of Insurtech Development in the USA, the UK, China and Russia. In *Vision 2020: Sustainable Economic Development and Application of Innovation Management from Regional Expansion to Global Growth Proceedings of the 32nd International Business Information Management Association (IBIMA) Conference in Seville* (pp. 3509–3516). Spain.

Prasad, E., Rogoff, K., Wei, Sh.-J., & Kose, M. (2003). Effects of Financial Globalization on Developing Countries: Some Empirical Evidence. *IMF Occasional Paper* No. 220.

Van den Berghe, L., & Verweire, K. (2000). Convergence in the Financial Services Industry. *The Geneva Papers on Risk and Insurance. Issues and Practice.* Palgrave Macmillan, *25*(2), 262–272.

Walsh, K. (2019). Regional Capability Emergence in an Entrepreneurial Ecosystem. *Journal of Entrepreneurship and Public Policy, 8*(3), 359–383.

Zorio-Grima, A., & Merello, P. (2020). Consumer Confidence: Causality Links with Subjective and Objective Information Sources. *Technological Forecasting and Social Change, 150.*

CHAPTER 8

International Investment Law: A Journey from the Past to the Future

Evgeny Popov

Introduction

Systems of international investment law have evolved over centuries as a result of various political and economic reforms. In the formative years of international investment law, the traditional idea of "laissez faire", alongside with the principle of unrestricted free enterprise, gave way to the neoliberal concept of foreign investment management for solving global problems, such as (for example) improving citizens' welfare. All this resulted in a situation where international investment law came to be seen as an integral and inseparable part of the structural global task for providing a world order founded upon international law.

E. Popov (✉)
Moscow State Institute of International Relations (MGIMO University), Moscow, Russia
e-mail: e.popov@inno.mgimo.ru

J. Kovalchuk (ed.), *Post-Industrial Society*,
https://doi.org/10.1007/978-3-030-59739-9_8

Methodology

According to Labin, there is a fundamental difference in the interpretation of international investment law as a part of private international law, compared to the Western doctrine which interprets international investment law as part of international law (Labin and Solovyova 2017). This research is aimed at studying the development of international law, and the context in which international investment law has been developing. The author does not set out to criticize the concept of international investment law.

In the 1960–80s, developing countries turned to international mechanisms to regulate foreign investment, rather than to customary international law (Schrijver 1994). The reason for this is that foreign investors (including multinational corporations) who deal with hosting state investments were imposed with certain obligations: to use local raw materials, to hire local staff, and not to interfere in the internal affairs of the state. However, in the 1990s, these developing countries started to oppose the regulation of foreign investments under the auspices of the World Trade Organization (WTO). It was developed countries who voted against regulating foreign investments in the framework of UN mechanisms, stating that the involvement of international regulatory mechanisms would create a sustainable system prioritizing those states that receive investments. In the 1990s, an attempt was made, through the mediation of the OECD, to formulate a comprehensive, universal, international agreement on foreign investments, but this initiative was not supported by developing countries. No significant international organization is involved in developing a global agreement on international investment law.

Results

International investment law cannot remain detached from the changes in the international environmental law, in the international law concerning human rights, or in the system of corporate social responsibility and good corporate governance (Leader 2006). There is a need to establish a proper balance between the competing principles of international law. Moreover, it is also necessary to promote human rights and sustainable development. All these and many other problems can be gradually resolved by building relationships between foreign investors and host states. This must be done in such a way that international investment law is accepted by both parties as the most effective tool: helping the interests of states and investors to both be taken into account, and ensuring sufficient attention to other competing principles of the international law is paid.

Bilateral investment treaties (BITs), free trade agreements, the WTO Agreement, and other agreements, governed by customary international law, seek to impose restrictions and obligations on states that receive investments. There is no single, legally binding, international instrument that imposes the same obligations on foreign investors or large multinational companies (MNCs) (Konina 2018). In the absence of agreed international rules governing the responsibility of MNCs for human rights violations or environmental damage, it turns out that courts of different jurisdictions can come to conflicting conclusions based on separate legal principles or "soft law" principles.

Initially, international investment law regulated economic relations in the field of investment activities and assumed the protection of their citizens abroad. However, today, investment law is more focused solely on protecting private investors in international arbitration tribunals for claims against states that accept investments.

The main tasks of international investment law are to protect investors against political risks, increase the economic efficiency of the countries that receive investments, and stimulate economic growth in these countries, creating other conditions for attracting investments including legal certainty for foreign investors.

International investment law affects the country that received investments; it defines the international standards and the legal regime of foreign investors, and also provides additional protection for them such as, for example, access to independent international tribunals (particularly for those investors dealing with poor and developing states with relatively weak legal systems). In cases of conflict, foreign investors who deal with infrastructure projects in such countries may be subject to an unfair and hostile attitude on the part of the state receiving investments. Therefore, the possibility of appealing to an independent international arbitration tribunal is the only way to protect the investor's rights. The probability that an investor will receive significant compensation as a result of a court decision is one form of deterrent for the state receiving the investment.

Conclusions/Recommendations

The countries concerned are increasingly aware that the current state of affairs is unsatisfactory. The main purpose of most investment agreements, both bilateral investment treaty (BIT) and under WTO agreements, is to protect the rights of foreign investors, which often happens at the expense of social values or international soft law. Besides, there is no balance between protecting the rights of investors and preserving public policy space, which is extremely important for those states that are both importers and exporters of foreign direct investment (FDI).

International investment tribunals often violate generally accepted principles of international economic law, such as the state's right to permanent sovereignty over natural resources or the principle of economic self-determination, which to some extent distorts the international legal order and leads to judicial decisions that are not accepted by the developing states as a measure of legal certainty (Schultz and Dupont 2015).

In the absence of a global agreement governing foreign investment, the current rules of international investment law are still based on customary international law, which gives international investment tribunals the power to interpret the rules to apply and make decisions as they see fit. In most cases, investment tribunals focus exclusively on the commercial aspects of the proceedings when making decisions, thus ignoring other competing principles of international law. When conducting proceedings, investment courts and tribunals must pay equal attention to competing principles of international law and to public and private interests.

Existing and growing discrepancies and disagreements about the key principles of international investment law are extremely disadvantageous to both the host states and the international investors, including MNCs. All parties are interested in conducting objective and consistent proceedings, whilst also ensuring the rules and regulations are applied consistently regarding the treatment of foreign investors or citizens. The main aim of the international investment law is to provide opportunities for "playing fairly" under clear and predictable rules within the overall structure of international law. This will improve the quality of relations between the host countries and the foreign investors, making them more stable, predictable, and coordinated, and will also make international law more important. International investment law should become a more open, fair, and rule-based transparent system, if it is to play the same role as the WTO system does in international trade.

Investment courts and tribunals should also demonstrate a greater desire to recognize the rights of the investment-receiving states, especially in allowing them to independently take the necessary regulatory measures to ensure that the activities of foreign investors within these states comply with the principles and objectives of their social, environmental, and economic policies. The law should not protect foreign investors from political risks, or others, in the territory of the state receiving them. In the Oscar Chinn case, for example, the Permanent Court of International Justice ruled that "favourable business conditions and goodwill are transient and inevitably changing circumstances, and therefore they are not subject to protection" (Chinn 1934).

Political and socio-economic conditions in the host country constantly change, so investors should take these circumstances into account when making decisions. Governments seek to meet the needs of society, for example, by carrying out economic reforms, improving the efficiency of the tax system, improving the quality of health and education systems, and dealing with other important issues such as the environment, raising the minimum wage, and creating safe working conditions. All these changes inevitably affect how foreign investors act.

The system of international law, and the system of international investment law in particular, has undergone significant changes in recent years. Those countries that were previously supportive of investors, such as the United States, now protect sovereignty; conversely, those who used to defend sovereignty, such as China, are now increasingly protecting foreign investors. China, for example, is expanding investment activities abroad; Bolivia and Venezuela have withdrawn from International Centre for the Settlement of Investment Disputes (ICSID); other states are returning to the Calvo doctrine, which requires foreign investors to file claims in the state court of the host country before applying to the international tribunal cases a conflict (Report of the South Centre 2005). Such countries as India and Australia plan to amend, or have already amended, their existing bilateral trade agreements by removing the provisions that allow a foreign investor to apply to international courts and tribunals to resolve disputes with the host state (Aisbett et al. 2016).

According to the ICSID rules, the system of international investment proceedings also requires major changes, especially in increasing transparency of proceedings, accountability, openness, and ensuring equitable geographical representation of arbitrators and the proceedings themselves.

Critics of the current system of proceedings under the auspices of ICSID drew attention to the fact that the investment proceedings, with elements of public law, should not be heard by randomly appointed arbitrators. Such proceedings should be held in the permanent courts, which have the authority and the competence to examine different actions of the state and to make the decisions that directly affect state (public) policy (Van Harten 2017).

The traditional distinction between developed and developing countries are smoothed out when it comes to improving the existing mechanisms for resolving international investment disputes. These mechanisms were originally created for settling a small number of private disputes by a group of lawyers specializing in commercial law (Carim 2015).

Existing mechanisms, such as ICSID, have their advantages (objectivity, speed of dispute resolution and flexibility), which it is advisable to maintain when implementing reforms within the dispute resolution system. At the same time, they have to function effectively within the broader framework of the rule of international law.

As for the Dispute Settlement Body (DSB) of the WTO—which resolves trade disputes between state governments within the framework of those multilateral trade agreements that fall within the scope of the agreement on rules and procedures for dispute resolution—this mechanism deserves closer study. In contrast to investment ad hoc tribunals that operate under the ICSID rules or other arbitration rules, DSB proceedings are more efficient and transparent. In September 2015, the European Commission published amendments to Chapter II of the Transatlantic Trade and Investment Partnership (TTIP) agreement, which proposed creating a new transparent system for resolving disputes between host countries and investors (the so-called Investment Court System) in the image and semblance of the WTO DSB. This system could replace the existing ICSID mechanism in future EU investment agreements. Both the court of first instance and the court of appeal, the authors of the TTIP agreement assumed, were supposed to become a part of the new system. Mediation and consultations will be offered to these parties as pre-trial proceedings, as in the WTO DSB (EC Press-Release 2015). All this is an attempt to improve the mechanism for resolving disputes between investors and the state through reforms and transformations, the essence of which is to form an official judicial system instead of arbitration. As is known, the TTIP parties (both the United States and the EU) have recognized the lack of relevance of continuing consultations and discussions regarding the TTIP agreement, but for academic purposes, the analysis of the aforementioned draft agreement is nevertheless of interest, since it demonstrates the current trends in the development of the international legal mechanism for regulating investment activities and resolving disputes that arise from such activities. In October 2015, negotiations on the Trans-Pacific Partnership agreement (TPP) with the countries in the Asia-Pacific region were completed, and countries including Mexico, Chile, and Vietnam, as well as Japan, New Zealand, and Australia, agreed to use an improved mechanism for resolving disputes between investors and the state. Thus, when it comes to settling disputes over the most relevant and sensitive issue in international investment between investors and the state, both developed and developing countries agree that they need to improve the mechanism for regulating investments. Again, even though TPP has not entered into force, the very fact of its presence—that a multilateral agreement was made, and an improved mechanism for resolving disputes between an investor and a state was agreed upon—should be recognized as a step forward in creating an international legal treaty regime.

Developed countries acknowledge that, since they are also receiving investments, their corporate headquarters can be located in countries with emerging markets; issues of international arbitration are also relevant for them. This is why developed countries have begun to restrict the investment protection regime: to protect their interests and to provide greater freedom of manoeuvre for state regulators (Schwebel 2014). The United States refused to provide full protection to foreign investors, which was reflected in the revision of the Model US BIT in 2012. It was a vivid example of the above.

The convergence of interests of states receiving investments and FDI-exporting countries, as well as both developing and developed countries, show that there is a need to develop a comprehensive international convention on protecting investments (Wellhausen 2016). The difficulties of establishing an appropriate balance between competing principles of law and the interests of all parties should not be underestimated. Addressing all these important issues requires a coherent and coordinated international approach to ensure consistency, transparency, fairness, legitimacy, and predictability in the complex relations between foreign investors and the countries receiving investments. There is still a hope that the global investment agreement will be based not only on the previously concluded International Investment Agreements (IIAs) between developed and developing countries, but also on the IIAs between developing states.

In the absence of a comprehensive international agreement regulating foreign investments, a well-written new Multilateral Investment Agreement (MIA) or a revised MIA may be useful to resolve the issues of international investment law by determining the nature and scope of investment protection principles and the protection of the regulatory system of the states receiving investments. Furthermore, it is necessary to clearly define the conditions under which foreign investors can sue states receiving investments in international courts and tribunals.

References

Aisbett, E., Busse, M., & Nunnenkamp P. (2016). *Bilateral Investment Treaties Do Work; Until They Don't* (Working Paper, No. 2021). Kiel Institute for the World Economy.

Carim, X. (2015). *International Investment Agreements and Africa's Structural Transformation: A Perspective from South Africa* (Investment Policy Brief, No. 4, p. 4).

Chinn, O. (1934). *PCIJ Reports* (Series A/B, No. 63, p. 65).

European Commission Press-Release. (2015, September 16). Available at: http://europa.eu/rapid/press-release_IP-15-5651_en.htm. Accessed 21 Jan 2020.

Konina, N. (2018). Evolution of the Largest Multinational German Companies. *Sovremennaya Evropa, 2*(81), 49–59.

Labin, D. K., & Solovyova, A. V. (2017). Mesto investisionnogo prava v sisteme mezhdunarodnogo prava [The Place of Investment Law Within the System of International Law]. *Moscow Journal of International Law, 3*(107), 40–51.

Leader, S. (2006). Human Rights, Risks, and New Strategies for Global Investment. *Journal of International Economic Law, 9*, 657–659.

Report of the South Centre. (2005, February). Development on Discussion for the Improvement of the Framework for UCSID Arbitration and the Participation of Developing Countries. South Centre Analytical Note. SC/TADP/AN/INV/1.

Schrijver, N. (1994). Developments in International Investment Law. In J. Macdonald (Ed.), *Essays in Honour of Wang Tieya* (pp. 703–720). Dordrecht: Martinus Nijhoff.

Schultz, T., & Dupont, C. (2015). Investment Arbitration: Promoting the Rule of Law or Over-empowering Investors? A Quantitative Empirical Study. *European Journal of International Law, 25*(4), 1147–1157.

Schwebel, S. (2014). In Defense of Bilateral Investment Treaties. *Columbia FDI Perspectives, 1*, 35.

Van Harten, G. (2017). The Use of Quantitative Methods to Examine Possible Bias in Investment Arbitration. *Yearbook on International Investment Law & Policy*, 2011, Paper 33.

Wellhausen, R. L. (2016). Recent Trends in Investor-State Dispute Settlement. *Journal of International Dispute Settlement, 7*, 117–135.

CHAPTER 9

"Who Will Rule?": Institution of State in the Transformation Process of the Twentieth and Twenty-First Centuries

Vladimir Osipov

Introduction

In the twentieth and twenty-first centuries the most significant processes and events in human history have occurred that have had a direct and most significant impact on the change in the institution of the state. As a result of two world wars, the collapse of a number of empires of the past, the emergence and decomposition of a bipolar world, the formation of a multipolar world with an obvious hegemon and so on, the political map of the world has changed beyond recognition. Transformations of the institution of the state turned out to be so significant that some of the states ceased to exist at all, while others, on the contrary, appeared and are already having a significant impact on global development. The border between democratic states and states with extraordinary powers (authoritarian regimes) is increasingly visible on the political map of the

V. Osipov (✉)
Moscow State Institute of International Relations (MGIMO University), Moscow, Russia
e-mail: vs.ossipov@inno.mgimo.ru

J. Kovalchuk (ed.), *Post-Industrial Society*,
https://doi.org/10.1007/978-3-030-59739-9_9

world. The task is to determine the trajectories of the legal change of the institution of the state and its transformation into either a democratic or an authoritarian one.

D. Bell asked in his famous book, "Who will rule?" (Bell 1999). And this question is more and more actual at the time of the transformation process.

The result of the implementation of a legal norm, that is, the quality of citizens' behavior in the course of implementation, depends on the legal culture, legal awareness and respect by citizens of each other's rights and freedoms. In this case, the institute is a system of norms ensuring the equal rights of citizens. Hence the need for a more complete disclosure of the concept of democracy.

For our study, the definition of democracy given by the eminent scholar Joseph A. Schumpeter has a great importance. He suggested that democracy be understood as an institutional device for making political decisions, in which individuals acquire the power to make decisions by competing for votes (Schumpeter 1983). If democracy is an institutional structure, then we see no reason to refuse the same monarchy, aristocracy and other forms of state, even incorrect ones. The question is how a change in this institutional structure arises.

Methodology

The methodology of institutional analysis, the general theory of systems and the system-structural approach based on it were used in the chapter to identify and justify the connections of elements of systems.

An interdisciplinary approach has great importance for the research, because institutional theory is dualistic due to legal and economic sciences. Legal science laid the theoretical foundations of institutionalism, and economic science contributed to the implementation of the ideas of institutionalism in the practice of state formation and regulation of public relations.

A democratic state can be characterized by the following basic principles:

- the ruling elite does not have a monopoly on political activity;
- people who are not members of the elite have the right to participate in political activity;
- The activities of the ruling elite are regulated by laws;

- the existence of a legitimate mechanism for the transition of the supreme state power from the hands of one group of people to the hands of another;
- a change in the ruling elite does not imply *a coup d'état*.

Thus, the content of democracy does not overlap the form of implementation of the procedures, while often the opposite happens. Formal adherence to the procedure implies adherence to the spirit of the law, while this is not at all the case. The prevalence of form over content turns law into an instrument for establishing an authoritarian or a totalitarian state.

Currently, some countries, under the banner of democratic institutions, are establishing authoritarian regimes where human rights are violated in strict accordance with the formal procedure. Thus, the combination of a legal norm and the practice of its implementation, according to the level of legal culture in society, makes it possible to assess the real behavior of actors, the possibility of exercising rights and ways of forming legal relations.

Thus, in the democratic form of the state, institutional changes are permanent, but the scale of changes may be reduced, since the system of checks and balances we have already mentioned reduces the possibilities for institutional changes. It seems to us that institutional changes over time have the character of damped fluctuations. It turns out that the gauge effect also works like a pendulum oscillation, damps if the institution does not embed by regular use of the institute in similar legal relationships. If the institution does not embed, its action gradually weakens until its action ceases completely, as the pendulum oscillations decay.

Each new wave of oscillations is smaller in strength than the previous one, since the previous wave of changes has a limiting effect on the subsequent ones (Fig. 9.1). The new institutional change cannot surpass the previous one. The only way to break this chain of institutional changes with a "vetocracy" (Fukuyama 2011) at the end, where the fluctuations are minimal, is to revolutionize the shape of the state with the establishment of a new political regime. As we noted earlier, due to the path-dependence effect, some institutions will continue to operate, but they will not be provided with compulsory legal force of the state, which means that their action will gradually fade.

In connection with the competitiveness of political markets, it should be noted that it also arises between informal institutions and government

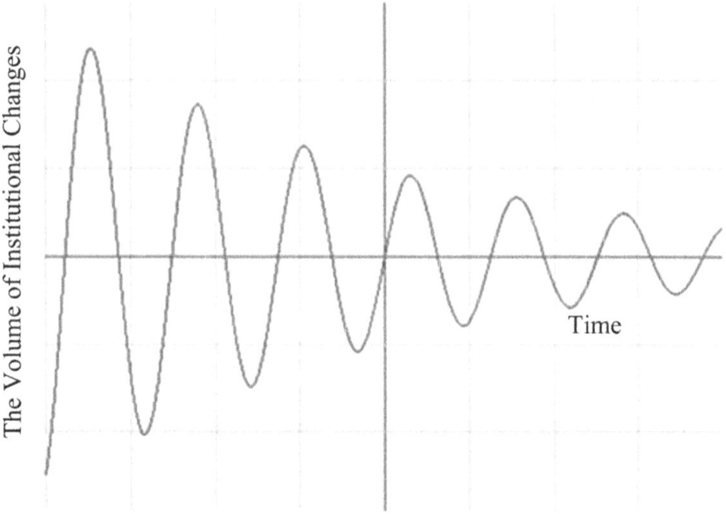

Fig. 9.1 Fading fluctuations in institutional change

bodies. If we turn to the manifestations of informal institutions in public administration and in socio-economic activity, we can see the following picture. Such institutions become a peculiar competitors of state and municipal bodies, officially established procedures, direct democracy institutions (Tikhomirov 2005a).

V. Lyubashits notes, that power is an integral property of the human community (Lyubashits 2002, 2012). As a social phenomenon, it appears as a perfect and objective regulator of social relations. Being generated by them, power, in turn, acts as a tool for organizing society, establishing discipline and order in it. This means that the fundamental, initial point of institutional change is precisely the change in power, that is, there is a sustainable pair of "power is changing – institutions are changing".

In another of his work, V. Lyubashits notes that there are four innovative stages in the legal institutionalization of modern political dominance: civil state, rule of law, democratic rule of law and social rule of law. The transition from a state of arbitrariness to a state of law is characterized by the institutionalization of private enterprise, as well as by the regulation of public administration (Lyubashits et al. 2015).

Results

To analyze the process of transformation of the institution of the state in modern conditions, it is necessary to determine the possible directions of changes in the institution from the origins of institutional theory.

The constitutional organization of power consists in the formation of a favorable organization of the internal authorities of the state institution for political freedom. It is important to note that in this case, Hauriou assumes the synonymy of the institution and organization, which will subsequently be changed as part of the development of the theory of institutions (Hauriou 1910). Corporate institutions shape political freedom through four characteristics of an organization:

1. the establishment of a representative organization of power and its centralization over the community;
2. decentralization and separation of powers with the priority of the legislature;
3. ensuring transparency to facilitate the accession of the general public to decisions of authorities;
4. registration of the constitutional system in the form of a law to ensure order in the community.

Hauriou gives the most important characteristic of an institution, its embeddedness (as Mark Granovetter would later call this property of institutions [Granovetter 1985]): "Every actual state that lasts in society seeks, precisely by virtue of its duration, to become a legal state; as an example, one can cite the institution of prescription, as well as the fact that emerging governments, even if they came to power through usurpation, are nevertheless recognized as legitimate as their domination becomes long-term" (Hauriou 1910). It is important for us to note here that Hauriou recognizes the possibility of legitimizing usurpation and the establishment of a state institution under the usurper, which clearly intersects with the opinion of Ludwig Gumplowicz on violence as a way of organizing the state (Gumplowicz 1899). Recall that M. Weber was also a supporter of this theory (Weber 1905). Gumplowicz and Weber obviously had the most direct impact on the formation of the modern concept of D. North's social order (North 1990).

Hauriou points out that the expansion and equalization of rights to occupy posts leads to very sad consequences, that is, he nevertheless adheres not so much to the democratic order of establishing legal relations, as he is an adherent of egalitarian transformations and, possibly, an aristocratic regime (Hauriou 1910). He also does not refuse attention to the dictatorship, considering it as a means of combating the crisis caused, for example, by war.

The dictatorship provides for the rejection of the principle of separation of powers, since all power is concentrated in the hands of the government. Otherwise, the dictatorship does not ensure the regime of self-preservation, as well as the stability of the institution of the state. For salvation, the Hauriou state considers it possible to sacrifice fundamental principles in order to overcome the crisis vigorously and quickly. It is not possible to allow any discussion of the actions of the authorities in this case. Thus, the institution of the state in a crisis is presented as the highest value, for the sake of which a sharp change in the institutional order is possible. Despite the general characteristic of centralizing power, he suggests distinguishing between three types of dictatorship. So, the actual dictatorship comes when it is not provided for by the constitution, but at the same time, due to extraordinary circumstances, there is a concentration of power in the executive branch. Since the actions of the dictatorship are usually quick, swift, the focus of power in the hands of the executive branch is the most common.

Hauriou provides for the possibility of combating the crisis of public administration not only with the dictatorship (although he clearly prefers the latter), but also with the help of ordinary business. The only difference in this case is the postponement of the election, that is, some extension of the powers of the body, which was supposed to lose them by the term of the election. However, such an extension is limited by the terms of the special situation in the state, that is, from the moment the threat to the state ceases, the elections must be held according to the previous procedure with the transfer of powers to the newly elected people.

The behavior of citizens or citizens of a state in which the authorities resort to extraordinary powers or the introduction of a dictatorship is also considered in the context of extraordinary circumstances. So, in France, the Constitutional Act of June 24, 1793 (Declaration of the Rights of Man and Citizen) states that when the government violates the rights of the people, rebellion constitutes for the people and for each part of it the most sacred of rights and the most urgent obligation (Duguit 1923). Leon Duguit paid great attention to these problems. Thus, comparing Articles 10, 11 and 35 of the Declaration of 1793 with one another and giving them a legal description, he noted, that it is a bitter irony that such principles were proclaimed by the assembly, which for two years oppressed our country with one of the most bloody tyrannies (Duguit 1923). Duguit correctly says that the law, just because it is law, does not become absolute truth. Demanding obedience to the law only because the law is law means trying to make people slaves. Obedience to the law is a social necessity, but the law should not become an instrument of tyranny.

It is difficult to imagine that the state voluntarily agreed, and even more so obliged its citizens to rebel against themselves in case of violation of the rights of the people. The main problem is what is considered a violation of the rights of the people. It is quite obvious that the state may not consider it a violation of rights, what citizens consider a violation of rights. This discrepancy can have the most adverse consequences for public order, because citizens will be guided by this rule in every case when it seems to them that their rights are violated. Thus, the probability of the onset of revolutionary events increases with the presence of such a norm on the one hand. On the other hand, this norm "protects" the state from taking controversial measures. The state will take a more balanced approach to the introduction of new norms and rules; it will be much more responsible in the development and adoption of new decisions that can worsen the situation of citizens. Thus, such a norm will not necessarily lead to a revolution, but it can also serve as a certain measure of checks and balances in the state. It is important to note that in France, revolutionary events (with certain periods of attenuation) lasted until the establishment of the Third French Republic.

There are two ways of institutional decline of the state. First, society prefers stability, from which conservatism arises in relation to political institutions. This "natural" conservatism does not allow the institution to change when external circumstances change (note that this is possible, even with highly adaptive institutions). Between the necessary change in the institute and the modern quality of this institute, a lag arises, which causes its decline. Secondly, when the actors are "captured" by the institute; that is, they do not imagine another direction of action than the institute provides; they cannot change the obsolete institute due to the fact that they do not notice the process of its obsolescence.

The second path of political decline is nepotism and favoritism, when political institutions patronize their clientele and relatives in business activities. We can observe this second path in almost all young democracies. The reason for this phenomenon is that political institutions lack confidence, which translates into transferring responsible areas of activity into the hands of loved ones, not professionals. A clientele in exchange for this patronage provides support to a political institution. At the initial stage of the formation of the state institution in a new form, this behavior is justified, but as the institution matures, the clientele is replaced by professional personnel. However, it is possible to extend the clientele system by transferring powers, activities and even positions to their children.

So, we can observe entire dynasties in the judiciary, in the executive branch, in state corporations and in universities.

Political systems and the configuration of power can be assembled into an interconnected structure, which Huntington did (Huntington 2006).

The democratic state, due to the strengthening of vetocracy, is losing the ability to quickly adapt to renewing (note, even faster) changes in the external environment, which results in a decrease in the effectiveness of public administration. On the one hand, everyone understands that changes are necessary, and on the other hand, no one admits changes so as not to upset the fragile balance of interests that has been established. Thus, the institution of the state of the republican democratic form of government, as well as constitutional monarchies, impedes the development of the institution of the state and the institutional conditions for conducting entrepreneurial and other activities on its territory, which entails increasing pressure from social movements to switch to another form of government. So, one can observe the emergence of authoritarian leaders in formerly democratic states. Authoritarian leaders, in turn, seek to destroy democratic institutions and translate the institution of the state into an authoritarian form of government. H. Arendt noted that "behind the seizure of power by a dictatorship, as a rule, a routine, predictable and" domesticated "state arises" (Arendt 1956). The transition to authoritarianism (dictatorship) resolves the conflict of interests of different classes and groups and makes the institutional transformation of the state. For a while it seems that the problems have been resolved, but the institution of the state is moving toward a new crisis and contradictions, because the previous solution was found through violence, which means it is ineffective—hence the fragility of authoritarian regimes.

Conclusions

From the side of the external environment, of course, the main challenge is globalization, which allowed organizations and self-organized groups of citizens to establish relationships at the expense of the information and communication network, bypassing territorial borders and quite often ignoring national legislation, which allows them to conduct entrepreneurial, political, social, and terrorist, criminal and any other activity, including those related to the undermining of existing national political institutions. Since such relationships are not connected with the territory, and also allow for the possibility of interethnic communication, then, provided that political institutions are ignored, such interaction networks replace or replace the state. One of the last bastions of the state, the monopoly on the production of banknotes, also fell due to scientific and technological achievements (blockchain technology) associated with the information and communication network. The state still continues to print national banknotes, but their value in the calculations is gradually decreasing, and the volume of electronic money circulation, on the contrary, is increasing. Defense is still a stronghold of nation-states, except for those states that are united in supranational unions. But, as we noted earlier, due to the impossibility of a new big war, the importance of defense can also begin to decline. And if we take into account the increasing military enrichment of terrorist groups, the armament of criminal groups that regular armies can no longer cope with, it becomes clear that the military forces of the state are also weakening.

In addition to the inability of the state to cope with terrorist and criminal groups, political institutions themselves erode their own foundations. So, the transition of public administration to the so-called service approach makes it easier for public administration to abandon the many functions that were previously performed by government bodies (Osipov et al. 2017). The desire to abandon part of the functions is dictated by the inability to respond to changes in the external environment; that is, the state, instead of the necessary modernization of political institutions, prefers to discard those functions with which it is unable to cope. Tikhomirov correctly notes that "the American method of deregulation is used in our other sense, as a" reset "of state functions" (Tikhomirov 2005b). The only clarification that should be made: such a "reset" is characteristic not only for our state, but for almost everyone who makes the transition to a service state.

References

Arendt, H. (1956). Authority in the Twentieth Century. *Review of Politics, 18*(4), 407.

Bell, D. (1999). *The Coming of Post-Industrial Society. A Venture in Social Forecasting*. New York: Basic Books.

Duguit, L. (1923). Traité de Droit constitutionnel. 2e édition. Tome III. La théorie générale de l'État.

Fukuyama, F. (2011, November 22). Oh for a Democratic Dictatorship and Not a Vetocracy. *Financial Times*.

Granovetter, M. (1985). Economic Action and Social Structure: The Problem of Embeddedness. *American Journal of Sociology, 91*(3), 481–510.

Gumplowicz, L. (1899). Grundriss Der Sociologie.

Hauriou, M. (1910). Principes de Droit Public. Librairie de la Société du recueil J.-B. Sirey et du Journal du Palais, Paris.

Huntington, S. P. (2006). *Political Order in Changing Societies*. London: Yale University Press.

Lyubashits, V. (2002). State Power: Concept, Features and Types. *Pravovedenie*, 6.

Lyubashits, V. (2012). Problems of Typology of Evolutionary Forms of State and State Power. *Yurist-Pravoved, 1*(50), 70.

Lyubashits, V., Kiyashko, E., & Timofeeva, A. (2015). *Social and Legal State as a Necessary Institutional Form of Legal Freedom. Socio-Economic and Humanitarian-Philosophical Problems of Modern Science* (pp. 42–43). Moscow/ Ufa/Rostov-on-Don: Ufa State University of Economics and Service.

North, D. (1990). *Institutions, Institutional Change and Economic Performance*. Cambridge, MA: Cambridge University Press.

Osipov, V. S., Skryl, T. V., Blinova, E. A., & Kosov, M. E. (2017). Dysfunctions of Public Administration System: Analysis of Institutional Reforms. *International Review of Management and Marketing, 7*(2), 123–129.

Schumpeter, J. A. (1983). *The Theory of Economic Development: An Inquiry into Profits, Capital, Credit, Interest, and the Business Cycle*. New Brunswick: Transaction Books.

Tikhomirov, Y. (2005a). Law: Formal and Informal. *Journal of Russian Law, 5*, 80–87.

Tikhomirov, Y. (2005b). Law and Selfregulation. *Journal of Russian Law, 9*, 88.

Weber, M. (1905). *The Protestant Ethic and the Spirit of Capitalism*.

CHAPTER 10

"New Generation" EU Free Trade Agreements: A Combination of Traditional and Innovative Mechanisms

Anastasia Makarenko and Lyudmila Chernikova

Introduction

Free trade agreements have become a significant part or the global trading system over the past 30 years. Such agreements have increased tenfold since the 1990s. The question still stands, however, as to whether making such agreements is a reasonable step, especially as multifaceted trade liberalization offers an alternative path

It is currently hard to ignore the fact that the global trading system is in a state of crisis. Economic sanctions and trade wars are merely two prominent political processes which undoubtedly negatively affect global trade. Globalization is also taking effect: the emergence of digital technology, social unrest in many states, and climate change create new

A. Makarenko (✉)
Moscow State Institute of International Relations (MGIMO University), Moscow, Russia

L. Chernikova
Financial University under the Government of the Russian Federation, Moscow, Russia

J. Kovalchuk (ed.), *Post-Industrial Society*,
https://doi.org/10.1007/978-3-030-59739-9_10

opportunities, but also new challenges. All of these factors lead to new world trade tendencies taking place. Many experts nowadays identify four such new tendencies: manufacturing-sale chain development, services expanding trade (including digital and e-commerce), the growth of investments, and the increasing significance of developing countries. The key players of the world trade system are forced to adjust to these changes in terms of, among other things, foreign trade and external economic activity regulation.

In such conditions a unilateral approach is obviously the most destructive for international trade, because such an approach implies non-compliance with international law and support for protectionism. It can, however, be observed that the multilateral approach has to some extent also failed to meet expectations, being based on the activity of international organizations and their respective multilateral instruments. This is proof of the World Trade Organization's (hereinafter WTO) lack of efficiency, acknowledged even by its head, Roberto Azevedo, having already led to a deadlock in its mechanisms for rulemaking and dispute resolution, with reforms of the latter being a subject of discussion among the organization's member-states.

In this context, bilateral free trade agreements seem, perhaps, to be the most effective means of trade relation regulation between an individual state and the rest of the world. It must be noted that this does not imply the prevalence of the bilateral approach. The multilateral approach is preserved through its transformation into an "omnilateral" one. This means it is important for states to not simply enter into individual free trade agreements but also to conclude such agreements with their key regional partners, which, thus, creates a sort of "network" consisting of their trade partners from all around the world. The European Commission website states as much, with the Commission insisting on using the term "trade network" in relation to all of the EU's trade agreements with other states.

The European Union (hereinafter the EU) currently enjoys the largest trade network in the world, with its 41 trade agreements with 72 countries. In spite of the harsh economic climate, European companies continue to actively make use of the opportunities that the largest trade network in the world provides. The EU's free trade agreements allow companies to access new markets thanks to the lifting of tariffs, the simplification of administrative procedures, and more synergy among goods and services trade standards and rules.

Generally speaking, a free trade agreement is a contract entered into by two or more states (or groups of states) for the purposes of creating a legal order in which any customs tariffs, import quotas, export restrictions, and other trade barriers are abolished in cross-country trade relations. It was these agreements, aimed at the abolition of any goods trade restrictions, that the EU had entered into up until 2006, when the European Commission adopted an instrument called "Global Europe—World Competition," a strategy stipulating that the Union must open up its services and investment markets, and not simply liberalize its trade of goods, in order to achieve an appropriate level of economic growth, taking into account all changes in the global economy. As a result, from 2006 onward, the EU started entering into so-called new-generation trade agreements: agreements concerning not only ordinary trade of goods matters, but also service provisions, investment matters, state procurement, competition, and sustainable development.

It is the new-generation trade agreements that are of interest in terms of EU foreign trade relations regulation and their effect on the world trade system, taking into account its aforementioned development tendencies in the modern era. Despite such agreements representing the bilateral approach to trade regulation, they often affect third parties, that is, states which are not parties to the agreements. A question arises: how do we make trade agreements, including EU free trade agreements, into "building blocks" and not "stumbling blocks" for the world trade system? It is becoming more and more difficult to find an answer to this question. Before, it was possible to estimate how trade agreements affect third parties with the help of economic indicators (on the basis of which conclusions could be made regarding whether access for foreign companies to a specified country's market was limited in some way), but nowadays, due to the agreements becoming increasingly more complex, it has become too difficult to account for any effects in regard to third parties. It is, however, obvious that it is the complexity of the "new generation" agreements that allows the EU to react accordingly to the challenges posed by the current state of world trade, thanks to combining both traditional and innovational trade relations regulations methods.

By "traditional" trade regulation goods trade regulation is meant. The EU's free trade agreements contain standard provisions on giving access to parties' goods markets on a mutual basis, on ensuring national treatment for them, on simplifying customs and trade procedures, and on regulating trade protection methods, technical barriers in trade, sanitary and phytosanitary measures.

In comparison, the provisions of "new generation" trade agreements regulating other trade aspects appear to be more modern and contain certain novelties. Some of these aspects and chapters dedicated to them were not included into "first generation" agreements. This chapter will examine individual regulation areas, making use of innovational regulation methods not present in a multilateral system. In particular, matters of e-commerce, investment dispute resolution and the relation between trade and labor and environment protection standards' observance will be analyzed.

Methodology

This study was conducted with the application of common scientific methods alongside special methods for exploring legal and economic phenomena, as well as different processes in the area of international economic and trade law: a systematic-structural analysis, social and legal phenomena synthesis, and comparative analysis and formal logic.

Results

Originally, regarding the first aspect, services trade did not fall under the scope of the EU's bilateral agreements; this can be explained by noting that the Union was taking shape, so services did not play a big role in the EU's trade at that time. Nowadays, however, according to the European Commission's data, services trade constitutes almost 70% of the member-states' economic activity. "New generation" agreements place services trade much higher, which is due to the fact that the WTO General Agreement on Trade in Services (GATS) is in need of improvement. As per the EU's free trade agreements, the liberalization of trade in services occurs on the basis of ensuring a national or preferential treatment for service providers, as well as with the help of so-called positive and negative lists of services. A "positive" list, in this case, is a list of service types which are allowed in the EU market, included in the agreement (the European approach, which is favored by the majority of such agreements). A "negative" list implies that the agreement provides access for all of the parties' services to their respective markets, excluding services listed in the trade agreement (the North American approach).

Another difficulty is the existence of two opposite approaches to e-commerce, regarding whether the subject matter of such commerce is a *product* or a *service*. On the scale of the WTO, this matter has been partially resolved through the *Antigua and Barbuda v. USA* case (the matter at hand was the provision of gambling services on the internet). The dispute resolution body found that online service provision is the first type of service supply as per GATS: it is a transnational supply of services. However, some of the WTO member-states—the United States among them—view goods as the subject matter of e-commerce and, in doing so, apply General Agreement on Tariffs and Trade (GATT) to relations arising from it. The EU supports the WTO's position in viewing e-commerce as a special type of wholesale and retail trade in services.

The regulation of e-commerce in the EU's free trade agreements is based on the abolition of custom duties and tariffs on services provided with the help of electronic means. Also, the agreements set forth provisions declaring e-commerce to be a global phenomenon and, thus, that parties agree to conduct negotiations on the following matters: the recognition of contracts concluded in an electronic format, electronic authentication, and certification; intermediaries' liability in the supply of services by electronic means; consumers' data and personal information protection; non-discrimination concerning service provision by means of e-commerce; and the fight against online fraud and other unfair practices. These provisions are included in the EU's agreements with Canada, Singapore, and Japan, among others. Unfortunately, many pre-existing differences in national laws prevent the EU from including more specific and binding provisions in its free trade agreements. However, the inclusion of e-commerce provisions, taking into account the developed European legislation in this field, is thought to greatly affect this area's regulation on a multilateral plane, which would serve to further liberalize e-commerce in such agreements. Steps in this direction have already been taken: on April 26, 2019, the EU presented its proposals, reflecting the aforementioned provisions in its free trade agreements in more detail concerning mutual obligations in the field of e-commerce, to the WTO. This proposal is on the WTO's agenda on the rules of e-commerce, with more than 70 states having already joined in on the discussion.

The innovations proposed by the EU's free trade agreements include investment regulation cooperation. On an international level, such cooperation is based on bilateral investment treaties (hereinafter BITs). With the help of such treaties, foreign investors are guaranteed unobstructed investment activity, with the main guarantees being national or preferential treatment, the protection of investments from expropriation or similar measures, equality and fair treatment of investments, and a ban on restricting investment payments abroad. The majority of such treaties include provisions on dispute resolution, should any such disputes arise between the host state and foreign investors. In accordance with these provisions, an investor has the right to take legal action in a competent national court of the host state, or to appeal to the International Centre for Settlement of Investment Disputes (ICSID), or to go into ad hoc arbitration in accordance with the United Nations Commission on International Trade Law (UNCITRAL) arbitration regulations.

Originally, in the EU, matters of foreign investments were addressed by both the Union and its member-states. As the EU developed, it strived to provide access for foreign investors to its market, in order to increase European business competitiveness and to create new jobs. The Lisbon treaty successfully achieved this by allocating foreign investments to the EU's exclusive competence as part of the Union's general trade policy.

The main difference of the EU's "new generation" free trade agreement is that the agreements, and not the BITs, regulate the Union's investment policy toward third parties. The agreements provide the same warranties to foreign investors as BITs, with the main novelty being dispute resolution. Previously, the main investment resolution method was investor-state dispute settlement (ISDS), that is, a mechanism for the settlement of investor-state disputes. ISDS is basically an international public law tool, utilized in a number of BITs and in some international trade agreements as well. Should an investor from one state invest into another state (the host state) but the host state infringes on the rights of the investor as per the treaty, with both having agreed to settle their disputes in accordance with ISDS rules, then the investor may go into arbitration with the host state. Despite ISDS sometimes being associated with international arbitration based on ICSID rules (the World Bank's International Centre for Settlement of Investment Disputes), in reality most investment disputes are resolved in international arbitration tribunals in the framework of other norms or other international institutions. Such tribunals include the London Court of International Arbitration, the Hong Kong International Arbitration Centre, and the International Chamber of Commerce.

A number of criticisms toward ISDS, made by the civil society of EU member-states, prompted the Union to reform the system. Among the main flaws of the ISDS were the following: (1) states were wary of losing their sovereignty in the settlement of such disputes: the ISDS rules state that the parties may choose between international and national arbitration courts, and in many cases, the parties favor an international arbitration court due to fears of national courts favoring the host state; (2) foreign investors may attempt to create more favorable conditions for themselves by transferring their HQ into a particular state (or by making a subsidiary there) in order to use a specific BIT to their advantage and to settle any potential disputes in the court which provides the best chances at winning the case (scholars have named this approach "forum-shopping" or "national planning"); (3) arbitration costs are not covered by the losing party, but are distributed between the parties, which creates a disproportionate situation where the state's expenses greatly outweigh the investor's expenses in the case of a loss; and (4) due to confidentiality being one of the main features of arbitration, ISDS procedures are not transparent.

Consultations on the matter began during the negotiations on the Transatlantic Trade and Investment Partnership (TTIP) between the EU and the United States, and, as they continue, have led to the EU's proposition of a new investment judicial system. Despite the negotiations on the TTIP having reached a dead end in light of a number of political events, the EU managed to realize its idea—the Comprehensive Economic and Trade Agreement (hereinafter CETA) between the EU and Canada became the first agreement to implement the system.

According to CETA, a new judicial system (consisting of two instances) has been established: the arbitration investment court, consisting of 15 publicly appointed judges and the court of appeals. As opposed to the previous system, the judges are not appointed by the parties but rather by the CETA Joint Committee. The 15 judges would include five EU representatives, five Canadian representatives, and five representatives from third countries. In proceedings the three judges hear the cases, with the possibility of a single judge resolving the dispute on the condition that the parties have agreed upon this thereon. The judges are elected from the entirety of the court's judges by the presiding judge based on rotation. A similar system is in place in the court of appeals.

The agreement reserves the rights for the parties to choose where their case will be heard: in national or international arbitration, or in accordance with the new system. A mediation procedure has also been implemented. By itself, the dispute resolution procedure begins with one of the parties requesting consultations with the party providing justification for their request in terms of which CETA provisions have been supposedly breached, as well as the legal and factual justification for their claim. If the investor had originally sought remedy in national courts, the request must be filed within the two years after the case had been discontinued, yet not later than ten years after the investor became aware of the breach. If no agreement has been made as a result of consultations, the investor may file a suit in an investment court not earlier than 6 months and not later than 18 months from the moment of filing the consultation request. If a suit is not filed in due time, the case will not be heard. Moreover, the investor is denied the right to file a request to determine the respondent (the latter, however, can inquire whether the Union or a member-state is in breach of its obligations), and also will not be able to file a new claim on the same basis. In cases when a suit is filed by an investor, the other party (the EU or an individual state) has to express its consent to settling the dispute before the court is formed. States can veto the hearing of a case based on the provision denying benefit to a third party. The provision's meaning is that the EU or a member-state may deny an investor the hearing of a case, should an investor own a business or control it in a third country, and on the condition that the host state has taken measures to prevent or to prohibit any transactions with said business for the purposes of maintaining world peace and security.

As such, three conditions must be met for an investor to gain the right to file a suit:

1. An investor's written request to settle a dispute in court (consultations being the first stage).
2. The 180-day time period from the moment of filing the consultation request must expire as must, if applicable, a 90-day time period from the moment of filing a request to determine the respondent.
3. Any ongoing trial in national and international courts on this matter must be dismissed.

Non-compliance could mean the suit being prematurely dismissed.

According to CETA, a ruling issued within the scope of the judicial system is binding for all parties involved in the dispute regarding their respective cases. The losing party must recognize the ruling and execute it. Moreover, Article 8.39 of CETA defines the remedies provided by the court. The court may award damages with interest, as well as a restitution in property.

Thus, the following advantages of the new system could be identified:

1. A permanent dispute resolution mechanism will be put in place, including a court of appeals.
2. The proceedings will be transparent, and the hearings will be public.
3. The system will stop cases of investors choosing the more advantageous case settlement method for themselves.
4. Unsubstantiated claims will be subject to dismissal.
5. Proceedings may be accelerated with the help of mediation.

The social area has also been affected by certain novelties about the EU's free trade agreements. The trade policy in many countries, including the EU, has been subject to criticism on the part of the population recently, with the latter claiming that state interests more often than not infringe on society's interests. This concerns mainly labor and environment issues which, in turn, give rise to many disputes during negotiations regarding the conclusion of free trade agreements. This has led to the EU having undertaken an adjustment of its trade policy, beginning in 2015, with the aim of fulfilling Sustainable Development Goals. These goals were set by the UN in its World Development Agenda, and include 17 fundamental tasks—such as the elimination of poverty and famine, ensuring high-quality education and decent labor conditions, and more in this manner—that the member-states have undertaken and strive to achieve by 2030. As one means for fulfilling these goals, the EU started including chapters on trade and sustainable development into its "new generation" free trade agreements. The provisions in these chapters can be divided into two main categories: the parties' obligations in the field of labor protection, and obligations in the field of environment protection. The parties undertake to observe and efficiently implement fundamental multilateral agreements into the respective fields, as well as to create such conditions in bilateral trade that would prevent the level of standards in international treaties from being lowered. Moreover, the EU's free trade agreements set forth the parties' obligations to maintain proper national labor standards and not to make use of labor standards for protectionist purposes in trade, as well as to communicate and cooperate by means of institutions specifically created for such purposes (including institutions in civil society), and to monitor and control the observance of the provisions contained in the chapters related to regulation of labor. In order to ensure efficient application of trade and sustainable development chapters, a joint committee may be created as per the agreements, consisting of representatives from both parties, as well as consultative groups consisting of representatives from business associations and non-governmental and scientific organizations.

When it comes to environmental protection regulation, the EU's free trade agreement provision can be subdivided into three main categories. The first group is aimed at preventing both national and international environmental legislation standards from being lowered for the purposes of promoting the parties' trade and investment goals. The second group sets forth inter-state cooperation in the field of so-called green technology. The third group includes provisions on undertakings to exchange information concerning environmental protection and climate change. It has to be noted that the EU has excluded environmental matters from its general dispute resolution system established by the agreements. Consultations by special committees on trade and sustainable development, consisting of expert groups specializing in environment protection, are proposed as an equivalent. A novelty in this context would be the involvement of civil society in settling environmental matters made official by the agreements. These representatives of civil society would have the right to participate in the expert group's activity at any stage of dispute settlement, and could make proposals on the efficient implementation of trade and sustainable development chapter provisions. It must be noted that such a manner of communication between the civil society and the authorities—established by the EU's free trade agreements with its partners—is already in place, and is being actively utilized in relations between the EU and South Korea, Peru, Columbia, and Central American countries, as well as Georgia and Ukraine.

Conclusions/Recommendations

The European Commission acknowledges that the EU's "new generation" free trade agreements are its trade policy tool, designed to attend to the needs of European businesses in the modern era without ignoring civil society. In doing so, the agreements must positively affect not just the EU market, but also markets in other countries with which the agreements have been entered into, to fully facilitate trade liberalization without violating world peace and security and fundamental human rights. "We are showing the world that it is possible to become better and stronger by working together. We are inspired by the idea of trade not based on barriers and tariffs, but on our values and principles, on a search for mutually beneficial solutions which leave every participant of the process victorious," stated the then president of the European Commission, Jean Claude Juncker, in 2018.

In this context, European values and principles play a key role. Europe is widely considered to be the Old World, synonymous with traditionalism. However, from the trade policy's point of view, the EU, along with other states and integration communities, has been forced to respond to new challenges and tendencies over the past few decades by creating new regulation mechanisms. Such tendencies have mainly taken the form of an increase in the complexity of trade, the appearance of new technical trade methods, and the increase in the role of developing countries on the world trade stage. The EU is expected to be able to develop institutions and legislation, allowing it, among other things, to reasonably combine innovation with tradition. It is for those purposes that the Union has reviewed its bilateral economic relations policy by beginning to enter into trade agreements covering a number of issues, with some of them being indirectly tied with trade activity. One of the advantages of this "new generation" trade agreements is that it allows the EU to harmonize its more modern rules and standards in the sphere of trade (services, government procurement, investments, and intellectual property) with the respective rules and standards of other countries in order to promote these uniform rules in the future on a multilateral basis. With this, the EU has given a negative answer to the question of whether it is attempting to substitute a multilateral trade regulation with a bilateral one. Even in 2006, a direct answer to this question was given by the EU "Global trade" strategy, when it was stated that free trade agreements enable the development of new standards based on WTO rules and other international norms due to these agreements being aimed at a faster and a more thorough economic integration which covers matters that the parties are not yet ready to discuss on a multilateral basis. The EU has confirmed its position countless times, with an emphasis on free trade agreements which represent the bilateral approach to trade regulation, not being in breach of, or substituting, the multilateral approach, but simply adding to and developing it. This is further evidenced by the majority of the EU's free trade agreements being based on the parties' commitment to WTO rules governing specific areas, which demonstrates, among other things, a traditional approach to regulating different aspects of trade in such agreements: the parties employ the currently employed practices on the multilateral level, yet the EU and its partners have also (as has been stated) been known to go beyond this traditional approach, albeit slightly, by suggesting new solutions. This combination of tradition and innovation is the main feature of the EU's external activity as a whole and its trade agreements in particular.

Regarding the matters analyzed in this chapter, the following effects of combining traditional and innovational mechanisms in the EU's "new generation" free trade agreements can be traced. Firstly, the agreements serve to produce rules on a bilateral level that could later be implemented on a multilateral level. For example, e-commerce regulation is a relatively new area of trade regulation, and therefore certain aspects of it, such as the need to recognize electronic contracts, electronic authentication, and its other novelties, are currently being discussed in the WTO and may very well take the form of binding rules for its member-states in the future. Secondly, the EU is proposing completely new regulation formats in addition to the currently existing ones; it should be noted that, with that in mind, the parties privy to the agreement reserve the right to choose either the traditional or the innovational approach. Thus, the EU has developed a new mechanism to settle investment disputes, established in large part by its trade agreement with Canada. A new system of investment courts entails an increase in permanence, transparency, and impartiality. Certainly, the effectiveness of any novelty must be evidenced by its effective realization, which is why the investment court clause is not mandatory, but rather one possible option for settling disputes between an investor and a host state. However, the system which was eventually adopted after many rounds of negotiations and consultations between parties (in particular between the EU and Canada) seems to have a high chance of meeting expectations, and later in being reflected in upcoming trade agreements, including some not merely within the EU. Thirdly, the "new generation" agreements include the most pressing matters for the international community, such as the globalization of the world trade system. This also concerns the labor and environmental fields. With that being said, the EU in its free trade agreements seeks to take into account not just global and national interests, but also the interests of its citizens. "New generation" agreements make participation in the negotiations on their conclusion mandatory for the parties, as well as for representatives of the civil society, during their implementation stage. In practice, this mechanism is already functioning: based on current agreements (e.g., between the EU and South Korea, or the EU and Singapore) expert groups have been created consisting of members of society working and conducting research in their respective areas. The groups' reports are heard during governmental consultations, are monitored and recorded, and are open to the public. As such, basically every EU citizen may express their opinion on a particular topic.

All of these conclusions make it possible to assume that the EU's "new generation" free trade agreements are performing their task of liberalizing trade to its absolute maximum potential at the current stage, taking into account the interests of its partner states as well as those of European companies and EU citizens. Moreover, the agreements have turned out to be the means of suggesting new approaches and regulation mechanisms for trade relations, which might be utilized by other world trade system players on a multilateral level, among other things.

References

Baetens, F. (2013). Preferential Trade and Investment Agreements and the Trade/Investment Divide: Is the Whole More than the Sum of Its Parts? In R. Hoffmann, S. W. Schill, & C. J. Tams (Eds.), *Preferential Trade and Investment Agreements: From Recalibration to Reintegration*. Baden-Baden: Nomos.

Castellarin, E. (2013). The Investment Chapters in the New Generation of the EU's Economic Agreements. *EU, Investment Treaties, and Investment Treaty Arbitration – Current Developments and Challenges, TDM Special, 10*(2).

Communication from the Commission to the Council, the European Parliament, the European Economic and Social Committee and the Committee of the Regions. Global Europe: Competing in the World. A contribution to the EU's Growth and Jobs Strategy, Brussels, 4.10.2006 COM (2006). Available at: https://eur-lex.europa.eu/LexUriServ/LexUriServ.do?uri=COM:2006:0567:FIN:en:PDF. Accessed 30 Jan 2020.

Comprehensive Economic and Trade Agreement (CETA) Between Canada, of the One Part, and the European Union and Its Member States, of the Other Part, Full Text. Available at: https://eur-lex.europa.eu/legal-content/EN/TXT/?uri=CELEX:22017A0114(01). Accessed 30 Jan 2019.

Cottier, T., et al. (2012). *Analysis of the EFTA Model Chapter on Trade and Sustainable Development*. Legal Opinion Prepared for the Swiss Federal Office for the Environment.

EU-Singapore Free Trade Agreement, Full Text. Available at: https://trade.ec.europa.eu/doclib/press/index.cfm?id=961. Accessed 2 Feb 2020.

Garcia-Duran, P., & Leif Johan, E. (2018). Squaring the Circle: Assessing Whether the European Union's Pursuit of Bilateral Trade Agreements Is Compatible with Promoting Multilateralism. *Journal of Self-Governance and Management Economics, 6*(1), 7–32.

Joint Statement on Electronic Commerce. EU Proposal for WTO Disciplines and Commitments Relating to Electronic Commerce. Communication from the European Union. Available at: https://trade.ec.europa.eu/doclib/docs/2019/may/tradoc_157880.pdf. Accessed 30 Jan 2020.

Kabanov, I. (2015). E-commerce: From the WTO to Mega-regional Agreements. *MOSTI, 8*, 1.

Leal-Arcas, R. (2011). The Fragmentation of International Trade Law: Is Now the Time for Variable Geometry? *Journal of World Investment and Trade, 12*(2).

Report from the Commission to the European Parliament, the Council, the European Economic and Social Committee and the Committee of the regions on Implementation of Free Trade Agreements, 1 January 2018–31 December 2018, Brussels, 14.10.2019 COM (2019). Available at: https://ec.europa.eu/transparency/regdoc/rep/1/2019/EN/COM-2019-455-F1-EN-MAIN-PART-1.PDF. Accessed 1 Feb 2020.

Svoboda, O. (2019). The Common Commercial Policy After Opinion 2/15: No Simple Way to Make Life Easier for Free Trade Agreements in the EU. *CYELP, 15*, 189.

CHAPTER 11

Value Creation by the Sharing Economy in the Post-industrial Society

Igor Stepnov

Introduction

Economic exchange has always been known to develop society. Many perceive exchange as a phenomenon secondary to the production of goods, and often underestimate its role and significance. However, no market economy could operate without voluntary exchange, and its role in the distribution of, and access to, resources and goods is more important for any society than the production of such goods. Societies of all types (current or former) secure social coherence through exchange in one form or another, thus achieving social stability within a certain historical period. Sharing as a common pattern of resource distribution and access becomes one of the forms of exchange in societies. In this regard, it should be kept in mind that exchange is a social as well as an economic category, since there is not a single individual who lives outside a social community.

I. Stepnov (✉)
Moscow State Institute of International Relations (MGIMO University), Moscow, Russia

Financial University under the Government of the Russian Federation, Moscow, Russia

J. Kovalchuk (ed.), *Post-Industrial Society*,
https://doi.org/10.1007/978-3-030-59739-9_11

Therefore, any discussion regarding sharing must include both the economic and the social element.

The sharing economy (SE) has become the subject of a broad debate in the circle of politicians and economists, who consider it a potential new approach towards economic development. It is beyond doubt that the SE is so popular not only (and no so much) due to the economic benefits of this approach, but also due to the acceptance of this phenomenon by society and non-economic bodies (Zboron 2020). The SE's advantages and benefits include, inter alia, its ability to better perceive social and ethical issues (Albescu and Maniu 2017). Online communications, coupled with distributed registry technologies, have undoubtedly expanded human capabilities and, in doing this, created flows of both tangible and intangible assets, being exchanged, donated, leased, or granted for temporary use.

In recent studies, the term "collaborative consumption" was coined in 1978 by Felson and Spaeth in their article "Community Structure and Collaborative Consumption: A Routine Activity Approach" (Felson and Spaeth 1978), and since then it has become widely accepted, thanks to the spread of the internet and digital technologies.

Over recent years, as the world moves towards its post-industrial phase or a "second machine age" (Brynjolfsson and McAffe 2016), the number of digital business solutions heavily relying on the advantages of various asset sharing has been steadily rising (Acquier and Carbone 2018). A number of authors seek to find approaches in order to understand the SE correctly (Curtis and Lehner 2019) and, in doing so, naturally pay more attention to its economic substance. The SE is most often viewed as a new business model of the digital age, which ignores the fact that the asset-sharing pattern itself has a longer history of shifting from the economy of ownership towards sharing. Nevertheless, some reviews forecast that the global revenues generated by this business pattern will reach $335 billion in 2025 (PWC 2015), although such reviews emphasise "consumption" rather than "use". This increases the relevance of the SE, since consumption continues to be a decisive factor in the economic growth of nations. It should be noted, however, that verified data on the SE are scarce, since, as of today, there is no common approach towards understanding and presenting data on it, making it statistically difficult to identify the SE's contribution to GDP growth. Therefore, most assessments are just expert estimates; for example, as estimated by the World Bank, China is the global leader, the volume of its sharing economy being estimated at more than $230 billion, or 1.67% of the country's GDP, in 2018 (David 2017).

The key dilemma, however, refers to the fact that the SE's effect on GDP is ambiguous: on the one hand, households generate added value that contributes to GDP growth; on the other hand, shared consumption pushes down the demand for products to be purchased, thus leading to production decrease and GDP growth slowdown (Analytical Center under the Government of the Russian Federation 2019). In addition, it is worth repeating that economists ignore the fact that the SE has become a social phenomenon, and this largely results in erroneous conclusions. For example, the conclusion that collaborative consumption is based on the "underuse" of assets adequately explains the attractiveness of Bla Bla Car, but offers a very superficial or, to be more precise, one-sided explanation for the model of car sharing (Yandex). The growing economic significance of the SE is more due to the positive opinions of consumers, and their desire to develop a model of this type, than to the classical model of return on resources used. In 2018, according to Statista, 54% of the population utilised services through collaborative consumption in the United Kingdom, 47% in the United States, and 60% in China. This demonstrates public acceptance of the new form over its economic advantages. In this regard, it should be noted that the relevant business initiatives, when practically implemented, go beyond any conventional forms and result in various conflicts, including legal ones. SE is also characterised by the low transparency of its business solutions, the need to develop new methods for predicting future consumption, and, in many aspects, lower social responsibility of businesses.

When studying the SE, it is important to note that the new solutions unevenly penetrate business practices in various sectors. It is traditionally perceived that the SE is primarily about transportation and apartment rental services, but collaborative consumption has already expanded to entertainment and trade: for instance, collaborative consumption accounts for more than 44% of the retail trade segment in Turkey (PWC 2018) and, overall, more than 27 initiatives are believed to exist in the SE field (Acquier et al. 2019).

Therefore, this study is intended to identify the specific features of value creation within the framework of collaborative consumption, and to understand whether this value is always economically measurable—or whether it can be social, environmental, or political in its nature—in order to enable us to address many issues related to both the quality of services (which are of importance for the consumer) and taxation (which are of importance for state regulation and budgetary revenue projections).

Methodology

This chapter covers the theoretical aspects, and provides a critical analysis of the scholarly debate regarding the SE: its definitions, substance, and value description.

The analysis is concerned with the duality and synergism of collaborative consumption in light of the economic prospects of the digital society. In this regard, we refer to the fact that the objectively existing reality of the SE has been created by collective experience. Therefore, economic theory alone provides insufficient provisions to describe the SE phenomenon and SE practices, as well as their secondary effects, which themselves require comprehensive investigation. Therefore, system analysis, given its multidisciplinary nature and its ability to create behavioural models, becomes the principal methodology for this study.

The value-driven approach is of special significance, since through it, both the process of collaborative consumption itself and its performance can be assessed as fully as possible.

The subjective component of system analysis allows one to ascertain different researchers' attitudes towards collaborative consumption, whereas their common ground in the value aspect could be identified using the techniques and methods of system analysis, relevant to objective reality. In this regard, the subject matter of this study can be defined as the business model of collaborative consumption, assuming that the social component is involved in a dual manner in the interaction arising in the implementation of the business model. Through analysing the business models for collaborative consumption, it becomes possible to identify the primary value offers (within the framework of a single social community) and the secondary value offers (which use confirmed signals of interest in collaborative consumption for business purposes).

The method used herein allows us to compare different researchers' approaches towards describing the phenomenon, to find a common ground among them (taking into account the dual perception of collaborative consumption), and to eliminate the impact of any declarations to the effect that collaborative consumption leads to a shift from capitalist relations to socialist ones, because such declarations reflect a subjective attitude towards the phenomenon rather than the discovery of the substance of any new type of social relations.

Results

When discussing the SE, we should undoubtedly assume that, from the standpoint of the Clark-Fisher three-sector model (Fisher 1935; Clark 1940), the SE is included in the tertiary sector (service provision). The quaternary and quinary sectors carved out by Bell from the tertiary sector do not alter the substance of the sectoral approach, but, nevertheless, highlight those areas in which SE business models have already taken root (transport and utilities, financial services, insurance and real estate dealing, health care, education, leisure and entertainment, scientific research, public administration) (Bell 1999). Incidentally, it should be noted that the universal trend for replacing goods with services is at least an accompanying, if not encouraging, the trend for the SE. It is beyond doubt that globalisation has played an important role in these processes, as the location from which goods are sourced is now insignificant for consumers, provided that the quality of the relevant service is the same as before.

For the purpose of further analysis, it should be kept in mind that the SE is based on services and, consequently, heavily depends upon both the primary and the secondary sector, while generating supply for these sectors. The author of this chapter has failed to find any example of collaborative consumption models focused on the transfer of title to an asset. In turn, it transpires from this failure that the very phenomenon of collaborative consumption has clear limits, constitutes a new and independent economic process, and actually transforms property relations.

Despite the specific features mentioned above, the SE remains primarily a free market phenomenon (Sundararajan 2016) rather than a tendency for distribution-based or planned-economy relations; therefore, in our opinion, the value-driven approach is applicable to the SE. According to European Union documents, collaborations in the economy are distinguished by new business models under which digital platforms allow "temporary access" to goods rather than to "sell" them (European Commission 2016).

In addition, the SE further strengthens the consumer indifference between production and distribution by putting a firm emphasis on consumption as such, rather than on the solution making the necessary asset available (Mair and Reischauer 2017). Traditionally, with respect to any goods, economic studies treat industrial enterprises as producers, trade and service entities as suppliers, and private households (or their individual members) as consumers.

With the aid of real-time information on any available or requested resources, individuals currently perform the new functions of service/

goods providers in their peer-to-peer networks. In fact, an individual can be, with respect to certain resources, the supplier and/or the consumer—the role that has been called the "prosumer" (Kotler 2010). This new quality means that the SE reforms social relations by utilising the value of social contacts (Schor et al. 2015). The SE allows certain individuals to assume the role of service providers, provided that they own the requested goods underlying the service to be provided. Such an initiative essentially modifies the structure of the economy by building recognised social communities and allowing individuals to act as entrepreneurs in an area where they were previously supposed to be employees, thus significantly reducing the social responsibility of both the organisers of such communities and governments. The broadest opportunities for service provision on an individual level are offered by digital relations, which provide both control and certain guarantees as to the quality of such services. This is why practically all business model of collaborative consumption include feedback mechanisms reflecting the behaviour of individuals with respect to both consumption and provision of goods.

Another aspect, which should be discussed and which, possibly, also demonstrates growing trends of post-industrial society, is the contradiction between consumption and saving. The ownership of assets and their accumulation are part of saving processes, and almost all researchers believe this to be a fundamental economic principle (Habib et al. 2020). The SE, however, replaces this principle with the yielding/generation of revenues or with other (social) valuables (such as Instagram likes). Without discussing whether Instagram likes represent capital accumulation or some result of saving, it can still be concluded, however, that, for a person who sees value in mere popularity, there is no economic sense in acquiring assets instead utilising them. In addition, whether the new phenomenon of collaborative consumption is connected with asset depreciation, in economic as well as social terms, is a question that can only be answered after addressing the following key problem: how does collaborative consumption create value?

When considering the value aspect, we should, as yet another premise, refer to the fact that the SE is based on actual demand in many economic sectors; therefore, we can conclude that the SE is rational, since it meets the demand with a much lower supply and, in doing so, directly affects pricing. This situation results in the fact that the costs of a consumer involved in the sharing of services are considerably lower, and this leads to a significant reduction in the profits of the producer, as well as to a lower, but still significant, reduction in the profits of any intermediaries. In addition, considering the situation of a market forecast error, the collaborative consumption model will mitigate any erroneous projections due to the greater volume of services provided per unit of goods/assets used.

One of the common errors in SE theories is the assumption that each subsequent user generally gets the same service quality as the preceding customer. From the perspective of intangible assets, this assumption is true, but when it comes to tangible assets involved in collaborative consumption (e.g. car sharing or bicycle sharing), this assumption is not so true. The consumer is entitled either to expect that the usage price of a more worn-out asset will be reduced for them, or to expect fairness in the fact that this quality reduction is already reflected in the average price of collaborative usage. The problem of tangible asset depreciation in the SE significantly affects the value of the offer, and requires further research. In existing business models, the depreciation of the tangible component is addressed not through price reduction, but, on the contrary, through introducing various types/classes of service provision (from "standard" to "premium") and increasing the price of the shared service under premium offers.

Furthermore, temporary access is granted by means of value creation chains and, therefore, the implementation of collaborative consumption techniques becomes the decisive factor for profit extraction and value creation. In this regard, a key business model must answer the questions of what its value offers are, who the customers are, who the suppliers are, and why the business model is financially attractive (Blaschke et al. 2017). Most scholars believe that such value offer suggests the obtaining of any required benefit solely to the extent so required, instead of acquiring an entire product unit. In addition, for the social community to which the consumer belongs, the value of saving will be increased by the value of obtaining this benefit in this manner. The intermediary, most often represented by a platform, creates virtually no value (or such value is near-zero).

In order to identify the value aspect of the SE, the first step should be to classify the business models of collaborative consumption. The most appropriate method is to divide the business models into the following types:

- the providers of common infrastructure—ecosystems (e.g. the internet or transport means);
- publicly accessible platforms (the provision of "temporary access"—e.g. apartments to rent);
- intermediaries (also represented by platforms, such as Avito, that also offer temporary access);

- social groups implementing an entrepreneurial model in disguise (such as crafts);
- individual private initiatives.

In this regard, it should be noted that the offered value of one and the same service may be identical in all five types of models, but financial attractiveness may be very different. A transportation service can be provided under any of the business models listed above, but its cost, taxation, and transparency will vary significantly (e.g. Uber, Bla Bla Car, or just a fellow traveller).

Nevertheless, a free market tries to equalise the value of services received, and digital technologies play an important role in this process by acting as an intermediary, in order to reduce operational costs, and enhance uninterrupted communications between the providers of services and/or goods offered for collaborative consumption and those who wish to obtain them. First of all, it should be noted that, despite statements by most authors regarding the digital component of the SE, this component does not always constitute its indispensable prerequisite. Surely, the digital economy makes its contribution to the SE as regards monitoring whether collaborative consumption is fair and whether it is consistent with the payment made and the original arrangements. It is digital technologies (blockchain, clouds, financial technologies, etc.) that significantly facilitate the implementation of collaborative consumption and help ensure that revenues are proportional to the value created. It should also be understood that digitalised benefits can be most easily adapted to the SE. In addition to offering technology infrastructure for information exchange, digital technologies have created new forms of social ties that can be expanded to the level of social relations sufficiently reliable for the purpose of doing business. The role of such technologies has meant that the SE has become inseparable from digitalisation and, accordingly, value creation in the SE is inseparably connected with digital transformation at the current stage, whereas its non-digital forms are on the decline.

As regards the SE, most scholarly concepts are aimed at increasing the performance of assets and household cost savings with an appropriate decrease in production (that, in its turn, results in, for instance, enhancing environmental friendliness). Such concepts allow for job cuts and lower GDP figures. Importantly, however, at least two major business models supporting the growth of both producers' profits and national budgetary revenues have emerged by now.

The first model is actually based on maximising the use of assets. It can be initiated either by the owner of such assets or an intermediary (typically a platform) that implements the creation of new relations (this is typical for the apartment rental market).

The second, younger, model assumes that, since the idea of the SE is already embraced by the society with respect to a certain market segment (due to increased asset utilisation), it is advisable to create further business models on the basis of collaborative consumption. This two-tier approach makes it possible to accumulate the achievements of social groups, and to use them in real business in an efficient manner. In this regard, the most remarkable progress should be expected in those areas where segmented models have been adopted (such as aircraft or car manufacturing): production, sales (including mediation), financing/leasing, and operation. As a result of this approach, producers have become dependent upon a vast array of intermediaries. In the immediate future, it should be expected to see manufacturers (including those making aircraft or motor vehicles, especially unmanned ones) significantly influencing the evolution of the SE by creating an ecosystem for collaborative consumption, while retaining control over their income-generating assets. It is this hybrid model that is expected to achieve product value creation through increasing the performance of tangible assets, while introducing an intellectual component available to those involved in collaborative consumption.

Under both models, the utilisation or consumption of a resource should appropriately be deemed a service from the perspective of both the actual dealings and taxation. Otherwise, surrogate transactions—disguised as social exchange or conditionally free access—can appear, and this would result in a distorted picture of economic activities and create opportunities for tax avoidance.

If collaborative consumption is recognised as service, five cashflow channels will be possible:

- a cashflow proportional to the market value of any service provided;
- indirect payment in the form of exchange;
- a combination of the first and second channels;
- an incidental cashflow;
- free access.

For instance, free access to many library systems will be granted either for a subscription fee or to those who have posted their own content, and this amounts to a combined business model. Another form of indirect payment occurs when a platform grants free access in exchange for authorisation to use personal data (including for targeted advertising). In addition, indirect payment can take the shape of charging part of the intermediary fees to the owner of the relevant asset or product.

As a result, we propose to use two components in determining value in the SE context:

$$SE\ service\ value = Economic\ value + Social\ value \qquad (11.1)$$

Economic value in the context of SE can be defined in two ways: (a) either as the aggregate of the benefits enjoyed by the consumer when using collaborative consumption, (b) or as the maximum amount of costs that the consumer is willing to bear when choosing one model or another of collaborative consumption. Given the individual nature of the first alternative, it cannot be used to estimate economic value, since it is impossible to compare the results obtained for different consumers. Therefore, we propose relying more on the cost-based approach, which involves determining the lower limit of the consumption value being created, entrusting the end consumer with free choice, and assuming that his or her behaviour is economically reasonable (i.e. that they will refuse the transaction if the costs exceed the values to be created by the relevant service). The cost measure of the value so created will be derived from the aforementioned cashflow channels:

- direct payment;
- estimated cost of conditionally free access;
- estimated cost of generating an incidental cashflow;
- estimated cost of infrastructure access;
- estimated cost of coordination (with respect to delegating the coordination of the consumer's own choice to an external party).

Therefore, a reasonable consumer will choose the service that provides the consumer with a value greater than the aggregate of the costs referred to above. However, this amount may be subject to adjustment depending upon the activity of the user, since the service provider would also take into account usage frequency.

For tangible assets:

$$EV^* = \frac{EV}{(1+r)^z} \times K_Q, \tag{11.2}$$

where EV^* is the adjusted economic value;
EV is the economic value as determined using the cost-based method (lower permissible limit);
r is the rate of return applicable between service requests;
z is the number of service requests over the asset's service life;
K_Q is the service quality deterioration rate for each subsequent request with respect to the same asset.

For intangible assets:

$$EV^* = \frac{EV}{(1+r)^z} \times K_Q, \tag{11.3}$$

where EV^* is the adjusted economic value;
EV is the economic value as determined using the cost-based method (lower permissible limit);
r is the rate of return applicable between service requests,
z is the number of the intangible asset's updates before its replacement;
K_Q is the intangible asset's update frequency coefficient.

The social value and the economic value can only be measured within a single system of coordinates in the form of relative measurements. For this purpose, we propose acknowledging the empirically estimated significance of a shared service alongside the influence of its social value, as determined by experts, in the form of an industry-specific multiplier, thus refining the formula (11.1) as follows:

$$SE\ service\ value = Economic\ value \times K\ Social\ value \tag{11.4}$$

In order to determine the social value multiplier, it is necessary to conduct empirical research, the results of which will be presented in further publications. This research should be rather social in its nature, since it is intended to identify the motivation involved in the consumption of any service.

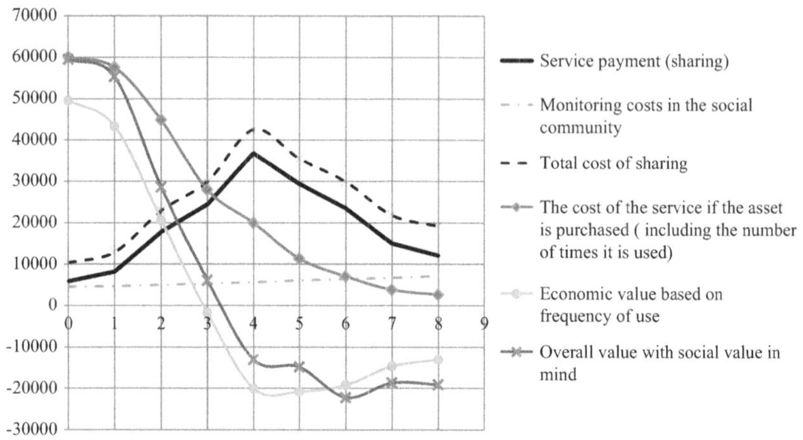

Fig. 11.1 Conditional SE value estimates. (*Source*: Developed by I. Stepnov)

A general representation of value creation is shown in Fig. 11.1; it includes notional values obtained by using the Monte Carlo method. In our model, we assume that social value shifts the choice line of collaborative consumption (as shown in Fig. 11.1) rather than generates new value. This hypothesis is supported by the fact that social choice, once recognised, does not require any economic substantiation, having a linear pattern when choice is available and a non-linear pattern when choice is shrinking.

Therefore, the models described herein demonstrate that the additional contribution produced by coordination has a greater influence than economic or social choice—a fact that fully correlates with current Big Data studies.

Conclusions/Recommendations

The sharing economy has a positive social effect by providing broader groups of society with access to a number of services that were previously unavailable to them. The inclusion of value aspects in studying the characteristics of social phenomena enables a better structured approach towards evaluating the consumer's choice in collaborative consumption practices. Having reached the conclusion that the sharing economy develops on the basis of consumer signals in the form of social approval (or social initiative), it is possible to put together a two- or three-stage model for evaluating the value that it creates: the receipt of a signal from a social community (an initiative or testing), the formation of a business model, and evaluation as to whether shared use by end consumers is beneficial (the lower limit). Such a model shows that digital platforms act as a facilitating element in the sharing economy by enabling prompt action upon consumer signals and supporting the scalability of services offered.

References

Acquier, A., & Carbone, V. (2018). Sharing Economy and Social Innovation. In N. M. Davidson, M. Finck, & J. J. Infranca (Eds.), *The Cambridge Handbook of Sharing Economy and Law*. Cambridge: Cambridge University Press. https://doi.org/10.1017/9781108255882.

Acquier, A., Carbone, V., & Massé, D. (2019). *How to Create Value(s) in the Sharing Economy: Business Models, Scalability, and Sustainability*. St. Louis: Federal Reserve Bank of St Louis.

Albescu, O., & Maniu, M. (2017). Sharing Economy: Evaluating Its Structural Dimensions for Policy Design Purposes. *On-Line Journal Modelling the New Europe, 22*, 85–103. https://doi.org/10.24193/OJMNE.2017.22.04.

Analytical Center under the Government of the Russian Federation. (2019). Personal Consumption of Goods. *Bulletin on Current Trends in the World Economy, 47*, August (In Russian). https://ac.gov.ru/archive/files/publication/a/21585.pdf

Bell, D. (1999). *The Coming of Post-Industrial Society. A Venture in Social Forecasting*. New York: Basic Books.

Blaschke, M., et al. (2017). Designing Business Models for the Digital Economy. In G. Oswald & M. Kleinemeier (Eds.), *Shaping the Digital Enterprise* (pp. 121–136). Cham: Springer. https://doi.org/10.1007/978-3-319-40967-2_6.

Brynjolfsson, E., & McAffe, A. (2016). *The Second Machine Age. Work, Progress and Prosperity in Time of Brilliant Technologies*. New York: W.W. Norton and Co.

Clark, C. (1940). *The Conditions of Economic Progress*. London: Macmillan.

Curtis, S. K., & Lehner, M. (2019). Defining the Sharing Economy for Sustainability. *Sustainability, 11*(3). https://doi.org/10.3390/su11030567.

David, M. (2017). "Sharing Economy" Only as One Part of Exploding Collaborative Economy in China. *Daxeuconsulting*. https://daxueconsulting.com/exploding-collaborative-economy-in-china/

European Commission. (2016). *Communication from the Commission to the European Parliament, the Council, the European Economic and Social Committee and the Committee of the Regions. A European Agenda for the Collaborative Economy*. Brussels, 2.6.2016. COM (2016) 356 final.

Felson, M., & Spaeth, J. (1978). Community Structure and Collaborative Consumption: A Routine Activity Approach. *American Behavioral Scientist, 21*(4), 614–624. https://doi.org/10.1177/000276427802100411.

Fisher, A. (1935). *The Clash of Progress and Security*. London: Macmillan.

Habib, M. M., Stracca, L., & Venditti, F. (2020). The Fundamentals of Safe Assets. *Journal of International Money and Finance, 102*, 102–119. https://doi.org/10.1016/j.jimonfin.2019.102119.

Kotler, P. (2010). The Prosumer Movement. In B. Blättel-Mink & K.-U. Hellmann (Eds.), *Prosumer Revisited* (pp. 51–60). Wiesbaden: VS Verlag für Sozialwissenschaften. https://doi.org/10.1007/978-3-531-91998-0_2.

Mair, J., & Reischauer, G. (2017). Capturing the Dynamics of the Sharing Economy: Institutional Research on the Plural Forms and Practices of Sharing Economy Organizations. *Technological Forecasting and Social Change, 125*, 11–20. https://doi.org/10.1016/j.techfore.2017.05.023.

PwC. (2015). *Sharing or Paring? Growth of the Sharing Economy*. https://www.pwc.com/hu/en/kiadvanyok/assets/pdf/sharing-economy-en.pdf

PwC. (2018). *Share Economy 2017: The New Business Model*. https://www.pwc.de/de/digitale-transformation/share-economy-report-2017.pdf

Schor, J. B., Walker, E. T., Lee, C. W., Parigi, P., & Severud, K. (2015). On the Sharing Economy. *Contexts, 14*, 12–19. https://doi.org/10.1177/1536504214567860.

Sundararajan, A. (2016). *The Sharing Economy: The End of Employment and the Rise of Crowd-Based Capitalism*. Cambridge, MA: MIT Press.

Zboroń, H. (2020). Sharing Economy in Axiological Perspective. *Ekonomia i Prawo, 19*(1), 187–201. https://doi.org/10.12775/eip.2020.013.

CHAPTER 12

Change of Tax Policy Model as a Base for Innovation Development While Transferring from the Pre-industrial to the Industrial Society

Anna Shashkova and Michel Verlaine

Introduction

Tax policy and the choice of a common approach to taxation are among the most important issues in the formulation of tax legislation and the modern tax system, and ultimately the revenue side of the budget.

Professor V.A. Kashin identifies several approaches to the study of issues of taxes and tax relations: "fiscal administrative law, criminal accusation, political, socio-economic and sociological approaches" (Kashin 2009).

A. Shashkova (✉)
Moscow State Institute of International Relations (MGIMO University), Moscow, Russia
e-mail: a.shashkova@inno.mgimo.ru

M. Verlaine
Commercial Institute of Nancy (ICN) Business School, Nancy, France
e-mail: michel.verlaine@icn-artem.com

J. Kovalchuk (ed.), *Post-Industrial Society*,
https://doi.org/10.1007/978-3-030-59739-9_12

The fiscal administrative law approach prevails in the Russian Federation. The criminal accusation approach means that according to the norms of the current Tax Code of the Russian Federation, any citizen or businessman can be accused of violating tax laws. All official comments and explanations in the Tax Code of the Russian Federation are built on the criminal accusation approach. The political approach is not developed in the Russian Federation and its influence is minimal. The socio-economic approach is developed by individual authors, though the official science does not recognize it (Etudaiyae-Muhtar et al. 2017). The sociological approach is known in its vulgar version as polls of taxpayers "satisfied" and "dissatisfied" with the payment of taxes (Yin and Wang 2018).

The present chapter adheres to the invisible political approach and the socio-economic approach leading to innovational development and forgotten in the official science. The author considers how the general approach to taxation changed with the transition from a pre-industrial to industrial society and what changes took place in countries where this transition happened a century later than in Europe and America.

Methodology

The subject of the study is based on the regulatory legal acts of the Russian Federation and Vietnam. The legal basis of the research is in the norms of constitutional, financial, administrative, and civil law, including the Constitution of the Russian Federation, the Budget Code of the Russian Federation, the Tax Code of the Russian Federation, the Civil Code of the Russian Federation, federal laws of the Russian Federation, regulations of the Russian Federation, regulatory legal acts of the Ministry of Finance of the Russian Federation, acts of other ministries and departments, as well as regulatory public contracts and others. The legal bases of the research is represented as well by decrees of the government of Vietnam, Vietnam's National Assembly laws, acts of the Ministry of Planning and Investment of Vietnam, acts of the Plenum of the Central Committee of the Communist Party of Vietnam.

The theoretical basis of the research represents the scientific works of domestic legal scholars in the field of financial law, constitutional, administrative, civil, and international law, as well as the theory of the state and the law, scientific and educational publications on public corporations, and law enforcement practice materials. The sources of the research were studied in the archives of the State Library of the Russian Federation, OECD library, Law Library of Congress, funds of the National Library of the Russian Federation, scientific library of the Moscow State University, and the President Library.

The following general scientific methods represent the methodological ground of the present research: analysis, synthesis, abstraction, and generalization (Alekseeva and Lebedeva 2016). The research also uses a number of particular scientific methods: historical-legal, system-functional, formal logical, and statistical. The present research uses sectoral legal methods, such as the formal legal method, complex method, and doctrinal comparative legal method.

Results

The Concept of Pre-industrial Society. Transfer to Industrial Society

A pre-industrial or traditional society is the process of direct interaction between a human being and nature. A human being relies on his physical strength (Marx 1844). At the same time, labor productivity in agriculture is low and does not give an opportunity to free up workers for other sectors of social production. A pre-industrial society is a system of a closed economy, a subsistence economy, which practically does not use machinery. Here, the internal needs of society are satisfied, and the conditions of the economy are produced on the farm itself. Such conditions of the economy are reproduced and reimbursed directly from its gross product. In pre-industrial societies, up to 70% of the created product is redistributed.

The transition from a pre-industrial to industrial society leads to a change in economic interaction within society: the development of commodity-money relations grows, money begins to play a decisive role as a common equivalent of values, barter transactions are supplanted, and market operations receive a wide scope. The borders of states expand by colonial wars, and the possibilities for investment in unexplored regions increase, and trade becomes legally protected and ordered.

The basis of an industrial society is private property: this is a sacred and inalienable right. At this particular stage, both private and state monopolies are formed, industrial and banking capital merges, and a world market emerges (Golesorkhi et al. 2019). The struggle of the main economic classes (the proletariat and the bourgeoisie) among themselves reaches its peak (Schumpeter 2008).

Transfer of the Tax System on the Border of Pre-industrial/ Industrial Society

With the transition from a pre-industrial society to an industrial one, the approach to taxation is changing in a key way. Land rent was considered as a source of taxes in a pre-industrial society. The emphasis is now shifted to profits and wages in an industrial society. The emphasis on wage taxes shifted to entrepreneur profits. The ground for the transition to a newly formed industrial approach to taxation was prepared by the works of Adam Smith, *The Wealth of Nations*, and the work of his follower David Ricardo, *On the Principles of Political Economy and Taxation*.

A new theory of taxes emerged. Such theory relied on the following formula: all taxes are paid out of the final result from the capitalist's profits and only some out of the land rent. The latter form of taxes is insignificant. Such a theory of taxation made it possible to justify all taxes, putting emphasis only on taxes directly falling on entrepreneurs.

The transition to an industrial society opened up opportunities for the rapid development of tax systems and the intrusion of taxation in all aspects of life. The value-added tax (VAT) is the peak of the development of the financial thought of an industrial society (Janzhul 2002). The VAT is levied at all stages of production with tax accounting for almost all operations. The VAT could not appear in a pre-industrial society that would never agree with "all-pervading" taxes. The socio-economic rationale for VAT began to take shape only by the 1930s, when the state turned from a property guarantor into a force ensuring the production process. The idea that the state provides, among other things, private production factors, through education, science, infrastructure construction, and so on, has taken root in the public consciousness.

Even though the fundamental works and ideological shifts that served as the basis for the transition from a pre-industrial to industrial society belong to the nineteenth to early twentieth century, the transition from the pre-industrial model to the industrial model in some countries took place at the edge of the twentieth and twenty-first centuries. That happened a century later than in the majority of the countries of the world. It is logical that the transition from a pre-industrial to industrial society differs in this case of a modern economic system from what it looked a hundred years ago (Shashkova et al. 2019). The field of taxation is not an exemption.

The socio-economic and ideological context of the transition from a pre-industrial to industrial society has changed (Galbraith 2007). First, the idea of encouraging foreign investment appeared and spread. At first, the state used a pre-industrial approach in attracting foreign investments: non-interference in the activities of companies. And only at the moment when foreign capital forced the industrialization of a specific sector of the economy did the state restructure relations with corporations with foreign capital and introduced enhanced control with "pervasive" taxation. That means that the state moves to a completely modern industrial approach: reducing tax rates but increasing control. Secondly, the preparation of public opinion for the introduction of diverse and "pervasive" taxes is carried out differently: there is no need for long work with public opinion or theoretical studies on economics. It is quite enough to refer to the developed economies of the world. Thirdly, in the arsenal of the modern state, there are all the tools of financial technology, tax equipment, and methods of collecting a variety of taxes (Kudryashova 2015).

Vietnam as an Example of Tax Transfer Modern System

An example of such a late transition and symbiosis of different systems is a modern economic system of Vietnam. In fact, this country combines three societies at once: pre-industrial, industrial, and post-industrial. In the present study, pre-industrial and industrial societies are researched.

Nowadays, the state in Vietnam has become a force that creates factors of production growth: the state invests in personnel training, industrial and service restructuring, and industrial and export zones. The encouragement of foreign investment is traced in Vietnam. Such an element represents the modern transition to an industrial society. Vietnam creates favorable conditions for interaction between the state and corporations: it is allowed to open enterprises with 100% foreign capital. On the one hand, the interaction between the state of Vietnam and corporations is based on the principles of private international law, which are known to foreign investors. On the other hand, Vietnam has socialist legislation, which is in the process of moving from administrative-command to market relations. It was only in the mid-1990s that the state recognized the possibility of owning private property (Pond 2018). Nowadays, enterprises owned by foreign capital account for 70% of the total exports of the state. Thus, a policy of rapid industrial growth was laid. At the same time, the state agreed with the low-income level of the population: about $1.5 a day per person in the mid-90s. Such a situation was one of the most important conditions for accelerated industrialization. Here one can observe the policy of non-interference or minimal state intervention in the activities of corporations, which is a characteristic of the pre-industrial society.

Vietnam attracts foreign capital by different types of business participation in the Vietnam market: joint ventures, business cooperation contract, BOT (build-operate-transfer), BT (build-transfer), BTO (build-transfer-operate) contracts, or 100% foreign participation in the economy of the country. A foreign joint venture is understood as an economic entity with, at least, one foreign company partner. A business cooperation contract is regulated by the Law on Investment of the year 2005 and is a form of cooperation agreement between investors, including at least, one domestic (Vietnamese) partner. The government of Vietnam encourages the execution of BOT, BTO, and BT projects on such infrastructure facilities as roads, bridges, tunnels, railways and tramways, airports, seaports, river ports and ferry landings; water plants, water drainage systems, wastewater and waste treatment systems; and power plants and power transmission lines. Under a BTO contract, investors are given the right to operate the infrastructure facility within a certain period after transferring the built infrastructure facility to the state of Vietnam. For a BT contract, on completing the construction of the infrastructure facility, investors will transfer such facility to the state and the state will facilitate implementation of other projects by the investor in order to recover the investment capital and earn profit or the state will make payments to the investor under the agreement in the BT contract. A BOT contract means a contract signed between competent state authorities and investors to build and operate an infrastructure facility within a certain period. At the expiry of such time, the investors will transfer such facility to the state without compensation. According to the law of Vietnam, foreign investors can establish a 100% foreign-owned limited liability company, but not in all business sectors. Foreigners can own up to 100% capital of an enterprise, except for the following cases: if in Vietnam's World Trade Organization's (WTO) Commitment, it states a maximum proportion of capital that foreign investors can own or it concerns specific cases regulated in the Law on Securities and relevant regulations (Table 12.1).

In Vietnam, pre-industrial sectors remain. Due to the special economic importance for the state, traditional types of agricultural production have to get subsidies (Table 12.2). The state compensates rice farmers up to 70% of their costs in fertilizers and pesticides, and pays compensation to

Table 12.1 Forms of foreign capital ventures in Vietnam by October 2018

	Form of investment	*Number of projects*	*Total registered investment capital (million USD)*
1	Joint venture	3957	74,499,067
2	Cooperation contract	241	6,011,651
3	BOT, BT, BTO contract	18	14,221,238
4	100% foreign capital	22,430	239,320,256
Total		**26,646**	**334,052,211**

Source: Elaborated by author based on information of the Ministry of Planning and Investment of Vietnam. URL: http://www.mpi.gov.vn

Table 12.2 Foreign direct investment of Vietnam by sectors as of October 2018

	Sector	*Number of projects*	*Total registered investment capital (million USD)*
1	Processing, manufacturing industries	13,026	190,844,285
2	Real estate activities	740	57,361,912
3	Manufacture and distribution of electricity, gas, air conditionals	115	22,790,532
4	Accommodation and eating services	714	11,969,965
5	Construction	1559	10,081,675
6	Wholesale and retail; repairing automobiles, motorcycles, motorbikes	3278	6,885,749
7	Mining	109	4,905,922
8	Warehouse transportation	717	4,866,207
9	Education and training	437	4,324,861
10	Art and entertainment	131	3,398,818
11	Agriculture, forestry, and fishery	493	3,389,290
12	Informatics and communications	1832	3,370,136
13	Professional, scientific, and technological activities	2712	3,002,058
14	Water supply and waste treatment	71	2,630,213
15	Medical and social work activities	140	1,971,809
16	Financial, banking, insurance activities	377	890,722
17	Other activities	133	715,224
18	Administrative activities and supporting services	57	644,893
19	Household's chores employment activities	5	7940
Total		**26,646**	**334,052,211**

Source: Elaborated by author based on information of the Ministry of Planning and Investment of Vietnam. URL: http://www.mpi.gov.vn

farmers growing “wet” rice for $25 per hectare per year. Future plans of Vietnam concern modernizing these areas of production.

In March 2010, the 12th Plenum of the Central Committee of the Communist Party of Vietnam was held in Hanoi. A number of documents determining the further economic development of the state were discussed there. One of these documents is the Strategy of Social and Economic Development of the Socialist Republic of Vietnam for the years 2011–2020. As a strategic task, Vietnam plans to fully transform the country into an industrial state, thereby eliminating those pre-industrial roots that exist in the country today. The core issues are industry programs for the development of energy, processing, and the mining industry. At the same time, the service sector is developing: air and sea transport, tourism, communications, information technology, and medicine. The country adopted the Comprehensive Plan for the Development of Tourism in Vietnam for the period up to 2020 and the period up to 2030. The strategy of socio-economic development assumes to bring the share of industry and services in the structure of GDP up to 85%.

The state is restructuring and simplifying the current tax system. In 2010 the corporate tax rate and value-added tax rate were reduced, and the income tax on profit from the transfer of land use rights was eliminated. In 2011 the state decreased the corporate tax rate again, and in 2014, it increased the employers' social insurance premium rate (Huang 2018). In 2015 it reduced the corporate tax rate again.

In the 2000s, a discussion about the effectiveness of policies to attract foreign investment began in Vietnam. Such a discussion was typical for the entire Asia-Pacific region in the early 2000s and continues till today. The adoption of some new key documents was the result of the Vietnamese discussion on the most effective policy to attract foreign direct investment in the country (Le 2017). One of the most important provisions of the new course was the adoption on 26 November 2014 of the New Investment Law and the Enterprise Law, which entered into force on 1 July 2015. It significantly liberalized the activities of foreign companies in Vietnam. At the same time, in Vietnam, one can note a policy to tighten the regulation of the work of foreign corporations and strengthen control, including in the tax sphere (Table 12.3). Such changes are implemented simultaneously with the liberalization of the investment activities of foreign companies (Aksenova 2016).

Table 12.3 Vietnam foreign direct investment brief as of October 2018

	Index	*Unit*	*First 9 months of 2017*	*First 9 months of 2018*	*Compare to the same period*
1	Realized capital	Million USD	12,500	13,250	106.0%
2	Registered capital	Million USD	25,483,56	25,372,95	99.6%
2.1	Newly registered capital	Million USD	14,560,51	14,124,54	97.0%
2.2	Additionally registered	Million USD	6754,69	5544,20	82.1%
2.3	Contributed and shares purchased capital	Million USD	4168,37	5704,21	136.8%
3	Number of projects				
3.1	Newly granted	Projects	1844	2182	118.3%
3.2	Raise capital	Times of projects	878	841	95.8%
3.3	Contributed and shares purchased capital	Times of projects	3742	5275	141.0%
4	Export				
4.1	Export (excluding crude oil)	Million USD	111,547	127,838	114.6%
4.2	Export (including crude oil)	Million USD	109,335	126,170	115.4%
5	Import	Million USD	93,079	104,184	111.9%

Source: Elaborated by author based on information of the Ministry of Planning and Investment of Vietnam. URL: http://www.mpi.gov.vn

Conclusions

As the research shows, many trends in tax policy are becoming clearer in the context of advances in society and in line with general political and social processes of a modern economic system. The transition from a pre-industrial to industrial society has brought global changes in taxation, and one can observe this transition in a number of countries nowadays. Such transition is characterized with a new qualitative level. The concept of transition to an industrial tax policy model has changed, as was shown by the example of innovational development of a modern economic system of Vietnam. There are quite a few studies in scientific periodicals that place particular phenomena of politics, law, and economics in the global socio-political context; however, such studies undoubtedly provide a more complete picture and reveal the meaning of new realities.

References

Aksenova, E. M. (2016). Problema formirovanija pravovogo polja dejatel'nosti inostrannyh kompanij vo V'etname [The Problem of Forming a Legal Field for Foreign Companies in Vietnam]. *V'etnamskie issledovanija, 6*, 87–106.

Alekseeva, T., & Lebedeva, M. (2016). Chto proishodit s teoriej mezhdunarodnyh otnoshenij [What Happens with the Theory of International Relations]. *Polis. Politicheskie issledovanija, 1*, 29–43. (In Russ.).

Etudaiyae-Muhtar, O., Ahmad, D., & Matemilola, T. (2017). Corporate Debt Maturity Structure: The Role of the Firm Level and Institutional Determinants in Selected African Countries. *Global Economic Review*, 1–19.

Galbraith, J. (2007). *The New Industrial State* (p. 576). Princeton: Princeton University Press.

Golesorkhi, S., Mersland, R., Randoy, T., & Shenkar, O. (2019). The Performance Impact of Culture and Formal Institutional Differences in Cross-Border Alliances: The Case of the Microfinance Industry. *International Business Review, 28*(1), 104–118.

Huang, W.-Y. (2018). Influence of Transparency on Employees' Ethical Judgments: A Case of Russia. *Journal of Business Ethics, 152*(4), 1177–1189.

Janzhul, I. I. (2002). *Osnovnye nachala finansovoj nauki: Uchenie o gosudarstvennyh dohodah* [Bases of Financial Science: Research on the State Finance] (pp. 88–90). M.: Statut.

Kashin, V. A. (2009). *Nalogi i nalogooblozhenie. Aktual'nye problemy nalogovoj politiki i nalogovogo administrirovanija* [Taxes and Taxation. Current Problems of Tax Politics and Tax Administration].

Kudryashova, E. V. (2015). Nalog na dobavlennuju stoimost' vo vsej svoej universal'nosti [Universality of the Value Added Tax]. *Nalogi-zhurnal, 3*, 5–9.

Le, H. L. (2017). Prjamye inostrannye investicii v jekonomiku V'etnama 1988–2015 gg [Direct Foreign Investments to Vietnam Economy Years 1988–2015]. *Molodoj uchenyj, 14*, 164–167. https://moluch.ru/archive/148/41512/. Accessed 22 Dec 2019.

Marx, C. (1844). *Human Requirement and Division of Labour*, from https://www.marxists.org/archive/marx/works/subject/quotes/. Accessed 2 Jan 2020.

Pond, A. (2018). Protecting Property: The Politics of Redistribution, Expropriation, and Market Openness. *Economics and Politics, 30*(2), 181–210.

Schumpeter, J. (first published in 1934, 2008). *The Theory of Economic Development: An Inquiry into Profits, Capital, Credit, Interest and the Business Cycle*, from http://compaso.eu/wpd/wp-content/uploads/2013/01/Compaso2012-32-Croitoru.pdf. Accessed 3 Jan 2020.

Shashkova, A. V., et al. (2019). Questioning State Corporations as Special Forms of Legal Entities. *International Journal of Economics and Business Administration, VII*(Special Issue 1), 186–203.

Yin, N., & Wang, S. (2018). The Effects of Corporate Environmental Disclosure on Environmental Innovation from Stakeholder Perspectives. *Applied Economics, 50*(8), 905–919.

CHAPTER 13

Civil Liability Concept Transition in Post-Industrial Countries

Yuri Monastyrsky

Introduction

This work is aimed at tracing the changes in the theoretical concept of the legal regulation of relations when dealing with the repayment of losses, corresponding to the modern conditions of the post-industrial society of Russia. This could help us to clarify the methodological basis for improving the norms and practices of their application, protecting the rights and legitimate interests of participants in these legal relations.

Methodology

The methodological basis of the research included both private scientific (special legal, comparative-legal, historical) and general scientific (problem-theoretical, teleological, systemic) methods of analysis. The problem-theoretical approach is applied when studying fundamental issues. The specific scientific method of comparative-legal analysis is used to highlight

Y. Monastyrsky (✉)
Moscow State Institute of International Relations (MGIMO University), Moscow, Russia
e-mail: monastyrsky@mzs.ru

J. Kovalchuk (ed.), *Post-Industrial Society*,
https://doi.org/10.1007/978-3-030-59739-9_13

the peculiarities of various claims for losses and foreign regulation. The historical method was used for analysing the continuity of views on the conditions for the declaration and consideration of claims for losses in Russia's pre-revolutionary, Soviet, post-Soviet, and post-industrial periods. The main trends in the development of the ideology of compensation for losses and liability, alongside other aspects under discussion, as reflected in domestic and foreign studies, were approached using the methods of problem-theoretical and systemic analysis. The teleological method contributed to the establishment of current and future regulatory goals. General logical methods (abstraction, analysis, synthesis, analogy, generalization, etc.) were used for studying and comprehending specific legal issues.

Results

Summarizing the existing knowledge, this chapter made it possible to formulate a concept for the legal regulation of relations for protecting legal rights, and, in particular, loss indemnity. It has significant scientific and practical importance. Our findings could form the basis for further doctrinal research in this field within the framework of creating a modern Russian theory of loss reimbursement and so on. This will contribute to improving scientific ideas about the legal nature of the recovery of damages and a better understanding of the specific character of this important legal remedy, and establish its universal relevance and unlocking its potential.

The Origin of the Loss Theory

In Russian historical legal documents, property liability for any "insult" was sanctioned in the form of fines. In the nineteenth century, prominent Russian civil lawyers, who worked at leading Russian universities, worked at developing the general legal principles of damages, to make such laws more mature and sophisticated (Belyackin 2005). The starting point for writing conceptual works was primarily the research of German civil law theory and the legislative process, firstly in German states and later in a united Germany.

In the second half of the nineteenth century, industrial development provoked an increase in political demands in the case of harm especially personal injuries; thus, there were not so many claims based on these articles. The Governing Senate (Russian supreme judicial authority) heard up to several hundred cases per year. Of those, in 1871, only approximately

10% of claims were for compensation, whereas in 1910, such claims constituted approximately one-third of cases. They arose both from tort and from domestic and small-scale transactions.

The doctrine of losses did not exist at that time, and moreover, reviewers of the Senate's decisions sometimes directly referred to the works of top German legal experts and to the achievements of the German legislators (Zmirlov 1908).

Thus, we can see that the theory of losses itself only appeared at the beginning of the twentieth century. Since then, it has become possible to compare legal experts' viewpoints on the problem under consideration. Their works influenced how the relevant formulations of the Civil Law of the Russian Empire were drafted, although this was not adopted due to World War I. For the first time, civil responsibility for guilt was established.

German legal experts' legislative activity came to the following conclusion: no one has the right to realize their subjective intention for the sole purpose of harming another person.

As for the regulation of both tort and contracts, their non-fulfilment subsequently resulted in the single normalization, as established by Article 684 of the reprinted collection of legislation of the Russian Empire "on compensation for harm and losses resulting from acts not recognized as crimes and misconduct". This was particularly significant, as it included the conditions of exemption from liability—"the requirements of the law or government", personal defence (defensio propria), or an unavoidable circumstance. Although this Article was initially intended mainly for cases causing various property damage and harm outside of transactions, it began to be applied to contractual losses, along with Article 574: "Everyone has the right, in cases of non-performance under contracts and obligations, as well as in cases of grievances, damages and losses, to seek satisfaction and compensation through the court". In general, the legislative base was limited to this.

A necessary condition of liability in Soviet civil law was unlawfulness (*ubicunque est injuria ibi damnum sequitur*) (Alekseev 1959). Since a violation of obligations was recognized as the criterion of judicial response in the pre-revolutionary civil tradition, cases whenever a person does not receive or is deprived of what they can claim on the basis of participation in the relations within the scope of the rule of law had to be taken into account.

First of all, because of the planned economy, there was not the economic basis upon which such laws could be established; the division into positive damage and lost profits, in relations between organizations, was not possible. In the socialist system, the enterprise could not have such an indicator as “lost profit”, if only because the organization’s income was not a market but an accounting unit. The main task of business entities was to fit into the plan for the fiscal period. Failure of the boundary partner to fulfil their obligation (e.g. to supply high-quality raw materials) could lead to the following consequences: firstly, to the non-receipt of the total planned income; secondly, to the loss or reduction of excess profits; and finally, to direct damage to property, its reduction, impairment and so on. However, it was difficult to judge to what kind of losses a specific violation led to. Therefore, sometimes, if actions were not executed without harm to the aggregate national output, no measures were taken. If the violation affected the amount of planned income, the difference (*differentia est requisita*) was collected. As mentioned previously, if it reduced super profits, there would have been no measures taken. This practice did not contribute to the theory of losses’ development.

The normative category of losses in the well-known Decree of the Council of Ministers of the USSR of July 25, 1988 no. 888—“On approval of the provision for the supply of industrial products, the provision for the supply of consumer goods and the basic conditions for regulating contractual relations in the implementation of export-import operations”—is very indicative. The Soviet era was drawing to its end, and the way in which the issues of lost revenue were regulated in this document (paragraphs 74 and 65 of the first two provisions, respectively) shows that the institution of losses in the USSR had not been introduced properly. For example, as is noted previously, they could be determined in advance.

Legal Nature of Claims for Property Liability

In Russian courts, there used to be a negligible amount of loss cases, although the main task of law in general—legal regulation, judicial activity, and law enforcement agencies—is to bring cases to prosecution. Amendments to the Russian Civil Code, dated March 8, 2015, removed the main procedural obstacle for claims for damages, which once arose in the bowels of judicial lawmaking and consisted of the need for plaintiffs to adhere to the principle of adversariality to prove the exact amount of damages (Ioffe 1975). This disciplinary canon was dictated by the then-current legal ideology of the Soviet Union. The legislator ordered courts in paragraph 5 of Article 393 of the Civil Code to positively decide on the damages awarded, even if it is difficult or impossible to calculate them.

However, another fundamental difficulty for using this remedy is the understanding that the claim for damage and loss of profit is always a request for sanctions.

In case of non-contractual harm, its perpetrator is bound by an obligation not to compensate for losses but to eliminate the consequences of this harm. The postulate of the continental legal system is the following: first comes natural restoration, and only then can a monetary replacement be provided, as stated in Article 1082 of the Russian Civil Code. By virtue of regulation, an ex officio court may invoke the cause to be liable instead of natural enforcement. It is important to note that the restoration in kind implies fulfilling the obligation, while compensating for the losses due to regulation is the responsibility for guilty behaviour, for the assigned risk from a source of increased danger, or for conducting business operations.

Commentators sometimes argue that the moment of harm creates such an obligation (Shepel' 2006), and if it is not executed voluntarily, only then should a sanction (which does not arise immediately due to obvious malicious behaviour) follow. This is a peculiar feature of Russian regulation.

Responsibility occurs at the moment of violating the subject's rights. In the contractual area, it is related to the property expectations of the participants of legal relations. In the case of tort, the violation does not occur in the field of agreements, but because of the damage that has to be suffered not by the victim.

The main condition of loss is the presence of guilt. An exceptionally subjective understanding of intent and negligence needed to change, and this happened in 1994 when Article 401 was introduced into the Civil Code of the Russian Federation, linking guilt with the lack of a proper degree of care and caution in taking measures for the proper fulfilment of obligations "required ... by the nature of the obligation and the terms of the turnover". However, it was introduced only in the section on obligations, not next to the concept of good faith (Articles 1, 10 of the Russian Civil Code). The following conclusions suggest themselves: the subjectivity of guilt was left behind only when dealing with contracts or torts, but it does not apply to non-contractual duties, and when dealing with intellectual property, it applies to both contractual and non-contractual relations. It sounds paradoxical, but it is logical. When dealing with the unauthorized use of someone else's intellectual property or when obstacles to ownership are created, the compensation of losses does not arise from obligatory relations, but from other property relations, and in these cases, Section III of the Russian Civil Code should not apply.

EU Loss Compensation Approaches

The EU's Model Regulations of 2002 and 2009, adopted for the purpose of formulating the legislation of European countries, contain more flexible approaches to compensation of losses than in domestic legislation, its priority being a remedy. When dealing with delayed monetary obligations and violation of personal rights, the provisions of these documents imply a stricter liability than the "pure economic losses".

In Europe, unified acts have been adopted to implement the principles of European contractual law and the Principles of European Tort Law (PETL) in domestic legislation. These are considered the best documents, as well as the most recent, which include the greatest achievements of legal thought. The Framework or the Model Rules of European Private Law (DCFR) was adopted as a guideline in 2009. Except for non-contractual liability chapter this document is not perfect from the point of view of losses, but is nevertheless worthy of attention.

These acts are a compromise between the established views of common law and the decisions of the Romano-German or continental legislation. They contain a set of approaches which is useful primarily for Russian theorists.

In Russian law, guilt is an indispensable condition for imposing sanctions if something is damaged or a contract is not executed. Russian entrepreneurs are obliged to cover losses regardless of their *dolus* or *culpa*; indeed, their liability is even stricter than in Europe. Those who are aimed at profit-making do not pay losses only due to circumstances not under control—these should be extraordinary according to the prevailing point of view, and thus even if the phenomenon cannot be defined as rare (although harm cannot be prevented by any measures), the entrepreneur should compensate the missing profit. For example, a strike may be unpreventable, but it cannot be called an "extraordinary event". Europeans are exempt under a much wider range of circumstances that are merely "beyond the control of the debtor" and—it is important to underline this—they could not anticipate them. This category is most likely to include: power outage, currency exchange rate collapse, and, especially, unexpected actions by third parties. Meanwhile, this formula also gives room for the discretion of the court in each individual case.

However, a completely different approach was adopted in the Old World—the cradle of jurisprudence—in awarding damages due to tort. The main reason for this is guilt, hazardous activity (PETL), whatever it may be (Art. 1: 101. (2) PETL).

When regulating tort and contracts, one can see the English influence in prioritising awarding payments before the compulsory fulfilment of an obligation (Burrows 2007). At the same time, we have identified a number of fundamental approaches in this regard. In European law, tort does not give rise to obligations. This term is missing in PETL, but the corresponding legal relationship is declared when causing harm not to property and personality, as we have seen previously, but to interest. Hence, an important consequence emerges: damage correction, repair, replacement, or restoration of things can be a substitute rather than a priority remedy. Article 10: 104 of PETL states that, instead of damages, restoration may be required by the affected party to the extent that it "is possible and not burdensome for the other side" (Art. 10: 104. PETL). It can readily be understood that, because of the quoted legal provision, whether in the past or the present, and well into the future, potential claims for restoration in kind are conceivably quite rare.

The preference for monetary performance in contractual relations can be clearly traced as well. Despite the current breach of obligations, a creditor can always recover payments and a good equivalent in the full sense of the word in the form of interest on short-term unsecured loans at the location of the creditor (Art. 9: 508 (1) PECL).

Thus, greater cost and fulfilment of financial obligations in comparison with others are supported. To do this, the creditor must adhere to only two conditions (Art. 9: 508 in conjunction with Art. 9: 101 PECL): not to enter into a replacement transaction, and to continue to make a property provision to the debtor. However, there is a wide discretion within the courts as to whether such a performance by the creditor has become unreasonable (Art. 9: 101 (2) PECL).

In European law, it is not always possible to require in-kind performance under a contract according to the all the documents provided: it is impossible to be obtained from another source, it has become burdensome for the debtor, it has not been announced promptly and so on. (Art. 9: 508 (1) PECL). The institution of losses, its universality, its effectiveness, all are affected by the monetary obligation regime. It is enforced if the creditor has fulfilled their part, with the addition of the rate on the short-term loan (Art. 9:508 (1) PECL), while the implementation of the non-monetary claim occurs with reservations.

The European concept introduced a significant weakening of the fundamental principle of *pacta sunt servanda* (treaties must be respected) through a revolutionary revision of the institution of withdrawal from the treaty (Karapetov 2007). Continental national law means that assessment of whether the current deviation from execution was fatal or incurable, and whether it could be terminated upon request or not, is solely left to the prerogative of the court.

It must be said that European regulation has incorporated the decisions and institutions of the Anglo-Saxon legal system (Benjamin 1960), and we are not trying to judge whether this is good or bad; the usual tools have been radically transformed into some hybrid means that are already tested by the legal system, in which the precedent predominates in its diverse interpretation by practising lawyers, judges, lawyers.

Rethinking the Role of Losses Institute

The potential of this universal legal instrument is not fully realised by law enforcement agencies for a number of reasons. At first glance, the institution of losses can be considered unconventional for the domestic legal system. The restoration function of civil law is understood in its framework, first and foremost, as the performance of what is due in kind: that is, in the form in which it arose due to legal facts.

However, the obligation ignored by the defendant is often no longer of significant value to the victim in a dynamic legal and commercial environment in the post-industrial era. For these cases, only monetary satisfaction is appropriate as the only acceptable way to compensate for lost property or to replace non-received material goods.

The essence of economic turnover is that compensation for losses objectively becomes the main means of protecting subjective civil rights. At the same time, the dispute settlement bodies cannot cope with its use and, in some cases, either refuse to sue or, as mentioned, reduce the number of requested amounts for various reasons.

Wrongfulness is not a necessary basis for imposing the burden of loss. Such consequences may arise from both the accepted risk and the direct legal establishment. The logic of the economic turnover regulation has already allowed liability in contractual relations without fault and unlawfulness, when a causal relationship determines the number of reimbursable losses of the principal, the customer with the permitted withdrawal from the contract of their counterparties, the attorney and the service provider (paragraph 3, Article 978, paragraph 2, Article 782 of the Civil Code of the Russian Federation, etc.). Nowadays, it is necessary to proceed from a generalization of liability without unlawfulness, following the *de lege lata* legislative establishment, long known from the norms of the Russian Air Code on compensation for the loss of baggage by an air carrier (n. 3 of Art. 118). In accordance with paragraph 1, part 3, Article 1064 of the Russian Civil Code, compensation for harm, and even losses (Article 1082) arising from lawful acts, may be separately provided for in the legislation. This norm, however, was included in Chapter 59 on tort. In this regard, it makes sense to supplement Article 15 of the Russian Civil Code with the clause on the compensability of losses from lawful actions by virtue of the normative direction of the law.

Guilt is increasingly becoming not so much a liability condition as a significant determinant of the amount of damages claimed, including but not limited to the commercial sphere. In case of solidarity of the debtors, joint harm and negligence of the creditor, the amount of losses depends on the degree of the defendants' fault. In this case, a literal understanding of this phrase as three types of guilt—intent, mild and gross negligence—makes it difficult to identify the true legal influence of this important legal category to establish the amount of losses, the factor of which is the degree of guilty infliction. It happens to depend on the persons involved in their joint intent or carelessness, including the sphere of entrepreneurial relations.

The classification of losses in the form of real damage or lost profits, including in the amount not less than the income of the offender (paragraph 2, part 2, Article 15 of the Russian Civil Code), is supplemented by the cost of measures and preparations (part 4, Article 393 of the Civil Code), but this is not exhaustive, since it does not include other results of harm, the spread of false information and the like. Compared to different works on civil law, the definition by Pobedonostsev—"Any deterioration, decrease of values and forces, any damage on property is a loss" (Pobedonostsev 1896)—is the most relevant. The formula adopted by the courts allows for the absence of consequences if there has been an offence, but there is no real damage or loss of profit. The courts do not include future costs as a significant form of loss (part 2, Article 15 of the Civil Code).

In cases of loss recovery, all legal provisions on the obligations of Sections III and IV of the Russian Civil Code—which, as a result of increasing detail, no longer apply to the circumstances of the losses—are not applicable. Claims for the imposition of their burden are taken without evidence of a reminder of the need to repay them, as these are obligations that do not have a period of performance (paragraph 2, Article 314 of the Civil Code of the Russian Federation). Thus, if these are obligations, then all of them—without expiration of the execution time—are unaffected by the limitation period; this was not what was meant by the legislator and the developers of the Russian Civil Code. Rules—such as Chapter 22, Article 310, 311, 313, 315 and 328, and other rules from other chapters of Section III, Subsection 1 of the Civil Code—are incompatible with the recovery of damages. However, it is advisable to include a reference norm to Chapter 24 (Replacement of persons in obligations) on application to claims for losses in the general provisions of the Russian Civil Code.

Conclusions

The main feature of the civil liability's evolution is the changing ratio of losses' recovery and forfeit payment. At first, its variety (a fine) implied responsibility, but was charged only for guilt. The institution of losses began to increasingly replace fines and later spread to an innocent violation of rights. The forfeit in entrepreneurial relations began to perform the same function in the post-Soviet era, and by its legal nature, it approached the substitute for losses, and finally, in the post-industrial period of development, a request for property liability without fault and unlawfulness appeared as a means of restoring property balance.

There is no single legislative concept of compensation for losses in Russian civil law. The rules governing the implementation of the aforementioned requirements are located in different parts of the Civil Code and are not agreed among themselves in Sections I, III, IV and VII. There are many legal provisions on the possibility of recourse to liability in the amount of losses incurred; nevertheless, such claims can be used in other cases. Detailed regulation of damages should be placed in Chap. 2, "The Emergence of Civil Rights and Obligations, the Implementation and Protection of Civil Rights", of the Russian Civil Code, along with the chapter on obligations.

Claims for losses are more correctly defined as the cost of violated subjective civil law, and not just norms, and not only as real damage and lost profit, which, primarily as legal categories, are designed to calculate and vary sanctions.

The institution of recovery of damages is central to all civil law, and urgently requires development and improvement.

References

Alekseev, S. S. (1959). *Grazhdanskaya otvetstvennost' za nevypolnenie plana zheleznodorozhnoj perevozki*. Moscow.

Belyackin, S. A. (2005). *Vozmeschenie moral'nogo (neimuschestvennogo) vreda* (pp. 25–26). Moscow.

Benjamin, P. (1960). Penalties, Liquidated Damages and Penal Clauses in Commercial Contract: A Comparative Study of English and Continental. *The International and Comparative Law Quarterly, 9*(4), 600–627.

Burrows, A. (2007). *Oxford Principals of English Law: English Private Law* (3rd ed.). Oxford: Oxford University Press.

Ioffe, O. S. (1975). *Obyazatel'svennot pravo*. Moscow.

Karapetov, A. G. (2007). *Rastorzhenie narushennogo dogovora v rossiyskom i zarubezhnom prave*. Moscow.

Pobedonostsev, K. P. (1896). *Kurs grazhdanskogo prava. Chast' tret'ya: Dogovory i obyazatelstva* [The Course of Civil Law. Part Three: Agreements and Obligations]. St. Petersburg.

Shepel', T. V. (2006). *O legal'nom opredelenii ponyatiya viny v grazhdanskom prave*. Sovremennoe pravo, No. 7.

Zmirlov, K. P. (1908). *Voznagrazhdenie za vred i ubytki, vsledstvie smerti ili povrezhdeniya zdorov'ya, prichinennyh zheleznodorozhnymi i parohodnymi predpriyatiyami, po resheniyam Prayyam itel'stvuyushchego Senata*. St. Petersburg.

CHAPTER 14

Global Competitiveness of High-Tech Companies: Factors, Barriers, Government Support

Tatyana Kreydenko, Julia Bogdanova, and Dmitry Prozorov

Introduction

Connected with the use of high technologies, which determine the introduction of the most effective innovations from the point of view of socio-economic and geopolitical development (Konina 2018), modern changes

T. Kreydenko (✉)
Financial University under the Government of the Russian Federation, Moscow, Russia

Peoples Friendship University of Russia (RUDN University), Moscow, Russia

J. Bogdanova
Institute of Economics of the Russian Academy of Sciences, Moscow, Russia

Russian Foreign Trade Academy of the Ministry of Economic Development of the Russian Federation, Moscow, Russia

D. Prozorov
Moscow Aviation Institute (National Research University), Moscow, Russia

J. Kovalchuk (ed.), *Post-Industrial Society*,
https://doi.org/10.1007/978-3-030-59739-9_14

in the economy constitute the basis for increasing the competitiveness of both individual companies and national economies in general. The most significant development factors contributing to economic growth at the end of the twentieth century and the beginning of the twenty-first century are knowledge, innovation (including technological), and investment in human capital (Romer 1990). Comparison and analysis of the factors underlying the formation of technological and economic structures at the current stage of economic development make it possible to distinguish the main variables in measuring competitiveness of market actors, to determine the most significant barriers to development, and to propose mechanisms for stimulating economic growth.

In the second decade of the twenty-first century, a special role in socio-economic development belongs to digital technologies: cloud technologies, artificial intelligence, the Internet of Things, neural networks, boundary and quantum computation, blockchain, immersive technologies, and many more. They contribute to the emergence of new business models and enterprise ecosystems, and also create conditions for not only the fullest possible realization of their present potential, but also the formation of further strategic competitive advantages in new and traditional markets based on using new development tools (fintech, e-commerce, Big Data processing, digital platforms, digital twins, etc.) (Stepnov et al. 2018). Data-driven innovations, new business models, and digital applications are now becoming the basis of a high-tech transformation across all sectors of the economy.

The term "high technology" (hi-tech) appeared in the 1950s, but there is still a lot of uncertainty about both the concept and the criteria for being classified as such (Zhukova 2007; Glushak 2017). Among the most significant criteria for compliance with "high technologies", it is important to distinguish the following: the knowledge intensity of research (the cost of scientific research in total production costs should be at least 3.5%; for leading science-intensive technologies at least 8.5%), knowledge efficiency, innovation, and focus on commercialization of the results of scientific activities.

It is customary to view the following as the key characteristics of high technologies: the use of the latest materials and methods of production, high cost-effectiveness (providing an optimal cost-benefit ratio compared to previous technologies), a significant share of R&D costs, a short product life cycle and high rates of obsolescence and product renewal, high risk of implementation, and use of technologies (Berezina 2011).

It is also important that the very concept of high technologies is temporary, and reflects the level of technological development typical of a certain economic order. Not all values related to this concept have accepted criteria, and the list of the industries included is undecided, but despite this, high technologies are incorporated into all areas of the modern economy. Under the influence of high technologies, changes significantly occur, not just in the industry structure (new industries, technologies, goods, and services develop; there is a significant transformation of traditional industries through changes in business processes) but also in the spatial structure of the economy (new forms of spatial organization of the economy appear: free economic zones, clusters, urban agglomerations, smart city, etc.); the business processes of companies are also affected and have to adapt.

The modern transition period—from post-industrial to digital development—is characterized not only by the strengthening of the processes of the commercialization of science, but also by the use of the achievements of high socio-humanitarian technologies, called "hi-hume" (Zhukova 2008). Changing the structure of high technologies leads to a change in approaches to the differentiation of high-tech industries. In 2020, five high R&D-intensive industries (aircraft, computers, electronics, optical products, pharmaceuticals) and eight medium-to-high R&D-intensive industries (including chemicals [excluding pharmaceuticals], electrical equipment, motor vehicles) were included in the group of knowledge-intensive and technologically intensive industries by the US Science Foundation.

In 2018, knowledge-intensive and technologically intensive industries launched productions for a sum of more than $9 trillion (about 11% of global GDP) (Fig. 14.1). Almost a third of the world's production in high-intensity R&D industries is produced by US companies, whilst the largest producers in medium R&D-intensive industries are Chinese companies.

The role of high-tech companies in the global economy is determined not only by their ability to produce goods and services with a high degree of knowledge intensity, but also by their ability to consolidate and disseminate new knowledge, creating and implementing progressive technologies at all stages of value addition (Tsukanova and Dubitskaya 2018). It is high-tech companies that act as a locomotive for the development of the economy, bringing new and improved consumer and industrial goods to the market, thereby contributing to the creation of new goods, services,

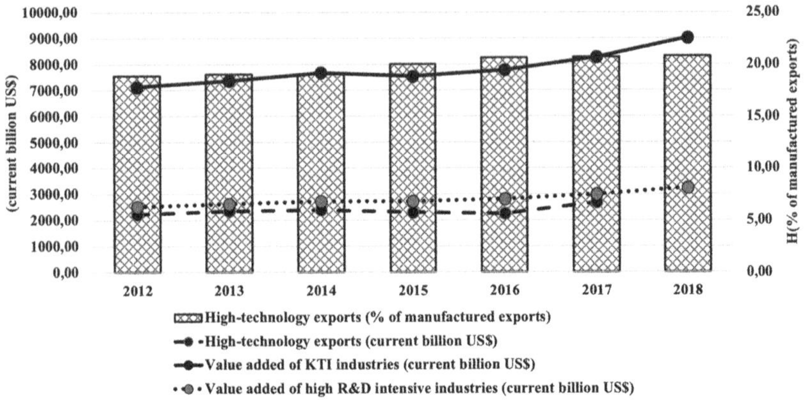

Fig. 14.1 Dynamics of the contribution of the high-tech sector to the world economy. (Source: Compiled by the authors according to the World Bank and the US Science Foundation)

and industries, whilst also improving the efficiency of traditional ones (Khalimova and Yusupova 2019). Analysing the factors of increasing such companies' competitiveness, not only in domestic but also in foreign markets, becomes crucial for the formation of competitive advantages in individual national economies.

Methods

The following general scientific methods serve the methodological basis of the study: system analysis, retrospective analysis of domestic and foreign literature on the international competitiveness of high-tech companies, a synthesis of knowledge gained, a systemically structured integration of the factors of international competitiveness and barriers that hinder the transition of companies to international markets, and, finally, measures of state support of their activities.

The development of the theory of competitiveness is based on an analysis of the leading factors determining the possibility of realizing competitive advantages. Until 1960 it was believed that an enterprise's competitiveness was determined by an organization's internal environment (production technology, the nature of the organization of production processes, the quality of labour resources, etc.). The key task of improving the organization itself was believed to be the effective use of material factors in production, due to which tactical superiority would be achieved at the technical and technological level of an organization (Matveeva 2017). The competitiveness of an enterprise was seen as its ability to create new technologies, new markets, and new ideas. In the 1960s–1990s, the external environment began to be actively considered as a leading factor to determine the competitiveness of an organization (Lischuk 2014). The formation of an organization's competitive advantages is associated with an organization belonging to a certain industry, its use of competitive strategies, product value chain (Stepnov et al. 2018), and executing key strategic activities (design, production, marketing, and distribution of products with lower costs or better quality than competitors). A firm's competitive advantage is based on its ability to use the conditions, innovations (including new technologies), new or changed customer demands, the emergence of a new industry segment, changes in the cost or availability of production components, or changes in government regulation (Porter 1990).

In this regard, in the second half of the twentieth century, researchers already were beginning to study not only the conditions for the formation of competitiveness, but also the process of forming competitive advantages itself, thus forming a resource-oriented approach. The emergence of the resource-oriented approach created the basis for analysing the external environment of enterprise development due to intra-company factors. The key idea of the approach is that the growth of a company takes place through the most efficient use of resources for the production of products, with a maximum added value for the consumer (Karlik and Platonov 2013). It was representatives of the resource-oriented approach who introduced the notions of "distinctive competencies" (on the basis of which special advantages can be created, both in individual parts of the product value chain and throughout the entire chain) and "dynamic competencies" (related to a firm's ability to change existing competencies in accordance with changing environmental requirements).

Thus, the modern, resource-oriented analysis of enterprise competitiveness is based on the assessment, diagnosis, and prediction of "the qualitative use of consumed resources" (Yendovitskiy et al. 2013).

The resource-oriented approach is also used in the definitions of competitiveness of a number of international and industry organizations. The "Europe 2020" strategy presents seven key aspects of competitiveness: the corporate environment, digital agenda, innovative Europe, education and training, the labour and employment market, social integration, and environmental sustainability (World Economic Forum 2014). This approach has been further developed in European Union policy documents, where competitiveness is defined as the ability of firms to mobilize and effectively use the productive resources necessary for the successful supply of their goods and services in the global economic environment. The competitiveness of a firm is determined by its ability to develop and adapt to changes through innovation. Achieving and maintaining competitiveness requires continuous improvement in productivity and constant adaptation in the conditions of the dynamic economic environment (European Investment Bank 2016).

In Russian economics, the resource-oriented approach only began developing at the beginning of the twentieth century, primarily in the theory of strategic management. The broad and diverse concepts of "competitiveness" and "the competitiveness of an enterprise" were reduced to the following direction: the "competitiveness of an enterprise" is based on the nature of a company's activities, the manner of the competitiveness of the goods produced, the combination of goods, and the production activities of an economic actor (Plotitsyna 2010).

In recent decades, international competitiveness has become one of the most complex phenomena of modern economic life, and has become one of the most important scientific and practical problems. The concept of a company's international competitiveness implies its ability to outstrip competitors in gaining and strengthening positions in national and global markets.

International competitiveness is a rather complex economic category which includes several levels. Specifically, while analysing the international competitiveness of a company, it is necessary to assess the advantages of the goods and services it produces, the distinctive features of the company itself, industry competitiveness, and the national characteristics of its home country. In general, the international competitive position of a company depends on several key groups of factors, which should include the resources and capabilities of a company, the competitive conditions of the industry, and national factors. The key factor in achieving high competitiveness is that the country has a "critical" number of firms capable of generating innovation in developing markets and eventually providing new types of employment. In order to achieve effective results, enterprises need to adapt to constantly changing conditions, which, in their turn, require the evolution of innovative concepts for the development of an enterprise and its competitiveness. In view of the above, the most important competitive advantages in the field of intangible assets are: patented technologies; unique technologies, goods and services; positive corporate reputation; well-established distribution means and so on.

Results

As there is no unified approach to the notion of "high technologies", we currently have no unified approach to defining "high-tech companies". Vostrikov suggests considering the following among their key characteristics: producing and commercializing products related to "high-tech"; the use of modern scientific achievements in the most important areas of the company's activity; high competence of employees at all levels; a high level of production research intensity and the subsequent need for continuous interaction with research units; economically feasible production profitability due to the uniqueness of products, high productivity, and labour quality; attractiveness for investors; speed in adapting to changes, improving products, technologies stimulating new research; and, cumulatively, generating innovative improvement and development (Vostrikov 2015).

Thus, high-tech companies can include the following organizations:

- high-tech industries (generating new knowledge and an innovative product based on R&D);
- medium- and low tech industries (not generating but actively introducing high-tech products using high technologies and innovations in their activities).

From this point of view, any high-tech company can be considered innovative, but not any innovative company is high-tech.

The analysis of the level of technological development, the competitive advantages formed by them, and the nature of the technological process in a company made it possible to distinguish several characteristics of each group, presented in Table 14.1.

The fundamental basis for the development of high-tech companies is "scientific and technical" and "scientific and technological" competitive advantages: a high level of the development of applied science and technology in the industry; special technical characteristics of production equipment; technological features of raw materials and materials used in production.

Table 14.1 Competitive advantages associated with "scientific and technical" and "scientific and technological" development

Industry	*Level of technological development*	*Implementation stage*	*Competitive advantage*
Medium- and low-tech	Medium-tech	Use of innovative technology	Technical
	Low-tech	Use of high-tech technology	Technological
High-tech	High-tech	Use of new knowledge to produce market-new goods or services, based on own R&D in existing knowledge	Scientific and technical
	High-tech based on leading knowledge-intensive technologies	Production of knowledge based on own R&D and creation of market-new products or services in the field of the 4th Industrial Revolution	Scientific and technological

Source: Compiled by the authors

The realization of "scientific and technical" and "scientific and technological" benefits is related to:

- the ability to introduce new developments and goods faster than other companies, as well as to quickly respond to changes in consumer demand (as a result, improving institutional management and streamlining production processes);
- the high scientific and technical skills of employees (as a result, improving an organization's activities, modernizing production, introducing new technologies, and attracting the best suppliers);
- production of unique goods;
- introducing innovations into the organizational structure that manages the operation of the machinery (this will aid with upgrading equipment and output growth);
- effective implementation of the investment strategy (which ensures a high rate of a company's economic development);
- a comprehensive solution throughout the life cycle, from the development of technology (production) to its use, which guarantees competitive cost;
- enterprises provided with a stable portfolio of technology (with the participation of foreign actors as well) and new products or services

(e.g. despite the European company Airbus, in 2017, losing in production volumes to its main competitor Boeing, it was able to bypass it in the market using firm orders that could not be cancelled).

However, if the ability to produce and apply new knowledge for the production of new goods or the provision of services becomes the main factor for high-tech companies, then for medium-tech industries the key factors are those that influence the nature of the deployment of high technologies into the production process.

As a result, 8 of the 11 most innovative companies in the world belong to high-tech industries. These companies spend on their R&D activities an amount of funding that is comparable to the levels of the R&D investments made by some states in totality (Table 14.2).

Generally, R&D expenditures among the 1000 largest companies has increased to $782 (an increase by 11.4% in 2018 compared to 2017). The R&D costs of companies connected with the hi-tech nature of products or services, or with pharmaceutical companies (Roche Holding AG, Johnson & Johnson, etc.) or the companies producing software or developing internet services and products (Microsoft Corporation, Alphabet Inc., etc.), may not raise many questions; the margin of leadership held by Amazon.com, Inc.—the largest company in the sphere of Internet retail—in R&D investments definitely attracts certain interest. Meanwhile, most of the investments in R&D are aimed at developing a cloud platform, Alexa-esque voice assistant, and computer vision technologies. Today, Amazon is not only an international trading platform, but also the world's leading provider of cloud computing, the first among internet companies to begin using predictive analytics (Marr and Ward 2019).

The peculiarities of modern high-tech companies are related to the fact that their activities are of a cross-sectional nature: deployment of high technologies into the organizational and technological process has become the basis for diversification (expansion) and deepening of their activities. The expansion of this activity can be connected not only with an increase in the number of economic activities, but also with an increase in the number of cooperative activities, both with consumers (expansion of the assortment of goods and services) and with counterparties (strengthening the role of integration processes within a company itself); this invariably, as the next step, leads to an increase in the share of internal production (depth of vertical integration). Therefore, in the most dynamic

Table 14.2 Cost comparison of the world's leading innovation companies with R&D public expenditures

	Company name	*Country*	*Industry*	*R&D expense (in USD billions)*	*Country*	*Gross domestic spending on R&D (in USD billions)*
1	Amazon.com, Inc.	United States	Internet and direct marketing retail	22.62	Spain	21.87
2	Alphabet Inc.	United States	Internet software and services	16.23	Israel	16.35
3	Volkswagen Aktiengesellschaft	Germany	Automobiles	15.77	Belgium	15.12
4	Samsung Electronics Co., Ltd.	South Korea	Technology hardware, storage and peripherals	15.31		
5	Intel Corporation	United States	Semiconductors and semiconductor equipment	13.10	Austria	14.66
6	Microsoft Corporation	United States	Software	12.29	Poland	14.07
7	Apple Inc.	United States	Technology hardware, storage and peripherals	11.58		
8	Roche Holding AG	Switzerland	Pharmaceuticals	10.80	Denmark	9.12
9	Johnson & Johnson	United States	Pharmaceuticals	10.55		
10	Merck & Co., Inc.	United States	Pharmaceuticals	10.21		
11	Toyota Motor Corporation	Japan	Automobiles	10.02		

Source: Compiled by the authors on the basis of Strategy & (2018)

technology companies in Germany, the average value added is about 40% (compared to 30% on average in the country) (Simon 2012).

Scientific literature has not developed a unified approach to determining groups of factors and the nature of their influence on the international competitiveness of high-tech companies as a complex, multifunctional, open, hierarchical, socio-economic system. Of interest regarding the basic factors of the development of high-tech companies are those companies that are working towards the development of innovative entrepreneurship, the removal of barriers that hinder the growth, and the creation of conditions that stimulate their development.

The international competitiveness of high-tech companies is connected with several groups of factors, the nature of which is determined, first of all, by the industry affiliation of the company. A comparison of these groups for high-tech companies of different industries is presented in Table 14.3.

Improving the competitiveness of high-tech companies in all industries is currently associated with the digitalization of their activities. This will require the use of all the instruments of the new economy, and will intensify the degree of the new groups of factors. In 2017, Boston Consulting Group experts, on the basis of the synthesis of the experience of advanced countries in the field of the digital economy, defined four new categories of instruments for socio-economic development (Boston Consulting Group 2017). An increase in the competitiveness of companies while implementing the "digital privatization" mechanism is based on eliminating the least effective segments in economic activities. The introduction of the "digital leap" mechanism is due to the creation of conditions for the development of production as a result of the development of certain digital technologies: Big Data, artificial intelligence, neural networks, blockchain. In the first and second cases, to support companies, the state itself initiates the introduction of digital tools into the company's activities, with the help of the application of incentives (stimulating demand for high-tech products, innovative activities, etc.).

The third tool helps to actively digitalize the activities of the state and companies with state participation. It makes it possible to increase the efficiency and transparency of all processes of interaction with the state, which simplifies doing business in the country. All this gives a wide multiplier effect for the economy. As a result, there is a significant increase in value added; a reduction in transaction costs in companies and significant cross-industry effects are the result thereof. With "digital reinvestment" the state is supposed to assume the role of an investor in the fundamental factors of economic development.

However, while entering high-tech industries, newly created companies face a number of barriers limiting their competitiveness, including in international markets.

Table 14.3 Factors of international competitiveness of high-tech companies of various industries

Groups of factors	*High-tech companies*	
	High-tech industries	*Medium- and low-tech industries*
Institutional and legal	State support for high-tech industries and innovation	State support for innovation
"Scientific-technical" and "scientific-technological"	High level of patent activity (intellectual property availability)	
	Development and use of new products based on the 4th Industrial Revolution technologies	Use of new products based on the 4th Industrial Revolution technologies
	Building competitive advantage across the life cycle—from new launch to global player (Dawson 2020)	
Economic	Venture capital funding	Investment funding
	Building the consumer value of new technology (Rydehell et al. 2018)	
Human resources	Advanced (professional) digital competencies of personnel	Basic digital competencies of personnel
	Having digital dexterity	Having soft skills
	Increased staff flexibility and adaptability requirements	
Organizational and administrative	Company management organization flexibility	
	Ability to develop and use new business models	Ability to use new business models
	Having an effective marketing strategy	

Source: Compiled by the authors

In foreign literature, one of the barriers to entering an industry is the cost of production, which should be paid by a firm seeking to enter the market (McAfee et al. 2004). The presence of this barrier allows firms already operating in the industry to set prices below average costs, which prevents newly created companies from making the same amount of profit (Lukyanov and Kislyak 2007).

Through the study it is possible to define the main barriers that limit entry into high-tech industries. The main barriers should include the existing "scientific and technical" and "scientific and technological" restrictions in the development and implementation of high-tech technology and products. At present, there is a tendency to significantly reduce the life cycle of high-tech goods, the development of which takes much longer; in the telecommunications industry, the life cycle of a product can be a year, whilst in mechanical engineering it is 3–4 years. Besides, the development of "high technologies" often takes place under conditions close to technological saturation, which is close to the boundary of the production capacity. Shifts are possible only in the long run (further development of sound transmission technology, video, etc.).

An important limitation is the resource availability of a newly created company. The existence of conditions created by the state for business development (tax relief and other preferences), the availability and adequacy of financing, and the development of an effective marketing strategy are significant advantages for companies in competition. Separately, free access to information, including industry information, should be noted under the conditions of the digitalization of the economy.

A significant barrier for a company to enter a high-tech industry is the shortage of human resources in the field of high-tech, management, and business development.

The monopolization of markets by transnational companies creates a number of constraints. The presence of such companies in the market often determines the stages of bringing technology and products to the market, which prevents other small companies—without the necessary targeted financing or breakthrough technologies—from introducing more advanced products within a shorter period of time.

Political restrictions on free competition can bar the doors for selling products completely (tabooing Huawei products in the United States, Europe, Canada, and Australia, or Apple products in China, etc.). As a result of the introduction of barriers, the principles of capital movement and the system of interaction in international markets in general are violated. This includes restrictions for reasons of national security and lobbying for the interests of states (the creation of the Mir payment system, boycotting Yandex by American government departments, etc.).

Institutional and management barriers should include the need for industrial cooperation in the field of "high technologies": very often the flow of output requires the organization of production in one place, then assembly and packaging in another, and then financing and management in a third. In general, this distributed production model can contribute to conflicts between states, create risks for suppliers, contribute to the emergence of technological dependence, and so on.

Among the emerging legal barriers worth noting are the problems of the need for copyright documentation. Intellectual property, on the one hand, protects the rights of developers and owners of technology, limits its use as a factor in production, and closes the market to competitors. On the other hand, the high cost of the patent procedure in some cases is not available either to small firms or to large ones as well. Besides patents, copyright certificates partially reveal the essence of innovation, contributing to the development of industrial espionage.

On the whole, the typology and nature of barriers to entering the high-tech industry depend on the size of a company, the specifics of the industry, and the national characteristics of the home country. Based on the results of the assessment of barriers, the attractiveness of the market is determined, a marketing strategy is developed, the business model of a company is adapted, and further steps are taken. Digitalization of the economy causes changes in traditional barriers to entering the industry, as production, warehouse, trade, and other traditional business principles are transformed.

Discussion

Analysis of foreign experiences in supporting the development of high-tech companies demonstrates the manner of emerging problems in different countries of the world. The choice of directions, mechanisms, and tools for solving these problems is determined on the basis of the specifics of their manifestation and the conditions of socio-economic, scientific, technological, and innovative development in the country. A number of states focus on active state support for scientific and technical developments; in other countries, tax incentives for developers come to the fore; the problem of supporting the creators of intellectual property results is solved, and so on. At the same time, it is possible to distinguish the general directions and solutions, including financial, administrative, tax, and a number of other mechanisms within the framework of which countries build strategies to support the development of high-tech national companies that are competitive in foreign markets.

The consolidated foreign experience provides examples in which state participation in business activities has been subject to detailed and balanced regulation, both through direct participation in the activities of companies and through indirect support and the development of innovative infrastructure, stimulation of consumer demand, and so on. There are several areas related to state support for high-tech companies:

1. targeted support for high-tech companies;
2. support for innovative entrepreneurship, including small- and medium-sized businesses forming the basis for the technological development of the economy (Saunila 2019);
3. support of sectoral development projects, including in high-tech industries;
4. support for certain activities (R&D, exports, etc.).

Innovative entrepreneurship takes many forms (commercial activities aimed at profiting from the creation of technical and technological innovations, the spread of innovation in all sectors of the economy, etc.). State support for this has become widespread in many countries, and itself takes many forms:

Institutional:	referring innovation policy to the competence of specially created state bodies.
Organizational and legal:	the right of state research institutes to be participants (shareholders, founders) in commercial innovative companies, stimulating the establishment of joint ventures by scientific institutions and business structures, and the use of innovative technologies at the level of small- and medium-sized enterprises (SMEs).
Infrastructure:	information and methodological support for innovation actors; support for technology parks and technology incubators.
Financial and economic:	direct financing of innovative enterprises (grants, loans on preferential terms, other financing programmes); financial support for venture capital enterprises; tax preferences to innovative enterprises.
Scientific and technological:	stimulation of patent activity (including international); additional payments to development authors in the commercial use of their inventions; granting permission for the employees of state research institutes to participate in commercial activities.

Economically developed countries around the world show, through their experience, the special effectiveness of supporting medium-sized fast-growing high-tech companies. These companies are recognized throughout the world as the main source of job creation and innovation support. To support their development in the domestic market, and for their access to outside foreign markets, special state structures and development institutions are formed, and a large number of programmes are being developed; these are meant to carry out direct subsidies of innovative projects and provide preferential taxation of high-tech companies, consulting services, training of specialists, analytical materials, assistance for participation in international congresses and exhibitions, and so on.

The most effective support programmes for fast-growing high-tech companies in Europe, the Asia-Pacific region, and the United States (world leader in the innovation process) are formed in a highly developed institutional environment. Such programmes include Growth Accelerator in the Netherlands, Mid-Tier Companies Development Programme in South Korea, programmes of the State Innovation Agency Callaghan Innovation of New Zealand, "Competitiveness Leaders–National Champions 2.0" in Kazakhstan, "Support of private high-tech leading companies" in Russia, and others in other countries. These programmes focus on soft support (implementation of educational programmes, organization of network communication between companies, consulting and marketing support, etc.), concierge management, assistance in developing a leadership strategy, and so on. At the same time, support is selective: assistance is provided to a limited number of companies on the basis of competitive selection, the winners of which are companies, not individual projects.

According to the results of the analysis, the most effective measures for the development of medium high-tech entrepreneurship adopted in international practice and possible for replication can include:

1. Tax relief to innovative small- and medium-sized enterprises in industries that are a major priority for the country's economy.
2. Simplifying the system of regulation of innovative medium-sized business, and updating the norms imposed on it.
3. Providing small- and medium-sized businesses with access to government orders.
4. Increasing government guarantees (and guarantee coverage) for SME investment loans.

5. The provision of targeted concession loans to innovative export-oriented enterprises.
6. The development of innovation voucher mechanisms as the most effective tool for innovation development and stimulating innovation.
7. The creation of a flexible system of state support which provides money for small- and medium-sized enterprises in an economic slowdown, and the development of a system of SME recovery.
8. Development of the national innovation system. The innovation system makes it possible to increase the intensity of the country's economic development by using effective mechanisms for obtaining, transferring, and using the results of scientific and technical activities in economic practice.

Conclusions

Modern high-tech companies are drivers of socio-economic, scientific, technological, and innovative development. An important condition for improving the competitiveness of high-tech companies in the current context is the presence of their critical mass, which has the ability to stimulate economic growth. The fundamental bases for the development of high-tech companies are "scientific and technical" and "scientific and technological" competitive advantages. However, the support of any innovation can become a catalyst for the high tech development of both companies and countries in general. A special role here belongs to the digitalization of all production processes of companies of any industry.

Among the factors determining the success of companies in global markets, there may be, on the one hand, the possibility of successfully including companies into global value chains (these create conditions for companies to participate in global production, specializing in the segments in which they have a comparative advantage but not in the production of the whole product). The experience of the most efficient fast-growing high-tech companies shows that it is much more important to expand one's presence in different regions of the same industry rank than to introduce products to different markets within the same region. But, on the other hand, the role of vertical integration of companies (implementation of all production processes) is growing. There are also emerging business risks associated with the geopolitical situation between states, technological dependence, and other bodies.

Under such conditions, a significant change in the requirements for employee competencies takes place: there is a gradual decrease in demand for professions associated with the performance of formalized repetitive operations; the life cycle of professions is reduced due to the rapid change of technology; the competency profiles of certain categories of personnel are transformed due to changes in the operational tools; new professions are emerging, based on the increased requirements for flexibility and adaptability of staff.

Dynamic and comprehensive responses to the rapidly changing market requirements—to both the need to produce new knowledge and the deployment of new technologies into all structural elements of a company's business processes—is the key to a company's high competitiveness in both domestic and foreign markets.

A comprehensive and coordinated system of state measures to support high-tech companies across all sectors of the economy is essential for the realization of all factors.

References

Berezina, A. A. (2011). *Modern Tendencies of the International High-Tech Market Development*. PhD thesis, Moscow.

Dawson, P. (2020). Establishing a High-Tech Company in a Global Competitive Market: A Sociomaterial Process Perspective. *Industrial Marketing Management, 86*, 233–244.

European Investment Bank. (2016). *Restoring EU competitiveness*. http://www.eib.org/attachments/efs/restoring_eu_competitiveness_en.pdf P.11

Glushak, N. V. (2017). On the Issue of the High-Tech Sector Complexes Distinction. *Creative Economics, 4*, 497–508.

Karlik, A. E., & Platonov, V. V. (2013). Analytical Structure of the Resource Oriented Approach. Part 1. *The Problems of Theory and Practice of Management, 6*, 26–37.

Khalimova, S. R., & Yusupova, A. T. (2019). The Influence of the Regional Conditions on the High-Tech Companies' Development in Russia. *Region: Economics and Sociology, 3*, 116–142.

Konina, N. (2018). Issues of Modern Geoeconomics. *Mezhdunarodnye Protsessy, 16*(2, 53), 186–196.

Lischuk, A. A. (2014). The Evolution of the Theory of the Competitive Ability and Competitive Advantages: The Becoming of the Value Networks Concept. *The Problems of Modern Economy, 53*(4), 172–176.

Lukyanov, S., & Kislyak, N. (2007). The Sector Entrance Barriers as a Significant Tool of Limited Competition Policy. *Economic Affairs, 2*, 101–110.

Marr, B., & Ward, M. (2019). *Artificial Intelligence in Practice: How 50 Successful Companies Used AI and Machine Learning to Solve Problems*. Chichester: John Wiley and Sons.

Matveeva, Y. A. (2017). *The Assessment of the Strategic Opponent Advantages of an Industry Company in the Social Responsibility Context*. PhD thesis, Ekaterinburg.

McAfee, P. R., Mialon, H., & Williams, M. (2004). What Is a Barrier to Entry? *The American Economic Review, 94*(2), 461–465.

Plotitsyna, T. (2010). *The Definition of a Company's Competitive Ability* (The Tambov State Technological University Gazette No. 1).

Porter, M. E. (1990). *The Competitive Advantage of Nations*. New York: Free Press.

Romer, P. M. (1990). Endogenous Technological Change. *Journal of Political Economy, 98*(5, Part 2), 71–102.

Russia Online. (2017). *The Four Priorities for a Breakthrough in Digital Economy*. The Boston Consulting Group. https://image-src.bcg.com/Images/Russia-Online_tcm27-178074.pdf

Rydehell, H., Löfsten, H., & Isaksson, A. (2018). Novelty-Oriented Value Propositions for New Technology-Based Firms: Impact of Business Networks and Growth Orientation. *The Journal of High Technology Management Research, 29*(2), 161–171.

Saunila, M. (2019). Innovation Capability in SMEs: A Systematic Review of the Literature. *Journal of Innovation & Knowledge*. https://doi.org/10.1016/j.jik.2019.11.002

Science & Engineering Indicators. (2020). National Science Foundation. https://ncses.nsf.gov/indicators/reports

Simon, H. (2012). *Hidden Champions. Aufbruch nach Globalia*. Frankfurt/New York: Campus Verlag.

Stepnov, I. M., Kovalchuk, Y. A., Ishchenko, M. M., & Lukmanova, I. G. (2018). Design Office as a Tool to Overcome the Entry Barriers into the Industry (on the Example Textile Industry). *Izvestiya Vysshikh Uchebnykh Zavedenii, Seriya Teknologiya Tekstil'noi Promyshlennosti, 374*(2), 18–22.

Strategy &. (2018). *The Global Innovation 1000 Study*. https://www.strategyand.pwc.com/gx/en/insights/innovation1000.html#GlobalKeyFindingsTabs4

Tsukanova, O. A., & Dubitskaya, E. A. (2018). The Fundamental View on High-Tech Enterprises and Their Role in the Economy. *Journal of Legal and Economic Studies, 1*, 151–155.

Vostrikov, V. S. (2015). High-Tech Companies as a Local Economy Strategic Development Factor. *Creative Economics, 9*(4), 473–484.

World Bank official website. www.worldbank.org
World Economic Forum. (2014). *The Europe 2020 Competitiveness Report*. http://www3.weforum.org/docs/WEF_Europe2020_CompetitivenessReport_2014.pdf
Yendovitskiy, D. A., Lyubushin, N. P., & Babicheva, N. E. (2013). Resource Oriented Economic Analysis: Theory, Methodology, Practice. *Economic Analysis: Theory and Practice, 341*(38), 2–8.
Zhukova, E. A. (2007). *Hi-Tech: The Phenomenon, Its Functions and Forms*. Tomsk: The Tomsk State Pedagogical University Editorial House.
Zhukova, E. A. (2008). *The Problem of the High-Tech Classification* (The Tomsk State Pedagogical University Gazette No. 1).

CHAPTER 15

Intellectual Evaluation of the Economic Systems' Performance in Post-Industrial Society

Antonina Kazelskaya and Igor Stepnov

Introduction

The fatality of errors in the forecasts of economic systems remains a pressing issue. When analysing the complex processes of their functioning, decision-makers face various types of stochastic uncertainties, amongst others. The lack of a universal risk management methodology for different types of economic systems can be explained by the specificity of each organization's business processes. Most approaches do not address the issues of quantifying the damage caused by external and internal impacts on economic systems. There is no analysis of the sensitivity of damage

A. Kazelskaya
Audit of Your Business LLC, Ryazan, Russia

I. Stepnov (✉)
Moscow State Institute of International Relations (MGIMO University), Moscow, Russia

Financial University under the Government of the Russian Federation, Moscow, Russia

J. Kovalchuk (ed.), *Post-Industrial Society*,
https://doi.org/10.1007/978-3-030-59739-9_15

estimates to major disturbances or vulnerabilities. The choice of effective countermeasures to reduce risks is not always justified.

Thus, the intended effectiveness of economic systems' management tools on data analysis is far from actually being implemented (Glushenko 2017). There are virtually no methods to improve the management of those economic systems that support the correlation of data from external sources, risk management, and cognitive modelling, let alone that can assess their functioning. This research aims to increase the efficiency of economic systems' management.

We used the mathematical algorithms based on neuro-fuzzy networks and cognitive modelling; doing so, we were able to identify the threats of external influences and to determine the current state of the economic system.

Methodology

Cognitive concepts are based on the uncertainty of the economic systems' development (Papageorgiou and Poczęta 2017). This uncertainty is expressed through the diverse possibilities for the world may transform, within the existence of a set (usually an infinite number) of system states, in which the object (economic system) is considered in the dynamics. The concept of uncertainty concerning these economic systems characterizes a situation in which reliable information about the possible conditions of the internal and the external environment is completely or partially lacking. "Uncertainty" is considered to be an incomplete or inaccurate representation of various parameters in the future, caused by various reasons but, above all, caused by the incompleteness or inaccuracy of the information available about the terms of decision implementation, including costs and results.

This is why it is no accident that study into the problems of uncertainty, the searching and processing of information, and the management of expectations—which are of primary importance when there is only incomplete information—has become the main foundation for the development of economic theory. Nowadays, the definition of the modern stage of economic development as a transition to the "knowledge economy" is generally accepted.

Results

For managing the economic system despite the conditions of uncertainty, it is necessary to simulate the dynamic situation, in which an expert (a person who creates a subjective model of reality based on their observations, knowledge and experience) measures its parameters. When creating a subjective model, the expert identifies the most significant part of the situation from their point of view, then makes a qualitative description of their knowledge and its interrelation.

It makes sense to use fuzzy cognitive maps to influence a variety of destabilizing interrelated events (Averkin and Yarushev 2017). This is a kind of mathematical model that allows the description of a complex object, problem, or the system's functioning to be formalized, and also helps to identify the structures of cause-effect relationships between elements of the system and elements of the problem, and assesses the impact after influencing these elements or changing the nature of their linkages.

Cognitive graphs differ in clarity due to the transition from verbal information (or other symbolic paths) to a visual image (Carvalho and Tome 1999). Cognitive maps can be used to describe various situations, depending upon the analysis needed to identify the possible ways to develop the system (Olier et al. 2018). Their main advantages lie in the ability to visualize the factors of organizational development, and to interpret their mutual influence naturally.

Thus, a fuzzy cognitive map can be represented as an oriented, weighted graph; its vertices represent concepts, entities, factors, goals, and events, and its arcs represent cause-and-effect relationships and their impact. The influence is characterized by a certain threshold function based on expert evaluation, which is initially set in out through language.

Furthermore, the target factors include achieving the optimal order portfolio (matching production capacity to the order portfolio) and optimal capacity utilization; matching financial resources to the order portfolio; matching labour and material resources to the order portfolio; and matching actual indicators to the planned ones.

Formation is based on the following main factors: information obtained as a result of experts analysis of product availability; labour, financial and material resources; and the compliance of the order portfolio.

The basic factors are: the order portfolio, production capacity, the availability of financial and labour resources, and availability of material resources.

At the second stage of situational modelling, we will form a set of problem situations that arise while developing a production programme and which require certain management decisions to be made. One of the most rational approaches may be to form subsets of problem management situations by objects, that is, to determine deviations in a system from the target factors.

In this context, deviation from the target factor will be the expected as the non-fulfilment of output, due to the influence problem factors have upon the basic factors.

The list of problems includes the following:

- a lack of orders;
- insufficient production capacity; full load, resulting in wear and tear, and frequent failure or incomplete production capacity;
- production potential being mismatched to the order portfolio;
- a lack of financial resources;
- a lack of qualified personnel;
- a lack of material resources;
- failure to comply with the production plan;
- failure to implement the plan.

The next step is to identify the factors that negatively impact the problem factors (the negative impact is that its change leads to an undesirable change in at least one problem factor). To do this, symptoms were identified and noted for each of the identified problem factors. Based on observations and on in-depth interviews with experts, each management decision determines its symptoms and identifies its relevant problem factors.

Causes for this include:

- low demand; employing the wrong marketing policy;
- a lack of the equipment necessary for the market; "bottlenecks"; a lack of financial resources to re-equip the fixed assets; the need to modernize equipment; an insufficient portfolio of orders, or insufficient production capacity;
- high demand; insufficient production capacity, or an insufficient portfolio of orders, or insufficient resources of the enterprise;
- high interest rates; the growth or decline of the exchange rate; the absence of external investors; inflation or increased costs of the

enterprise; lack of management accounting; decrease in sales volumes; misuse of funds;
- a lack of university graduates; lack of targeted training programmes; ineffective retraining of personnel; insufficient personnel capable of working on new equipment; insufficient incentive system;
- the supplier left the market; a lack of financial resources; overplanned waste of raw materials; errors in the planning of delivery and storage; incorrect resource distribution;
- violation of plans for the supply of material resources; violation of financing plans by buyers or creditors; inefficient use of material and labour resources; disruption of the production process;
- insolvency of demand, or failure to comply with the production plan; failures in transport support.

The third stage includes: defining the structure of the problem, and systematizing the factors that contribute to the problem. This stage is where the strategy is determined.

This is followed by defining a control action that can change the situation. The system development model is analysed. A controlling influence is formed that improves the situation. It is necessary to consider the mechanism capable of reacting to the reasons analysed—this can be elimination or compensation. Elimination partially impacts the target factors by removing or weakening the factors causing them. Compensation involves identifying the control factors that positively impact targets despite persistent problems. The control effect is formed under either active or passive control.

Thus, the vector of control influence is formed by changing the conditions under which management decisions are made.

Established control effects include:

- those for a problem when creating an insufficient order portfolio or a full load portfolio: diversification of production; the search for new customers; improvements of marketing policy.
- those for solving the problem by creating insufficient production capacity: identifying and eliminating bottlenecks in production; re-equipping fixed assets; eliminating the shortage of financial resources;
- those for solving the problem of insufficient production capacity: solving the problem of an insufficient order portfolio;

- those for solving the problem of non-compliance with the order portfolio: solving the problem of insufficient production capacity or an insufficient order portfolio;
- those for the problem of a shortage of financial resources: lending; sale or lease of unused equipment and premises; the search for new investors; improvement of cash flow control; organization of management accounting;
- those for the problem of a shortage of financial resources: revising retraining policy; revising personnel policy; target direction; solving the problem of the shortage of financial resources;
- those for the problem of a shortage of material resources: searching for new suppliers; solving the problem of the shortage in financial resources;
- those for the problem of non-compliance with the production plan: retrofitting fixed assets; training employees; applying new technologies in production;
- those for the problem of non-compliance with the production plan: reviewing the marketing opportunities.

All authors who deal with the cognitive approach use cognitive maps—in the form of a sign or weighted graph over a set of factors—in which the vertices are the aforementioned factors, and the edges are the weight of one scale or another.

Different interpretations of vertices, edges, and weights, as well as different functions that determine the influence of connections on factors, lead to the creation of different modifications for cognitive maps, as well as the means to study them. At the same time, interpretations can differ both in terms of substance and in mathematical terms. Due to many modifications of cognitive maps, it is possible to see different types of models based on these maps.

Verification (establishing the truth of a cognitive map) is performed in various ways, including:

1. the method of alternatives: based on checking the obtained values in vertices or the model as a whole, using alternative approaches and mathematical or statistical methods such as the Monte Carlo method or simulation techniques;
2. the historical method: compare the output of each arc with real data from previous periods.

To check if the cognitive map is suitable for creating the production programme, the author has selected a method for analysing hierarchies, with which it is possible to

- provide a hierarchical representation describing the impact of changing priorities at the highest levels on the priorities of lower-level elements. Thus, a static analysis of influence is implemented; that is, the situation can be analysed by studying the structure of mutual influences using the cognitive map, highlighting the key factors that influence the target factors;
- enable direct and reverse hierarchical planning, and implement dynamic analysis (generating possible scenarios for the situation over time).

Each scenario describes the state of the system. Many state variables are used to understand and characterize them. These define the structure and threads of the system in this state. We have defined many state variables and used them to describe the result of our planning. These variables have been classified via different outcome aspects, such as: labour, production, material, financial resources, and portfolio security.

Each of the main scenarios is described using the language of change, showing how each of these variables differs from the status quo. The intensity of each of these variables is measured using a scale of differences, in the range -5 to +5.

A simple scale from 1 to 5 is an overestimation of the indicators for state variables, due to the influence control actions (as formed under the conditions defined by the scenario) have on the situation. Similarly, -5 to -1 as a scale understates indicators; 0 is a value indicator under the given scenario, whereby conditions does not change.

The following parameters of a direct process were defined:

I. Focus formation of the production programme.
II. The forces that influence the outcome. The main factors in the formation of the production programme include: labour, production, material, and financial resource security; the portfolio of orders.
III. Actors include: production capacity, portfolio of orders, material resources, human resources.

IV. Conditions for creating influences include: low demand, inflation, high interest rates, and so on.
V. Primary factors: re-equipment of fixed assets; lending, and so on.
VI. Three actions: overestimating indicators under the influence of wagering; underestimating indicators under influence; the real reflection of indicators.
VII. Scenarios:
- An increase in production programme indicators.
- A sequential increase in the security of labour and production resources, and so on.
- A simultaneous increase in the estimates of labour and production resources, and so on.
- Alternatively:
- Lower output from the production programme:
- The successive lowering of the labour resource security, production, and so on;
- A simultaneous decrease in available labour and production resources, and so on.

VIII. State variables:
- Endowment of labour resources
- Endowment of production resources
- Endowment of material resources
- Endowment of financial resources
- Portfolio security

To repeat, 1–5 is an overestimation of indicators of state variables due to influence; -1 to -5 is an underestimation; 0 means that indicators do not change.

The subject of the study is the values of the "Weights of Scenarios" and "Generalized Weights" patterns.

The study found answers to the following questions:

1. What management decision has the greatest impact on the formation of the production programme?

Currently, each pair of characteristics is compared in terms of their impact on the factors.

2.1 Which actor has the greatest impact on labour resources?

2.2 Which actor has the greatest impact on production resources?
2.3 Which actor has the greatest impact on material resources?
2.4 Which actor has the greatest impact on financial resources?
2.5 Which actor has the greatest impact on the security of the orders' portfolio?

The next step is to identify the conditions in which the actors operate and to identify the most characteristic conditions. The result is a custom vector that reflects the order and weight of the conditions.

3.1 What are the working conditions for credit institutions?
3.2 What are the operating conditions specific to the production capacity?
3.3 What working conditions are typical for customers?
3.4 What working conditions are typical for suppliers?
3.5 What working conditions are typical for investors?
3.6 What working conditions are typical of transport companies?

And so on.

We will determine what factors affect the actors based on the conditions in which they operate.

4.1 What factors affect production capacity when it is fully loaded?

And so on.

4.2 What is necessary to affect the customers in low demand?

And so on.

4.3 What effects on suppliers are necessary when the main supplier leaves the market?

And so on.

4.4 Each influence makes the actor perform actions that change the performance of the production programme. Therefore, for each influence, we define the actions of the actors to which they lead.

5.1 What "actions" of production capacity are likely to result in fixed assets being re-equipped when they are insufficient?

And so on.

5.2 What actions are likely to result in a change in marketing policy when demand is low?

And so on.

5.3 What actions by suppliers will likely result in the search for new suppliers when the main supplier is unavailable?

And so on. The last step necessary for obtaining scenario weights is to develop dominance matrices with respect to each action for the scenarios.

6.1 Which scenario is most defined by an increase in production capacity?

6.2 Which scenario is most defined by an increase in financial resource availability?

And so on. All in all, it is necessary to create a generalized scenario, which can be realized after the values of each characteristic have been determined using the generalized measurement scale.

The generalized scenario is interpreted as follows:

If the production programme is created, and certain actions that form certain goals for different actors are necessary, it is possible to change the indicators of the production programme. In particular, indicators of production and labour resources, as well as those of the order portfolio security, will be increased. Therefore, the results of evaluating financial resources have been significantly reduced. As for material resources, they will be virtually unaffected by the existing impacts.

A qualitative analysis of the cognitive model includes defining the routes, paths, and cycles needed to study the various cause-and-effect relationships in the system under study, as are displayed by the cognitive model. When managing socio-economic systems, it is necessary to know the forward and feedback cycles necessary for judging the system stability/instability.

Using a cognitive map to create the production programme, the influence of situation factors was found, evaluated, and obtained, based on the calculated influence of the forecasts.

Cognitive maps have a significant drawback—the need for painstaking expert work to identify cause-and-effect relationships between concepts in the system, as well as to adjust the weights of these relationships.

However, using a cognitive map makes it possible to make a qualitative forecast of the production programme, and to identify the most influential factors that can be used as inputs in the neural network. They include: crediting, re-equipment of fixed assets, changing the marketing policy.

Neural networks can allow the teaching of fuzzy cognitive maps. The training task is formulated to minimize errors in the prediction results of a fuzzy cognitive map.

Cognitive maps will be taught to represent their factors (concepts) as neurons, and contour parameters (synapses) as weights of the cognitive map's connections, which change so that they match the data as much as possible.

However, using a cognitive map means making a qualitative forecast of the production programme is possible, so the most influential factors that will be used as inputs in the neural network can be identified. These include: crediting, re-equipment of fixed assets, changing the marketing policy.

When choosing a network architecture, it is necessary to follow the requirements of the network operation accuracy, as well as the complexity and time of its training. As for forming a production programme, it is impossible to model neural networks with linear functions of neuron activation, since not all parameters are cumulative. This means that the characteristics of the production programme cannot change linearly when the input parameter vector is changed accordingly.

The next stage includes training the neural network, that is, determining the values of weight coefficients that provide a unique conversion of input signals to output.

By analysing the available input and output data, the network weights are automatically built to minimize the difference between the desired signal and the one obtained at the output after the simulation. This difference is called a learning error.

The error of a particular neural network configuration can be determined by analysing all available observations using the network, and comparing its output values with the desired target values. These differences make it possible to form a so-called error function (a criterion for learning quality).

It should be noted that, in general, it is impossible to guarantee that the global minimum of the error function can be reached for neural networks with non-linear activation functions.

In the case of a non-linear activation function for training neural networks, we propose applying the method of reverse propagation of the error.

Conclusions

Using a cognitive map for creating a production programme, the influence of situation factors was found, evaluated, and obtained, based on the influence of the forecasts calculated.

The neuro-fuzzy network allowed us to determine the quantitative characteristics of risk, such as the probability of implementing those factors identified in the cognitive map.

Therefore, following the dynamics of internal and external influences, changes in risks in the economic system were forecast. Using previously collected data allowed us to increase the accuracy of forecasts and risk treatment methods.

References

Averkin, A. N., & Yarushev, S. (2017). Hybrid Approach for Time Series Forecasting Based on ANFIS and Fuzzy Cognitive Maps. In *Proceedings of 2017 XX IEEE International Conference on Soft Computing and Measurements (SCM)* (pp. 379–381).

Carvalho, J. P., & Tome, J. A. B. (1999). Rule-Based Fuzzy Cognitive Maps and Fuzzy Cognitive Maps – A Comparative Study. In *Proceedings of the 18th International Conference of the North American Fuzzy Information Processing Society (NAFIPS99)* (pp. 115–119). https://doi.org/10.1109/NAFIPS.1999.781665.x.

Glushenko, S. A. (2017). An Adaptive Neuro-Fuzzy Inference System for Assessment of Risks to an Organization's Information Security. *Business Informatics, 39*(1), 68–77. https://doi.org/10.17323/1998-0663.2017.1.68.77.

Olier, A. J., Gómez, A., & Caro, M. F. (2018). Cognitive Modeling Process in Metacognitive Architecture. In *CARINA-2018 IEEE 17th International Conference on Cognitive Informatics & Cognitive Computing (ICCI*CC).*

Papageorgiou, E. I., & Poczęta, K. (2017). A Two-Stage Model for Time Series Prediction Based on Fuzzy Cognitive Maps and Neural Networks. *Neurocomputing, 232*, 113–121.

CHAPTER 16

Transit Economy in Global Post-Industrial Eurasia

Kobilzhon Zoidov and Alekxey Medkov

Introduction

Across the territory of Russia, other EAEU member states, and Global Eurasia, one urgent task is to ensure and enhance the competitive advantages of land and water/land transportation lines as transit routes, crossing these regions along the east-west and north-south directions, and their modifications.

Currently, the high urgency of the situation is caused by

- a reduction in global trade growth rates (Table 16.1);

This research was conducted with the support of the Russian Foundation for Basic Research, project 17-02-00482 OGN A.

K. Zoidov (✉)
Academy of Sciences of the Republic of Tajikistan, Institute of Economics and Demography, Dushanbe, Tajikistan

Market Economy Institute of the Russian Academy of Sciences, Moscow, Russia

A. Medkov
Market Economy Institute of the Russian Academy of Sciences, Moscow, Russia

J. Kovalchuk (ed.), *Post-Industrial Society*,
https://doi.org/10.1007/978-3-030-59739-9_16

Table 16.1 International trade of various countries worldwide (US$ billions)

	2000	*2005*	*2010*	*2015*	*2016*	*2017*	*2018*
				Export			
CIS	140.5	332.3	572.6	482.2	411.0	511.3	630.2
EAEU			485.4	419.1	349.3	439.0	548.8
OECD	4535.7	6478.4	8962.7	9370.7	9279.1	10150.0	11005.1
EU-28	2394.7	3976.7	5072.0	5244.4	5257.8	5766.0	6281.6
BRICS	479.8	1273.2	2485.4	3165.5	2948.4	3243.9	3525.2
USA	781.9	907.2	1278.5	1503.1	1451.0	1546.7	1664.1
China	249.2	762.0	1578.3	2282.4	2136.7	2280.4	2417.4[a]
Japan	479.3	595.0	769.8	624.8	644.9	698.2	738.2
				Import			
CIS	68.3	183.4	384.4	316.8	308.8	378.3	415.4
EAEU			301.9	251.2	242.7	300.3	320.5
OECD	4910.6	7208.4	9600.7	9992.9	9797.4	10771.9	11760.1
EU-28	2441.7	4065.4	5198.7	5112.4	5107.2	5650.2	6230.4
BRICS	395.9	1034.0	2247.0	2521.3	2351.9	2757.6	3056.3
USA	1259.3	1735.1	1969.2	2315.3	2250.2	2409.5	2614.3
China	225.0	660.0	1396.2	1680.8	1589.5	1842.3	2022.3[a]
Japan	379.5	515.0	692.4	648.0	607.6	671.3	748.3
				Balance			
CIS	72.2	148.9	188.2	165.4	102.2	133.0	214.8
EAEU			183.5	167.9	106.6	138.7	228.3
OECD	-374.9	-730.0	-638.0	-622.2	-518.3	-621.9	-755.0
EU-28	-47.0	-88.7	-126.7	132.0	150.6	115.8	51.2
BRICS	83.9	239.2	238.4	644.2	596.5	486.3	468.9
USA	-477.4	-827.9	-690.7	-812.2	-799.2	-862.8	-950.2
China	24.2	102.0	182.1	601.6	547.2	438.1	395.1[a]
Japan	99.8	80.0	77.4	-23.2	37.3	26.9	-10.1

Source: Compiled by the authors on the basis of UN Monthly Bulletin of Statistics, July 2019 (URL: http://unstats.un.org)

Source: OECD (URL: https://data.oecd.org)

- the reciprocal claims of key economic centres—the United States, the European Union, and China—against each other with respect to the fairness of their respective trade policies ("trade wars");
- growing reindustrialisation in developed countries;
- rising production costs and aggravating environmental problems in Southeast Asia; and
- the excessive container capacity of global sea container shipping services and other processes.

Due to the need to diversify the revenue sources of business entities, almost all Eurasian countries are calling for the development of their transit transportation systems (TTSs), preparing appropriate programmes and plans, and entering into alliances and infrastructure integration associations. In other words, they seek to develop, as far as possible, a transit economy in their territories.

In accordance with the authors' definition, the transit economy (TE) is an economic, industrial, and territorial system. One of the key sources for their welfare is revenues, which arise from numerous sources: from the transit of cargo and passenger flows, vehicles, energy, water, and information resources via the territory of the relevant country; from the provision of supporting services with respect to such transit; and from the development of related industries A significant number of the authorities, businesses, and individuals within such territories are involved in such revenues (Zoidov et al. 2018).

In this regard, particular attention should be given to the development of the industry and service sectors incidental to the transit of cargoes and passengers, and also to the passage of other resources, as an integral component of the formation of innovation and industry belts along twenty-first-century trade routes at the Industry 4.0 stage.

In addition, the movement of information resources—both in parallel to cargo flows and in the opposite direction—is an indispensable part of digital logistics that enables fast and seamless passage of transit cargoes, predominantly on the basis of unattended technologies increasing the reliability and efficiency of the shipping process and reducing risks of corrupt behaviour. It is reasonable to discuss the formation of digital trade routes within Global Eurasia from the very beginning.

The following three components—state regulation, the condition of industry and agriculture, and the innovative development of transport modes—are closely interrelated and mutually influence each other (Pak 2018). The German economist List notes, "everywhere, as manufacturing industry developed, transportation routes were improved, canals excavated, rivers made navigable, roads upgraded, railways and lines of steamers established – the necessary conditions for the development of agriculture and civilisation" (List 2017).

This relationship can be traced from ancient times. Paine notes that "the development of the sail gave the people of Upper Egypt a technological edge that enabled them to bring Lower Egypt within their political and economic sphere ... Without the development of river craft capable of travelling back and forth reliably and economically, commerce between Upper and Lower Egypt would have been intermittent and probably limited to small quantities of high-value prestige goods" (Paine 2017).

Changes in a political situation or state regulation can influence the characteristics of transport means and shipping patterns as well. For instance, "disputes over heresies undermined the cohesion of the Byzantine Empire in the seventh century and the resulting stresses are reflected in diminished activity that led to truncated or abandoned shipping routes, and fewer and smaller ships" (Paine 2017).

The relationship between the technical characteristics of transport means and the scope/focus of government support is also corroborated by the early history of Italian trade city-states—Venice, Genoa, Pisa, and Amalfi. Paine writes, "with less state support of maritime commerce, the inherent uncertainties of sea trade discouraged investment in large, expensive ships, and it behooved merchant-owners of relatively modest means to run ship that were small and easy to build. These comparatively inexpensive frame-first hulls also gave smaller polities such as the Italian city-states the opportunity to develop niche trades in which they could compete against more established maritime powers" (Paine 2017).

Today, the formation of an integral digital transport and logistics environment is the main route towards innovative development with respect to all transport modes. This process involves all of the aforementioned economic agents: the state, industrial and agricultural businesses, and transport companies. For instance, industrial companies increasingly operate without warehouse inventories—a practice imposing enhanced requirements upon prompt and reliable logistic support for production processes.

The formation of such an integral digital transport and logistics environment includes the implementation and operation of digital services, supporting interaction along the following lines:

- Businesses ↔ businesses
- State ↔ state
- State ↔ businesses

The goal of this chapter is to identify areas for the innovative development of all transport modes through the formation of an integral digital transport and logistics environment, and to find the most efficient methods for regulating the financial flows being generated by the transit movement of the most important economic assets.

Methodology

Mechanisms for the generation, distribution, and redistribution of revenues from the operation of a transit economy within Global Eurasia should be created and implemented, with due regard for certain dramatic expansions; this chapter contains the hypothesis that the innovative development of all transport modes should be focused on the processes of these dramatic expansions: automation, robotisation, digital transformation, AI implementation, and the transition to paper-free and unattended technologies. Against this background, the development of the transit economy requires the creation and implementation of mechanisms for the generation, distribution, and redistribution of revenues from its operation.

Tasks To develop and implement mechanisms for the generation, distribution, and redistribution of revenues from the operation of a transit economy within Global Eurasia against the background of automation, robotisation, digital transformation, AI implementation, and the transition to paper-free and unattended technologies.

The scientific and methodological basis of this study is made up by the methods of system analysis, the evolutional theory of institutions, the theory of industrial and technological balance in the economy, and the historical approach.

Results

The Aspects of Automation and Digital Transformation of Cargo Transportation by Rail Within Global Eurasia

Reducing the Time Required for Border and Station Procedures Border procedures have risks and drawbacks, such as their long duration, high complexity, and the potential for corruption; therefore, these constitute the most significant barrier for enhancing the competitive advantages of Eurasian land transportation routes being used for the transit of cargoes and passengers. Therefore, reducing the time required to complete border and station procedures should be the highest priority.

This is a bottleneck in the transit transportation systems (TTSs) in post-Soviet countries, and provides the key obstacle to the formation of Global

Eurasia from the infrastructural and institutional perspective. In other words, the innovative development of transport modes in this area should proceed along the following lines: (a) the acceleration of technological processes, and (b) the minimisation of human involvement.

As Klimovsky, GLONASS' Chief Commercial Officer, believes, the key issue today is not so the use of new technologies as the creation of a trusted tool for cross-border transportation (primarily from China to Europe). "In my opinion, one promising option is to automate customs inspection not through electronic documentation but through eliminating the very need for an inspector to approach the cargo. He or she could use only an electronic device that would display cargo details and information on the sealing/locking mechanism. Then the inspector, provided that all details are compliant, could allow the passage of the cargos, especially transit ones, through the border on a green corridor basis. Such a trusted environment, including the trusted tool, should be accepted by partners in China, Japan, and Korea" (Chernyshevskaya 2019a).

One innovative solution for accelerating customs clearance and minimising human involvement is the use of fixed and mobile inspection systems (ISs); for instance, an IS can be used to inspect a container train without opening any containers, without stopping the train; and at a speed of up to 70 km/h.

The transfer of containers from 1435 mm gauge platforms to 1520 mm gauge platforms and vice versa, without using container storage areas, shipping/logistic terminals, or cargo yards, is an innovative transportation and transhipment technology, ensuring the fastest possible passage of cargo flows between rail tracks with different gauges. Eliminating the processes of warehousing, storage, and accumulation of cargo shipments is a commonly used logistic technology consistent with Industry 4.0.

Another innovative technology in container shipping is the implementation of the XL-train project, which envisages the reassembling of trains coming from China for the 1520 mm track gauge on a "3 in 2" or "2 in 1" basis. The use of electronic data interchange (EDI) should also be mentioned. At the Port of Vladivostok, the implementation of the Intertran technology—allowing up to 30 operations to become paper-free—has worked in providing mobile workstations for freight clerks and tallymen, who count cargoes when loading or unloading aboard a vessel.

The passage speed of Eurasian transit depends on the *condition and innovative development of railway infrastructure in neighbouring states.* According to Vladimir Salamatov, general director at the International

Trade and Integration Research Centre, "whereas container trains move across the Russian territory at a rate of more than 1000 km/day, the speed in European countries drops to 300 km/day (Bashkanova 2019). Therefore, the fact that the European Commission provided Poland with two grants for railway infrastructure modernisation, totalling €604 million, in September 2019 should be welcomed; this will allow Polish Railways to implement a European traffic control system by 2023, thus eliminating the need to replace locomotives/equipment at border crossings (Gudok 2019).

The Automation of Carriage Processes and the Implementation of Unattended Technologies The automation of cargo and passenger carriage could be promoted by the implementation of "virtual coupling", a solution using a digital radio channel whereby the last car of a train is followed by a "radio tail" divided into limiting zones: "red" (the protective zone), "red/yellow", and "green" zones. In this case, the capacity of railway infrastructure depends not on the length of any block sections determined by rail circuits, but on the frequency and speed of actual movement.

A digital automatic train operation system featuring the function of intelligent automatic operation of cargo trains allows for a reduction in locomotive-to-locomotive distance from 4–5 km (when using standard signalling/centralisation/blocking (SCB) devices) to 1.5 km. This allows an increase in the capacity potential of the infrastructure, without capital investments.

Another innovative technology contributing to the adoption of unattended solutions for traffic operation, track status, or occupancy detection is the implementation of the "computer vision" system, which is a state-of-the art system for rolling stock positioning in the network, making it possible to generate a 3D picture of the surrounding space and identify items along the route of the train. It includes:

- signals from global navigation satellite systems,
- video cameras aimed at long distances (about 1.5 km),
- scanning lidars that are efficient at short distances (up to 200 m), and
- a thermal imager operating when the weather is bad.

Marshalling Yard Automation In order to arrange for unattended processes at marshalling yards for the technical examination of freight cars within its network, JSC Russian Railways is starting to implement a robotic unit (RTU) that uses a manipulator, a computer vision system, and other sensors in order to perform most of the operations now being performed by car inspectors/repairers, signallers, or yardmasters. The RTU will be used in addition to the Integrated Post of automated acceptance and diagnostics of rolling stock at marshalling yards (PPSS) in order to detect the technical condition of rolling stock and any cars requiring uncoupled repair (Kadik 2019).

An automated train/car inspection system, using laser scanning on rolling stock and cargo dimensions during the course of train movement, can identify any faults jeopardising traffic safety, such as substandard dimensions of rolling stock and its cargo, or failure to comply with the specifications for cargo fastening and positioning on open freight cars, The implementation of this will accelerate commercial inspection of cars and cargoes, increase capacity of marshalling yards, and eliminate the human factor.

The Automation of Track Infrastructure Maintenance and Repair This area features the following aspects of innovative development:

- the use of electronic track templates, recording any deviations from track maintenance standards and automatically delivering such data to the information system; and
- the implementation of the Mobile Workstation technology, allowing a railway employee, when working on a track section, to record any comments that would be automatically entered into the Unified Corporate Automated Infrastructure Control System (UCAICS), to make photos, and to deliver information to his or her colleagues.

According to Kuchin, Deputy Manager of the Central Infrastructure Directorate, "innovative solutions are in higher demand at the Eastern Segment railways. Whereas the railway network in western Russia is rather dense and some alternatives for the planning of a traffic campaign are available, the east of the country has only the Trans-Siberian Railway and, starting from Taishet, the BAM. So the problem of implementing modern technologies and equipment allowing maintenance periods to be reduced as much as possible is most relevant there" (Pasechnik 2019).

One promising way to enhance the safety of track infrastructure construction and renovation is the development and implementation of a video analysis system; this could inspect track maintenance personnel for the use of individual protective equipment, detect the presence of any personnel in a dangerous area when the lifting mechanism of a track laying crane is in operation, and block the operation of this mechanism until such personnel has left the dangerous area.

The creation of a digital operation control system, recording the amount of work completed, determining the quantity of materials used, and supervising process compliance, would contribute to the reduction and monitoring of track maintenance costs (Zubov 2019a).

The Evolution of the Regulatory Framework and the Innovative Development of Corporate Culture Digital transformation requires modifications to the regulatory framework and the innovative development of corporate culture. In this regard, Kirillova, member of the Research and Engineering Board of the Digital Transport and Logistics Association, notes: "JSC Russian Railways employs over 1 million people. In order to carry out digital transformation, we need to find, teach and develop change agents" (Gromadskaya 2019). In the opinion of Saratov, Head of RR's HR Department, "digital skills will become a mandatory component of personnel development. In addition, it is important to put together criteria for examining the digital readiness of our employees" (Gromadskaya 2019).

The Organisational and Institutional Tools to Overcome Negative Trends in the Market for Short-Life Cargo Transportation The transit carriage of short-life cargoes is a promising field of transit economy development within Global Eurasia. This primarily includes the transportation of fish and seafood from Japan, Southeast Asia states, and Iran to the EU. In this market, railway transport is quite capable of competing with air transport, but only if high-speed "cold trains", going in strict conformity with a clear dedicated schedule, are provided.

A very promising project is underway regarding salmon transit in containers along the Norway–Russia–China route. As Grishagin, CEO of Russian Container Company, says, "this new area of shipping has become possible due to the fact that last month Russia lifted its ban on transit shipping of a number of short-life products, including fish, which had previously been subject to sanctions" (*RZD*, 12 August 2019). Currently, all

Norwegian salmon shipments go to China by air, and their volumes grow fast. This transport mode is being criticised by Norwegian environmentalists due to its huge carbon footprint. The new initiative is closely monitored by Norwegian fish-farming companies that seek to demonstrate their green commitment.

Over the latest decade, the share of rail transport in short-life cargo shipping has dropped by 40%, and the share of road carriers has increased to 88% (Kudryavtheva 2019). Unfortunately, it should be said that consignors often choose their transport mode on the basis of freight costs rather than cargo safety. Unless the specifications for the carriage and storage of short-life goods are complied with, their shelf life can dramatically shrink. It is noted that, for example, the quality of fish and fish products, which are among the most challenging goods in terms of storage, can be affected by temperature fluctuations within the range of one or two degrees. According to Sinyov, President of the Refrigerator Car Operators Association, the Russian railways will proceed to test an end-to-end temperature control scheme with respect to fish transportation using the Mercury system (owned by the Russian Agency for Agricultural Supervision) and GLONASS during March–April 2020 (Zubov 2019a; b).

Kondratenko, Deputy CEO in charge of design activities and engineering policy at Eurosib SPb-TS, proposes taking the following measures to enhance the competitive advantages of railway transport over transportation by road in the field of short-life cargo carriage (Kondratenko 2019):

- To adopt stringent rules for the certification of transportation refrigerator equipment. Each refrigerator container must be subject to certification by the competent Russian bodies of agricultural and veterinary supervision to ensure that the equipment complies with temperature regime and heat conductivity standards.
- To tighten supervision over the circulation of short-life cargoes as to the observance and monitoring of in-transit temperature parameters. To this end, it is important to create a mechanism for monitoring a continuous cold chain for any cargoes requiring conformity with a certain temperature regime during their storage and carriage.
- To cut rates for short-life cargo delivery by rail using specialised refrigerator equipment. This measure is capable of turning dealers in fish, meat, and other products back to high-quality refrigerator equipment, such as is used by railway operators in their carriage

activities, from old, obsolete, and often incompetently adapted containers. This is the equipment these dealers currently use; such equipment is not prohibited as of yet.

- To impose a prohibitive salvage fee and other restrictions with respect to the import of foreign-made second-hand refrigerator equipment.
- To localise the assembly of refrigerator containers, using not only imported components, but also Russian-made components and materials.

As companies decommissioned or wrote off their specialised cars for rail transportation of short-life cargoes, they replenished their rolling stock by purchasing heavyweight refrigerator containers, foreign-made heat-insulated containers, and isothermal cars rebuilt from covered cars.

The Development and Manufacture of Innovative Rolling Stock for Cargo Transit In this regard, the following promising areas should be mentioned:

1. The launch of multipurpose platforms equipped with fold-back fitting stops that enable the transportation of both containers and other cargoes, thus making the use of rolling stock more efficient.
2. The development and wide application of interchangeable-body carriage solutions: a platform is equipped with car bodies that can be changed depending upon the type of cargo to be carried.

In general, this is required to enhance the flexibility of railway rolling stock in order to secure its competitive edge over road transport.

The Implementation of Electronic Sealing/Locking Devices (ESLDs) One of the key aspects of digital transformation in the field of cargo transit control is the creation of an ecosystem for electronic sealing/locking devices (ESLDs). The development and use of a cloud storage solution for data and internal memory is an integral part of ESLD implementation. For instance, the GLONASS-Transit software product processes all information coming from electronic seals to all supervisory authorities. In order to minimise the corporate costs associated with the implementation of this technology, it would be advisable to use an ESLD leasing scheme involving daily rental payments.

The Development of the Transit Economy on the Basis of Green Energy In order to meet the contemporary trends for reducing carbon dioxide emissions, the development of the national TTS should keep in mind the following concepts:

- supplying the power lines of electrified railways with electric power generated by hydroelectric power plants (HPPs),
- supplying power lines using solar panels or wind power units,
- using rolling stock equipped with batteries, and
- developing and implementing rolling stock using hydrogen fuel cells.

Supplying HPP-generated electricity to the power lines of electrified railways would be especially relevant for the main railways installed or planned in Central Asia, where such water-rich countries as Kyrgyzstan and Tajikistan are located.

In June 2019, the German state-owned railway company Deutsche Bahn adopted its Robust Railway (Starke Schiene) long-term strategy, envisaging that the company would completely switch to the use of electric power from renewable sources by 2038: 12 years earlier than previously planned (Gudok 2019).

It is peculiar that Scandinavian countries now see a public mood called "flight shame", which is felt by environmentally minded people when they travel by air instead of using more environment-friendly transport means (Gudok 2019). Such attitudes (being fostered by such PR activities as Greta Thunberg's statements) will be contributing to an increase in the share of railway transport in passenger flows and in carrying country, regional, and global cargo.

For those countries that produce liquefied natural gas (LNG), the green attitudes will favour wider use of LNG-powered rolling stock. For example, Sovkomflot's green LNG-powered tankers Lomonosov Prospect and Mendeleev Prospect shape a new standard of navigation safety: the use of LNG reduces the emission of sulphur oxides and soot by up to 100%, nitrogen oxides by 76% and carbon dioxide by 30% in comparison to vessels using heavy marine fuel oil (*RZD*, 03.10.2019).

Trends for the Innovative Development of Road, Sea, and Air Transportation Within Global Eurasia

The development of contrailer (railway/road) transportation, which is considered and developed in Europe as a more environment-friendly alternative to road transport, encounters a number of operational, engineering, organisational, and institutional obstacles in Russia. In order to eliminate these obstacles, it is required, inter alia, to make efforts in order to ensure the safety of trucks (wheels, glass, components, etc.) by covering the cabin with protective panels, and to arrange for driver transportation, since a heavy truck in Russia is formally owned by its driver and the driver must follow his truck (the situation is different in Europe where drivers change).

According to Alekseev, Chief Operations Manager at the Tochka-Tochka logistics company, "contrailer transportation will never become a segment of transport and logistics services until its technological, technical and market prerequisites are met and it has a strong lobby in the Russian transport logistics industry" (Lebedev 2019).

The "uberisation" of the market for cargo transportation by road (except for bulk cargoes) involves platforms that operate as digital brokers and allow consignors to find the best shipping terms available by automating the entire process, from request submission to billing. The use of predictive analytics algorithms allows cargo owners to get the best offers from carriers and provides the carriers with more orders, thus reducing the empty mileage of their vehicles.

In addition, the following is available as part of railway operations:

- the Cargo Transportation trading platform;
- Vagonline, a railway car aggregator similar to Yandex Taxi;
- Rail Commerce, a railway car exchange platform.

The common purpose of these platforms is to provide easier access to cargo transportation by rail, to ensure fair pricing, and to reduce losses for both the service customer and the rolling stock operator.

The Innovative Development of Sea Shipping The new standard of the International Maritime Organisation, IMO-2020, effective as from January 1, 2020, limits sulphur content in marine fuel and requires the installation of costly equipment to treat combustion products; as such it can make the shipping of cargo by sea less stable and more expensive for a certain period of time.

The commissioning of super large container vessels (carrying 23,000 twenty-foot equivalent units [TEU]) would reduce the shipping costs per container. However, the use of vessels of higher container capacity would require additional investment in port infrastructure and bottom deepening at berths, on the access routes to ports, in river estuaries, and in other areas.

Currently, the largest container vessels are about 400 m long, more than 60 m wide, and have a draught of up to 16.50 m. There are plans to build vessels 460 m long and 68 m long, capable of carrying up to 30,000 TEU. According to Bonz, head of the Port of Hamburg (UVHH) and of the European port federation Feport, "the operators of about 400 EU port terminals have agreed that this authorisation may only be reviewed on the condition that the maximum size of vessels visiting Europeans ports should be limited to their current maximum dimensions" (*RZD*, 05.08.2019).

It should be noted that Russian container terminals at ports are equipped with foreign-made machinery—Liebherr and Gottwald cranes, Colmar loaders, and so on.

The construction and commissioning of ice-class container vessels is a sea transport innovation relevant to Asia-Europe cargo shipping. The first high ice-class container vessel Norilsk Nickel was launched in 2005. It is designed to move without icebreaker support. In 2009, another containership of the same class, the diesel-electric vessel Talnakh, arrived at the port of Dudinka (Lobov 2019).

The nuclear-powered icebreaker Leader is at the design stage; its commissioning (scheduled for 2023) will accelerate the passage of the Northern Sea Route fivefold (Chernyshevskaya 2019a, b). However, it is impossible to predict when the project will pay back due to global warming and the cyclic nature of climate fluctuations.

The Innovative Development of Cargo Transit by Air In the field of air cargo transit, the following recommendations would be relevant:

- to use cargo carriers running intercontinental flights;
- to provide aircraft with technical landing facilities, primarily for refuelling purposes;

- to effect supplementary loading in order to increase the amount of cargo being carried by aircraft;
- to consolidate and distribute cargo flows across the territory of the Russian Federation and its federal districts;
- to develop cargo infrastructure at airports in accordance with market requirements, in particular to build refrigerator facilities ensuring the complete safety of high-value temperature-sensitive cargoes.

In this regard, it should be noted that contemporary aircraft can cover significant distances without refuelling; therefore, the expansion of cargo consolidation and distribution operations for the purpose of flying over Global Eurasia should be the main area of transit economy development with respect to air transport.

Conclusion

Slow implementation of unmanned systems in transport is due to the need to specify and allocate responsibility for their operation; nevertheless, the evolution of Industry 4.0 cannot be stopped. In this regard, the transportation processes involve—and will be involving—ever-decreasing amounts of human resources against the ever-increasing amounts of finance and assets. Therefore, the performance of any TE cannot be evaluated from the perspective of new job creation.

Since innovative TTSs will largely be based on unattended or minimally attended technologies, it is high time to develop and implement a mechanism for the generation, distribution, and redistribution of revenues from the transit transportation of cargoes and passengers. This mechanism should have a corporate format; the public-private partnership principle should be used. As regards Global Eurasia, a Eurasian Transit Transportation Company could serve as such a corporate entity.

However, the most efficient method for redistributing revenues from the operation of a transit economy to the majority of economic agents would be the development of businesses which provide related or auxiliary products or services on a high-technology basis, and the formation of an extensive innovation and industry belt along the trade route.

References

Bashkanova, V. (2019). Kaliningrad's Window to Europe. *Gudok*. Online at: https://www.gudok.ru/newspaper/?ID=1477530&archive=2019.09.19. Accessed 27 Sep 2019.

Chernyshevskaya W. (2019a). Can Provide End-to-End Monitoring for Multimodal Transportation? *RZhD-Partner*. Online at: https://www.rzd-partner.ru/zhd-transport/news/glonass-planiruet-predostavit-testovyy-dostup-dlya-rzhd/. Accessed 22 Nov 2019.

Chernyshevskaya, W. (2019b). Icebreaker Investments May Be Lost by 2050 Due to Climate Change. *RZhD-Partner*. Online at: https://www.rzd-partner.ru/wate-transport/news/vlozheniya-v-ledokoly-mogut-byt-obestseneny-k-2050-godu-iz-za-izmeneniy-klimata/. Accessed 04 Oct 2019.

Gromadskaya, Y. (2019). Effect Is Embedded in Strategy. *Gudok*. Online at: https://www.gudok.ru/newspaper/?ID=1484574&archive=2019.11.15. Accessed 21 Nov 2019.

Gudok (2019). *Issue #171 (26780) 19.09.2019 [Выпуск №171 (26780)] 19.09.2019*. Online at: https://www.gudok.ru/newspaper/?archive=2019.09.19. Accessed 03 Oct 2019.

Kadik, L. (2019). A Robot Will Uncouple Cars. *Gudok*. Online at: https://www.gudok.ru/newspaper/?ID=1477272&archive=2019.09.17. Accessed 02 Oct 2019.

Kondratenko, S. (2019). The Refrigerator Is on a Growth Track. *Gudok*. Online at: https://www.gudok.ru/newspaper/?ID=1481265&archive=2019.10.22. Accessed 22 Oct 2019.

Kudryavtheva, Y. (2019). Written Off as Scheduled. *Gudok*. Online at: http://www.gudok.ru/newspaper/?ID=1449655&archive=2019.01.15. Accessed 15 Jan 2019.

Lebedev, A. (2019). The Development of Transit Operations Needs Alliances of Multimodal Operators. An Interview with M. Alekseev, Tochka-Tochka's COO. *RZhD-Partner*. Online at: https://www.rzd-partner.ru/logistics/interview/dlya-razvitiya-tranzita-nuzhny-alyansy-multimodalnykh-operatorov/. Accessed 11 Nov 2019.

List, Friedrich. (2017). *The National System of Political Economy* (V. M. Izergin, Trans.). Moscow: Sotsium.

Lobov, V. (2019). Arctic Vector. *Transport Rossii, 37*(1104).

Paine, L. (2017). *Sea and Civilization. A Maritime History of the World* (I. V. Maigurova, Trans.). Moscow: AST Publishers.

Pak, Y. (2018). Public-Private Partnership in the EAEU Transit Economy: Russia and Central Asian States. *MGIMO Review of International Relations, 5*(62), 174–183. (In Russian). https://doi.org/10.24833/2071-8160-2018-5-62-174-183.

Pasechnik, Y. (2019). Automation Against the Human Factor. *Gudok*. Online at: https://www.gudok.ru/newspaper/?ID=1483346&archive=2019.11.06. Accessed 06 Nov 2019.

RZD-Partner. (2019a). *EU Ports Oppose Larger Containerships, 05.08.2019*. Online at: https://www.rzd-partner.ru/logistics/news/porty-es-vystupayut-protiv-dalneyshego-uvelicheniya-razmera-konteynerovozov/. Accessed 09 Aug 2019.

RZD-Partner. (2019b). *Norwegian Salmon Transportation by Rail to China Will Be 80% Cheaper Than Air Shipments, 12.08.2019*. Online at: https://www.rzd-partner.ru/zhd-transport/news/transportirovka-norvezhskogo-lososya-po-zheleznoy-doroge-v-kitay-oboydetsya-na-80-deshevle-vozdushny/. Accessed 27 Aug 2019.

RZD-Partner. (2019c). *Two Sovkomflot Tankers Go Via the Northern Sea Route from Primorsk to China, 03.10.2019*. Online at: https://www.rzd-partner.ru/wate-transport/news/dva-tankera-sovkomflota-otpravilis-po-sevmorputi-iz-primorska-v-kitay/. Accessed 04 Oct 2019.

Zoidov, K. K., Medkov, A. A., & Zoidov, Z. K. (2018). The Conceptual Foundations of Theory, Methodology and Practice of the Transit Economy. *Problems of Market Economies*, (3), 49–58.

Zubov, A. (2019a). Neuron Network Sees Everything. An Interview with A. Pikalov, Head of the New Projects Department, Central Track Maintenance Directorate. *Gudok*. Online at: https://www.gudok.ru/newspaper/?ID=1484071&archive=2019.11.12. Accessed 12 Nov 2019.

Zubov, M. (2019b). Comfortable Conditions for Fish. An Interview with M. Sinyov, President of the Refrigerator Car Operators Association. *Gudok*. Online at: https://www.gudok.ru/newspaper/?ID=1480216&archive=2019.10.10. Accessed 18 Oct 2019.

CHAPTER 17

Defining the Readiness for Smart City Concept: Russian Municipalities Study

Sergey Kamolov and Yulia Kandalintseva

Introduction

With regard to the public governance, "smart cities" concept implementation indicates that a state, a region or a municipality participate in the worldwide competition for talents who will define by their professional qualities local economic growth and future contours (Stepnov and Kovalchuk 2019). Owing to the so-called war for talent, local governance is forced to adopt strategies aimed at attracting and retaining citizens looking to develop their personality and the world around.

As a matter of fact the goal of any initiatives to implement the "smart city" concept should ultimately be confined to improving the quality of citizens life through greater efficiency of resource use (financial, energy, technological, human, etc.), the creation of multilateral partnerships, and active involving residents in the processes of urban governance.

The scientific community has not yet developed a generally accepted "smart city" concept. The analysis of 40 open-source definitions has been performed as a part of our study. It has been found that the concept

S. Kamolov (✉) • Y. Kandalintseva
Moscow State Institute of International Relations (MGIMO University), Moscow, Russia

J. Kovalchuk (ed.), *Post-Industrial Society*,
https://doi.org/10.1007/978-3-030-59739-9_17

presupposes a wide conceptual range: the framework comprises innovations and technologies, the environment components such as infrastructure, institutions and society, and citizen welfare improvement.

Figure 17.1 depicts the abovementioned variation of interpretations. The highest percentage of the selection is represented by definitions connected with "environment," which echoes the existing tendency among most providers considering the cities potential with the purpose of introduction of new technologies and methods of urban environment management.

The Russian Ministry of Construction has launched its a departmental project "Smart City" which is designed to accomplish a multifaceted range of tasks: competitiveness, safety, adaptability, comfort, efficiency, and people-centered development.

The past decade was marked by growing research related to the "smart cities" phenomenon, which can be clustered into five focus areas: conseptualists, comparativists, regional studies, school of administration in a digital environment, and technology-centered studies.

Conseptualists Urban strategist Boyd Cohen elaborated three generations of smart cities that differ in the purpose of applying technologies, the level of development of physical infrastructure, the degree of citizens engagement, and other stakeholders in urban processes (Cohen 2015):

Smart Cities 1.0: a technology-oriented city where technology is used in order to increase its stability, vitality, and controlla-

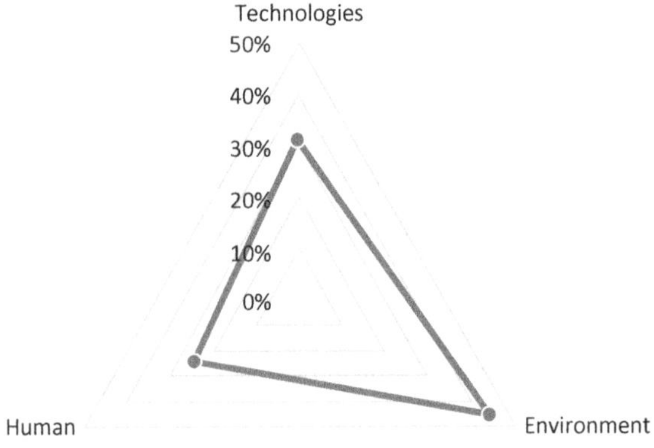

Fig. 17.1 Polars of the "smart city" concept

bility. The main stakeholders are companies—suppliers of technological solutions and services.

Smart Cities 2.0: a technology-enabled managed city where technologies improve the quality of life and solve problems in the field of healthcare, transport, environment, and ecology. The main role in the city development is assigned to the authorities, residents are involved in a limited way.

Smart cities 3.0: a highly intelligent integrated city that is characterized by a combination of technologies that stimulate the development of social integration and entrepreneurship. The single ecosystem contributes to the citizens involvement, making them active participants in the urban growth.

Many researchers have proposed various methods of smart city conceptualization from different perspectives. A triple-helix "smart cities" model was introduced by Leydesdorff and Deakin reflecting the relationship between business, government, and academic communities, namely, in the joint development of technologies and innovations (Leydesdorff and Deakin 2011). Lombardi et al. enhanced this approach with a civil society indicator group so as to evaluate the performance of smart city elements (Lombardi et al. 2012). Nam and Pardo offer their three-dimensional (3D) model—technology, society, and institutions—as the basis for "smart city" strategies (Nam and Pardo 2011). Glebova et al. designed smart city conceptualization building on five principle elements (public security, intellectual transport system, management of energy consumption, environmental protection, and ICT), whereas Zygiaris' "smart city" model comprises six layers (innovation, applications, integration, instrumentation, interconnection, and environment and city) (Glebova et al. 2014; Zygiaris 2013). According to Liu et al. key smart city activities should incorporate 33 elements, with another 27 considering as the supportive ones (Liu et al. 2014).

Comparativists At the present times cities are challenged with maintaining economic growth in tight competition. For that reason innovative means and tools are being created and applied as driving factors to enhance the metropolitan status. Significantly, the cities rising in major international ratings will eventually attract talented staff and greater investments.

Thus numerous ratings are extensively used and promoted. One of examples is the one created by Giffinger and Gudrun called "Smart City Rating," which can be used to identify cites' strong and weak points (Giffinger and Gudrun 2010). Ranking entails a system of benchmarks, according to which a comparison is made. Lee et al. presented a number of indicators to measure "smart city" components: technology, effectiveness of services, and relevant devices for access to services. (Lee et al. 2013). Other studies evaluate urban capacity with respect to city competitiveness (Singhal et al. 2013), good urban governance (UN Habitat 2014), size and global city performance (Kourtit et al. 2014), local government effectiveness (da Cruz and Marques 2014), and environmental and economic sustainability (Mori and Christodoulou 2012).

Regional Studies Several publications have appeared in recent years documenting the best world practices of "smart cities" and their features. T. Bakici et al. studied the Barcelona's transition from a traditional metropolitan area to the twenty-first century metropolis (Bakıcı et al. 2013). A. Mahizhnan examined Singapore's experience amid its successful shift away from an industrial economy to an information-based one (Mahizhnan 1999). The research works of S. Shwayri and G. Lindsay are devoted to the experience of the South Korean city Songdo, which was built from scratch (Shwayri 2013; Lindsay 2010). Vershinina proposes that "smart" model is quite attainable in the Russian Federation, while some regions are already effectively implementing it through a variety of technologies and innovations (Vershinina 2016), though there are still some serious administrative and technological obstacles that hamper concept's realization (Dolgikh et al. 2015).

School of Administration in a Digital Environment Barber convinces that creative and progmatic city administrators are vital to tackle global issues and states that "mayors rule the world" (Barber 2013). Landry has demonstrated that urban managers and local politicians should be guided by the aim of making their city not the best "in the world," but "for the whole world" (Landry 2012). As reported by Torfing, government policy plays a decisive role in the "smart cities" development while social problem-solving is not just a question of appropriate policy formulation, but a managerial issue of achieving better cooperation between the state and other stakeholders (Torfing et al. 2012). Within school of admimistration, the most interesting approach to this issue is the idea that effectiveness of the digital transformation will be defined by city authorities activities (Kamolov 2019). We argue that municipalities which fully understand the principal objectives of management digital transformation program and the role of a trained team and dedicated resources will provide a measure of success for cities transformation by the "smart" canons.

Technology-Centered Studies Although there is a debate about what should be at the core of "smart city" definition, the key common component of its diverse variations is the ICT, by which the quality of life of the urban population is improved. A number of modern cities are already deploying technologies to respond to existing challenges in ecology, safety, efficient management, and distribution of resources. Researchers identify various sets of digital technologies that are fundamental for building models of cities in the era of the digital revolution. The focus of recent research has been on such important innovations as the Internet of Things, artificial intelligence, blockchain, unmanned vehicles, bio- and nanotechnologies, Building Information Modeling (BIM) technologies, robotics, and 3D printing. The authors argue that to achieve the smart city goals just one technology or a smart solution is not enough. Based on global experience, researchers conclude that an integrated approach is needed, that is, the simultaneous and coordinated application of several "smart" solutions (Dobrynin et al. 2016).

Methodology

In this chapter, a new approach to determining the maturity degree of Russian smart cities is proposed. We assume that the task of assessing the readiness level will be to indicate readiness level of the management system at the stages of goal setting, planning, and programming.

The maturity of management systems should be reflected in the adop tion the "smart city" concept as regulatory and administrative documents by the local self-government executive and representative bodies. A specialized program or a strategy demonstrates that muncipal authorities carefully elaborated the "smart city" concept implementation on its territory in terms of goals setting and the availability of sufficient resources (infrastructure, personnel, budget, etc.).

Manville C. et al. developed an approach for assessing EU smart cities activities based on the online search for strategies, plans and programs, networks, solutions, and elements. (Manville et al. 2014). The authors identified four levels of maturity:

1. only a smart city strategy or policy;
2. level 1 + a project plan without implementation;
3. level 2 + pilot testing smart city initiatives;
4. a smart city with at least one fully launched initiative.

The research claims that in case of unavailability of smart city strategy, a city cannot be classified as "smart" and it will not involve any of the six characteristics (smart economy, smart mobility, smart environment, smart governance, smart living, smart people).

In many respects our approach is similar to the outlined above, however, our particular methodology focuses around governance aspects and the implementation of project management measures determined in the guidelines for the preparation of the regional project "Smart Cities." A content analysis, a comparative method, an expert assessment, and a statistical analysis method were used to analyze the sample of top 100 Russian cities with a population of 188,000 and up to 13 million people. We checked for the availability of regulatory documents at the municipal level directly or indirectly connected to the urban spaces digitalization of each city included in the sample and developed five evaluation criteria:

1. Smart city strategy (e.g., "Smart Moscow")
2. A section related to the "smart city" concept in the strategy for the development of a urban settlement
3. Highly specialized programs realized within the urban digitalization framework (e.g., "Smart Transport" or "Smart Meter")
4. Targeted implemented projects
5. Allocated budget

Results

Based on five criteria the cities were assigned to six groups, where the first group comprises the cities of the highest and the sixth one of the lowest readiness degree.

The first group comprises Moscow, St. Petersburg, and Chelyabinsk, which show the full compliance with five criteria. The second group is made up of cities that we could not belong to the first group due to the lack of data on the levels and sources of financing (Ryazan, Sevastopol, Naberezhnye Chelny, and Taganrog). The criterion of the third group is the unavailability of a strategy section relating to urban spaces informatization taking into account the presence of all other aspects (Izhevsk and Orenburg). The cities of the fourth group do not have specialized sections and a devoted budget (Yaroslavl and Rybinsk). The fifth group involves 36 reviewed municipalities without specialized strategy and budget, but which implemented "smart" solutions. This data revealed a significant multiplicity which proves extremely targeted nature of the digitalization of cities in the Russian Federation. Ultimately, we added 20 cities in the sixth group that adopted highly specialized programs and implemented projects within the framework of the "smart cities" concept.

The Ministry of Construction of Russia elaborated the methodological recommendations concerning regional projects management. In accordance with the provisions only seven cities of our sample created a project management body or office, four approved a project implementation plan for a three-year period, eight established a regional center of competence to digitalize urban spaces, and seven trained teams of municipalities and executive authorities of the constituent entities.

Conclusions/Recommendations

Summing up the experience of the most progressive cities in our study permits the formulation of the following recommendations:

- The city mayors should be persistent from an administrative perspective in the elaboration and official approval of the development strategy of their "smart city." The unavailability of this document can lead to strategically erroneous financing and integration of smart solutions.
- The strategic document adoption allows for planning an appropriate amount of the city budget expenditures for the "smart" technologies.
- It is crucial to ensure citizens' engagement in urban governance processes. Accordingly, authorities can benefit from social networks or specialized platforms capabilities, for example, "Active Citizen."

It is necessary to highlight the fact that the "smart city" concept realization in Russia will significantly impact the effectiveness of the national project "Housing and Urban Environment" and the national program "Digital Economy."

An important implication of the research findings is that all the cities in our sample implement technical solutions in a targeted way and perform a narrow range of tasks for urban systems digitalization with only three municipalities following the classification's criteria, which can reflect a high degree of readiness for a full-fledged adoption of the concept.

Studying the structure, content and focus of the "smart" strategies of various cities, we noticed that they tend to gravitate toward four main elements: data, technology, management, and citizen. The possible intersections of these areas and their practical implementation can be found in Fig. 17.2. From the outcome of our investigation it is possible to conclude that the cities themselves must determine which model is more relevant and what will drive their development.

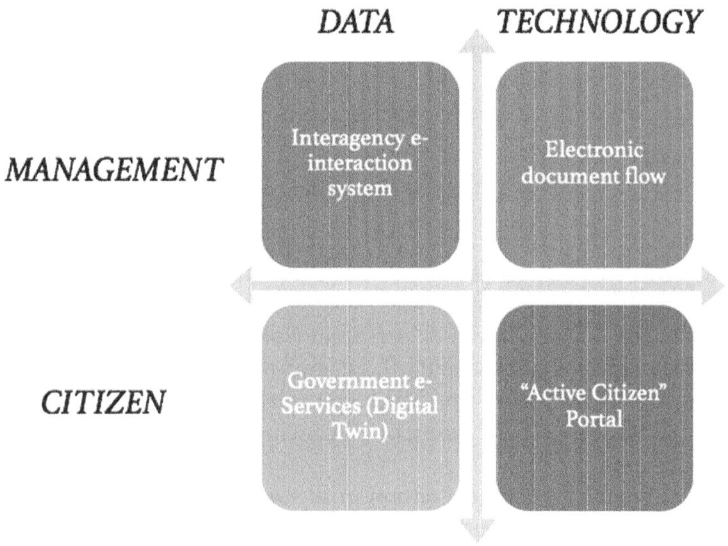

Fig. 17.2 The perception of "smart city" models

Therefore, we assume there will be four major types of smart cities across the country in the foreseeable future: (1) created around applied technologies easing the management process, (2) data-centered to enhance decision-making, (3) deploying technologies to create living environment for citizens, and (4) data-driven governance to assure that city management produces tailor-made decisions ensuring inclusiveness for all citizens. The latter we consider as the most sophisticated maturity level for smart cities.

At present the "digital divide" widens the gap between rich and poor cities, excluding the latter from the modern information economy. Within the framework of the "smart city," which is, mainly, a managerial project, urban settlements cannot overcome such problem only through technical methods. All municipalities require a proper management system.

There are substantial grounds for believing that the uneven readiness grades of management systems can lead to the outflow of talented staff to more promising cities. In other words, municipalities without formed and trained teams will be forced to face stronger opponents in the "war for talent." Accordingly the possible improvements should be directed not only toward the implementation of core "smart city" strategies or creation of specialized organizational structures, but also at raising the interest of the heads of municipalities in these changes.

References

Bakıcı, T., Almirall, E., & Wareham, J. (2013). A Smart City Initiative: The Case of Barcelona. *Journal of the Knowledge Economy, 4*, 135–148.

Barber, B. R. (2013). *If Mayors Ruled the World: Dysfunctional Nations, Rising Cities*. New Haven: Yale University Press.

Cohen, B. (2015, October 8). The 3 Generations of Smart Cities: Inside the Development of the Technology Driven City. *Fast Company*. https://www.fastcompany.com/3047795/the-3-generations-of-smart-cities

da Cruz, N. F., & Marques, R. C. (2014). Scorecards for Sustainable Local Governments. *Cities, 39*, 165–170.

Dobrynin, A. P., et al. (2016). The Digital Economy – The Various Ways to the Effective Use of Technology (BIM, PLM, CAD, IOT, Smart City, BIG DATA, and Others). *International Journal of Open Information Technologies, 4*(1), 4–11.

Dolgikh, E. I., Antonov, E. V., & Erlich, V. A. (2015). Smart Cities: Development Prospects in Russia. *Urbanistika i rynok nedvizhimosti* (Urban Studies and Real Estate Market), *1*, 50–61. (In Russian).

Giffinger, R., & Gudrun, H. (2010). Smart Cities Ranking: An Effective Instrument for the Positioning of the Cities? *ACE: Architecture, City and Environment, 4*(12), 7–26.

Glebova, I. S., Yasnitskaya, Y. S., & Maklakova, N. V. (2014). Assessment of Cities in Russia According to the Concept of "Smart City" in the Context of the Application of Information and Communication Technologies. *Mediterranean Journal of Social Sciences, 5*(18), 55–60.

Kamolov, S. G. (2019). On Epistemological Nature of the 'Smart Cities'. *Innovatsii i investitsii* (Innovations and Investments), *1*, 200–205. (In Russian).

Kourtit, K., Macharis, C., & Nijkamp, P. (2014). A Multi-Actor Multi-Criteria Analysis of the Performance of Global Cities. *Applied Geography, 49*, 24–36.

Landry, C. (2012). *The Art of City Making*. London: Routledge.

Lee, J.-H., Phaal, R., & Lee, S.-H. (2013). An Integrated Service-Device-Technology Roadmap for Smart City Development. *Technological Forecasting and Social Change, 80*, 286–306.

Leydesdorff, L., & Deakin, M. (2011). The Triple Helix Model of Smart Cities: A Neo-evolutionary Perspective. *Journal of Urban Technology, 18*(2), 53–63.

Lindsay, G. (2010, February). Cisco's Big Bet on New Songdo: Creating Cities from Scratch. *Fast Company*. https://longform.org/posts/cisco-s-big-bet-on-new-songdo-creating-cities-from-scratch

Liu, Y., Wei, J., & Rodriguez, A. F. C. (2014). Development of a Strategic Value Assessment Model for Smart City. *International Journal of Mobile Communications, 12*(4), 346–359.

Lombardi, P., Giordano, S., Farouh, H., & Yousef, W. (2012). Modelling the Smart City Performance. *Innovations, 25*(2), 137–149.

Mahizhnan. (1999). Smart Cities: The Singapore Case. *Cities, 16*(1), 13–18.

Manville, G., et al. (2014). *Mapping Smart Cities in the EU*. Brussels: European Union.

Mori, K., & Christodoulou, A. (2012). Review of Sustainability Indices and Indicators: Towards a New City Sustainability Index (CSI). *Environmental Impact Assessment Review, 32*, 94–106.

Nam, T., & Pardo, T. A. (2011). *Conceptualizing Smart City with Dimensions of Technology, People, and Institutions* (pp. 282–291). New York: ACM.

Shwayri, S. T. (2013). A Model Korean Ubiquitous Eco-city? The Politics of Making Songdo. *Journal of Urban Technology, 20*(1), 39–55.

Singhal, S., McGreal, S., & Berry, J. (2013). Application of a Hierarchical Model for City Competitiveness in Cities of India. *Cities, 31*, 114–122.

Stepnov, I., & Kovalchuk, Y. (2019). Digital Platform as a New Economic Agent in the Open Economy Model. *Drukerovskij vestnik, 2*(28), 5–13. (In Russian).

Torfing, J., Peters, B. G., Pierre, J., & Sørensen, E. (2012). *Interactive Governance: Advancing the Paradigm*. Oxford: Oxford University Press.

United Nations (UN) Habitat. (2014). *Urban Governance Index (UGI): A Tool to Measure Progress in Achieving Good Urban Governance*. http://mirror.unhabitat.org/downloads/docs/2232_80907_UGIndex.doc

Vershinina, A. (2016). Smart' Cities: Prospects for the Emergence and Development in Russia, Moscow State University Bulletin Series 18. *Sociology and Political Science, 22*(2), 163–175. (In Russian).

Zygiaris, S. (2013). Smart City Reference Model: Assisting Planners to Conceptualize the Building of Smart City Innovation Ecosystems. *Journal of the Knowledge Economy, 4*(2), 217–231.

CHAPTER 18

The Evolution of Fashion Consumer Perception in Post-Industrial Era

Natalia Konina, Igor Dolzhenko, and Monika Siennicka

Introduction

With globalization, and the formation of post-industrial society, there have been profound changes in how fashion is perceived and how consumers behave. This has resulted in the formation of a new global fashion market.

The relevance of this research is determined by the importance of the global clothing market for most economies. The production and marketing of clothes are an important source of employment, taxes, general development in the field of consumption, and all creative industries; the volume of the global clothing market was estimated at about $1.6 trillion

N. Konina (✉)
Moscow State Institute of International Relations (MGIMO University), Moscow, Russia

I. Dolzhenko
Fashion Group, Moscow, Russia

M. Siennicka
Giorgio Armani and Valentino, L'Oreal Luxe, Warsaw, Poland
e-mail: monika.siennicka@loreal.com

J. Kovalchuk (ed.), *Post-Industrial Society*,
https://doi.org/10.1007/978-3-030-59739-9_18

in 2019. The fashion industry determines the state and dynamics of the global retail trade to a great extent; it is not only the largest employment industry for a number of developing countries (China, India, Bangladesh, Vietnam, etc.), but also an important source of budget revenues for many countries, and an engine for the development of the economies of such countries as France, Italy, Spain, Turkey, China, and more.

In modern scientific literature, a fairly large number of researches have been described devoted to various aspects of the modern fashion industry and consumer behavior in the context of digital transformation. Some researchers note the impact of globalization on consumer behavior, and the fact that, now, consumers have more financial opportunities and shop more often (Hines 2001; Bulatov et al. 2019; Croll 2014). Quite a few authors consider fashion garments from the point of view of sociology, and emphasize the connection between fashionable goods and social life, participation in social contacts, social status, and features of social communication, noting how consumers connect image and personal characteristics, or their perception of fashion and their behavior (Solomon and Rabolt 2004; Solomon 2010). A number of researchers point out the democratization of fashion, and the fact that consumer expectations have shifted from the purchase of high-quality goods with less emotional reward through their experience as a consumer (Jain 2019). Researchers underline the use of new technologies in the industry (Stepnov et al. 2018) and the dominance of fast-fashion Transnational Corporations (TNCs) such as Zara, H&M, Mango, New Look, and Top Shop, which take what the leading brands present at luxury brand fashion shows and rapidly introduce design copies thereof to attract customers, who could associate their consumption with eliteness (Bhardwaj and Fairhurst 2010; Wang 2010; Cachon and Swinney 2011). A number of researchers note that modern consumers demonstrate both the desire for hedonism, perhaps the dominant model of consumer behavior, and for escapism, acting as a natural desire for individual freedom under the conditions of increased information pressure from the mass media and the whole technocratic sphere (Miller 2013). Researchers point out the problem of excess consumption: modern consumers have no physiological or psychological restrictions about the amount of clothes they would like to buy (Ma et al. 2012; Hill and Lee 2015). Considering this problem from the perspective of sustainable development, researchers note that Western consumers pay attention to the price rather than their ethical behavior (Castaldi et al. 2013; Clark 2008; Hur and Cassidy 2019). A number of studies are devoted to the impact of digitalization on fashion perception (Kawaf and Tagg 2012; De Veirman et al. 2016).

It should be noted, however, that in the works available, the fashion analysis is functional and narrow. Neither in foreign nor in domestic science, researchers are yet to stand at the crossroads of marketing, international business, and sociology; this would provide an interdisciplinary view of fashion in the post-industrial era and its perception by modern consumers.

Methodology

The authors studied a wide range of scientific works and articles on the perception of fashion across both the English and the Russian internet sites from December 2019 to March 2020. As a result, they complimented the established attitudes, and proposed their distinctive vision on this issue; modifying consumer perception of fashion in the post-industrial era is considered under the influence of globalization and digitalization. As an additional source of data, the authors used annual reports of the leading fashion industry TNCs for the period 2012–2019, and reviews of consulting companies devoted to trends in the fashion industry development.

The authors of this chapter attempt a comprehensive study of the modifications in the perception of fashion by the modern post-industrial consumer. The authors put forward the hypothesis that globalization, along with digitalization, radically changes the perception of fashion and its development trends. Under the influence of digitalization and globalization, all national fashion markets have been combined into a single global market, the dynamics of which are more and more determined by the information component. So-called fast fashion—the very existence of which is the result of modern post-industrial society and globalization, being generated by the processes of digitalization across all fields—is the dominant trend of consumption.

A systematic approach was chosen as the main approach to the study of this problem; thanks to this, such different elements as consumer behavior, the activities of the largest companies in the fashion industry, digitalization, and competition in the market were considered in an integrated manner. Accordingly, consumer behavior was studied during online shopping for clothes at the world's leading marketplaces.

The conducted analysis of the impact of globalization and digitalization in terms of dynamics and volumes of the world garment trade in 2010–2019 revealed positive qualitative and quantitative results. The main conclusions were drawn by means of generalization and synthesis of the data obtained.

Results

1. Fashion was greatly influenced and broadly changed by the transition to post-industrial society; the consumption model and economic globalization changed the sphere, and caused profound changes in fashion goods themselves, the methods of their production, marketing, and the global production system. Fashion permeates all spheres of modern society, and constitutes a very large segment of the economy. The volume of the global fashion market in 2020 is estimated at about $1.65 trillion. The clothes market consists of various segments, including both global discount retailers and the mass market and exclusive luxury brands. Fashion is connected with the consumption model, habits, traditions, and the functioning of the institutional factors of the external business environment.

In the post-industrial era, fashion has become even more dynamic and less predictable. Modern clothes are characterized by a shorter life cycle and the high volatility of the market demand. The consumer perception of fashion has changed significantly in the post-industrial era, because the fashion itself, the mechanism of influence transmission, and the consumer have changed. The post-industrial consumer is characterized by information dependence and highly impulsive purchasing.

The perception of fashion is connected not only with the human perception of needs (according to Maslow's hierarchy), and not only with the modern perception of beauty, but also with the culture and developed consumer tastes, as well as with the awareness of new trends and styles. Fashion still satisfies the need of the post-industrial consumer to be not like any other ordinary person, but like the most elite, most authoritative layers of a given society.

In the post-industrial era, consumers, as before, base their perception of fashion on the dominant morality, existing administrative rules and social restrictions, and traditions.

2. Over the past three decades, and all across the world, the perception of fashion and fashionable clothes has undergone profound changes, due to various shifts in lifestyle, culture, social life, and business, first of all, under the influence of globalization and information and communication technologies. Post-industrial society is characterized by the fact that—mainly due to the globalization and standardization of consumer habits—mass consumers demonstrate their interest in fashion: they are informed and very demanding, and prefer functionality to quality and exclusivity. The commercial success of Zara's polka dot staple dress in the summer of 2019 stands as convincing evidence; it was sold worldwide in hundreds of thousands of pieces, became a cult everywhere, turned into a popular meme that gathered more than 20,000 followers, and de facto became a symbol of the standardization of consumers' mood and taste.
3. Under the influence of globalization, the diversity and dynamics of the supply of clothes have increased; this is by force of the globalization of consumer habits and tastes. Fashion styling solutions have become more globally standardized, which is confirmed by the dynamics of sales growth of leading TNCs in the fashion industry—particularly, Inditex, Uniqlo, and H&M—in comparison with the dynamics of the general clothing consumption. The democratization of fashion, the widest instant dissemination of information on various fashion issues, and data accessibility to a wide range of consumers have led to a change in consumer views on novelty and uniqueness in clothes.
4. In the post-industrial era, consumer desires and behaviors have changed under the influence of a new environment, and perceptions of fashion have followed. In the post-industrial era, excessive and free information changes the source of influence of what is fashionable. The importance of seasonal shows in the world's leading fashion houses, which previously (along with fashionable historical images) were the principal reference point for the consumer, is declining. Earlier, in consumer attitudes, fashion trends were associated with the activities and creativity of a limited number of leading European high-fashion brands. In the post-industrial era, due to changes in consumer sentiment and desires, the perception of fashion trends has changed. On the one hand, fashion trends are created by the world's leading fashion brands, most of which belong to the largest TNCs in the field of luxury (LVMH and Kering); on the other hand, emerging fashion trends are picked up, imitated, and copied by fast-fashion TNCs, and through such imitators, tens of

thousands of small- and medium-sized companies from different parts of the globe are rapidly spread around the world. The formation of fashion trends is increasingly influenced by consumers themselves, as participants of the process of creating fashionable clothes and their socially active part are influencers and bloggers. An important feature of modern fashion is that it develops thanks to the strong influence of various subcultures and, particularly, such a phenomenon as urban fashion—streetwear.

In the post-industrial era, fashion became

1. global;
2. fast;
3. accessible to the general public and less elitist;
4. more and more technological;
5. more and more digital; at the same time, increasingly dependent on both digital technologies and the entire digitalization of society;
6. less connected with Western culture, more and more using the ideas and symbols of Eastern culture.

Fashion is becoming increasingly international; when searching for sources of inspiration, fashion brands often turn to the ideas and cultural symbols of different peoples and countries, to street wear, or to mass culture.

It is traditionally believed that the perception of fashion by modern consumers is influenced by such factors as exclusivity, compatibility of prices with expectations, risks perceived by consumers, the difference between quality and price, expectations and satisfaction in the process of consumption, and cost-benefit ratio. Demographic and socio-economic changes have led to a greater differentiation of fashion and changes in consumer behavior. Through buying fashion clothes of a certain brand, consumers want to express through this brand what social strata they belong to and what relationships are important for them.

5. Fashionable images, fashionable ideas, and modern trends are mainly revealed to the mass consumer by the fashion industry TNCs, which, on the one hand, are imitators and interpreters of the ideas of leading luxury brands, but on the other hand, due to the mass character of the production and marketing, are trend-setters for billions of people on the planet.

The increased speed of information dissemination, which stimulates the consumer thirst for new fashion ideas every season, has led to faster innovations and turnovers in product launches.

The modern consumer is looking for continuous innovation; instantaneous obsolescence is normal.

A characteristic feature of fashion in the post-industrial era is that fast fashion has become the main business model. Since 1999, fashion shows and catwalks have become public. When photographs of the latest fashion shows can be seen in magazines and on the internet, ideas of fashion instantly spread. Fast fashion has proven to be attractive for young modern women from diverse backgrounds. Modern technologies offer instant access to extensive information about recent trends or styles. The changed personality of the consumer, and their desire for innovation, underlie the modern perception of fashion. Consumers have become not only more informed; they have become more impatient, and largely want cheap, fashionable, disposable goods. At the same time, in the fashion industry there is always uncertainty about real consumer demands; flexibility and changeability are the optimal reactions of fashion companies.

Modern buyers are characterized by excessive consumption, which is associated both with the general consumerism of the post-industrial society and with the cheap clothes offered by fast-fashion TNCs, including Inditex, H&M, Topshop, and Uniqlo. This is proved by the numbers, since the average number of items of clothing bought by women has increased from 34 to 57 per year for the last decade. At the same time, 15% of the clothes purchased are never worn. Alongside overconsumption, fast-fashion supporters neglect the environmental component, as well as the problems of sustainable development. Even for young women, the sustainable development of the fashion industry remains a low priority—the Mintel agency found that 80% of consumers were mainly looking for low prices.

6. Perceptions are generational, and are more and more determined by new generations. Millennials or Generation Y—people born in 1980–1999—prefer more inexpensive, cheap, and fashionable clothes, compared to baby boomers, who would prefer to buy less but better-quality clothing.

Millennials are a very diverse generation in terms of education, religion, consumer preferences, life interests, and needs, a truism across developed countries. In this case, the main characteristic of this generation is that it has already grown up in a completely digital environment, under the colossal influence of digital media and advertising, and strongly depends on global brands in its perception of fashion. An average child in the United States, Great Britain, or Australia sees 20,000–40,000 television commercials per year. According to a study conducted by the National Consumer Council in the United Kingdom, an average ten-year-old child becomes familiar with 300–400 brands—twenty times more than wild birds they could name. At the same time, 70% of three-year-olds recognize the symbol of McDonalds, while only half of them know their own last name.

Consumers who grow up in the digital environment perceive fashion trends differently; they spend most of their free time surfing the internet, actively communicate on social networking sites, and increasingly shop online focusing on opinions being shaped by the digital environment. The influence of social networks increasingly determines consumer confidence and perception of risks, although an emotionally oriented spontaneous approach remains relevant for some consumers. Consumers of the post-industrial society are characterized by excessive conspicuous consumption of fashionable clothes and a wasteful consumption model designed to create an image of success and well-being. Modern man lives in the area of myths and mythical images, which is largely connected with an excess of information and various digital content. The abuse of digital devices and technologies alongside the increasing immersion into the virtual world leads to the fact that signs replace reality more and more. Fashion images occupy an important place among the images and styles spread by electronic media. The perception of fashion is more and more formed by digital means of mass media.

7. In the post-industrial era for an increasing number of consumers, the perception of fashion goes through the prism of sustainable development and environmental safety.

With the supporters of fast fashion in the modern digital society, against the background of growing ecological problems, the number of conscious consumers who are ready to pay more for environmentally friendly and sustainable clothes, slow fashion, green fashion, and organic clothes is increasing. Together with fast fashion, the phenomenon of slow fashion has originated in the twenty-first century; this should be ethical fashion, and represent everything that fast fashion is not. Even the fast-fashion TNCs like H&M, Mango, and Zara produce eco-friendly collections, and the largest European online store Asos has "an eco-section." It can be predicted that fashion brands associated with consumer perceptions of environmental friendliness and sustainable development will be more successful in the future.

8. The digital component, especially information flows and data exchange channels, has a growing influence on consumer behavior and perception of fashion. At the same time, new competitors—for example, Amazon (the United States), Aliexpress (People's Republic of China), Wildberries (Russia)—use the effect of platforms and often do not need specific assets.

The fashion industry is undergoing major changes as a direct result of technological developments and their impact on consumer behavior, and must adapt. The wide spread of social networks has led to the phenomenon of fashion bloggers and street fashion, which increasingly influences the perception of modern fashion by informed and responsible consumers.

The popularity of mobile and web technologies has transformed the consumer experience; where once it was simple viewing and buying, now it involves creating and distributing content through social networks. Around 389 female customers of the clothing store Fashion House were interviewed in Moscow in January 2020 in the framework of the study, the results of which showed that 13% of them are focused on image, demonstrate their significant interest in fashion, study fashion issues on the internet, prefer omnichannel shopping options, and would like to be aware of the latest innovations. About 85% of the respondents said they want to stand out from the crowd; self-expression is an important reason for buying clothes online. More than 65% of digital fashion consumers are actively using their mobile devices to search for fashionable clothes and view fashion-related materials.

An important feature of modern fashion perception is the change in the role of the consumer, from passive observation to conditional dominance and involvement, based on consumer experience in creating style and fashion. The active involvement of consumers into combined participation in creating fashionable clothes has been realized by the Zara brand throughout its history. Since the very beginning this brand has been orientated toward the production of models that are actually in demand. Every year, more than 300 designers work for the Zara brand and develop more than 40,000 stylistic solutions for various items of clothing, less than a quarter of which are launched into production on a mass scale. At the same time, the choice of specific models launched into mass production is determined by the final consumer during the study of sample models, is individual, and corresponds to the current consumer sentiment.

The vast majority of modern consumers use digital channels before, during, or after shopping. They want to interact, participate, influence, and communicate with the brands they buy and like.

Digital transformation allows consumers to actively participate in creating fashion on the basis of their experiences, and demonstrate their individuality.

Conclusions/Recommendations

The global fashion industry developed in the 1990s under the influence of globalization processes. Informed, selective, and responsible consumers cared about what they look like in public places. Now, in addition, they care about their appearance on social networking sites. The image of the goods themselves matter too. Consumers' attitudes toward fashion in a modern digital society have a complex and dynamic identity, reflect the consumerism of modern society, and are more and more formed under the influence of globalization and digitalization. Digitalization has many influences on fashion and style, consumers, and designers. Digitalization changes the perception of brands and fashion styles, making fashion more dynamic and democratic.

References

Bhardwaj, V., & Fairhurst, A. (2010). Fast Fashion: Response to Changes in the Fashion Industry. *The International Review of Retail, Distribution and Consumer Research, 20*(1), 165–173.

Bulatov, A. S., et al. (2019). *Prospects for Economic Globalization*. MGIMO: Moscow.

Cachon, G., & Swinney, R. (2011). The Value of Fast Fashion: Quick Response, Enhanced Design, and Strategic Consumer Behavior. *Management Science, 57*(4), 778–795.

Castaldi, C., Dickson, M., & Grover, C. (2013). Sustainability in Fashion and Textiles. In *Values*. Sheffield: Greenleaf Publishing.

Clark, H. (2008). Slow + Fashion – An Oxymoron – or a Promise for the Future...? *Fashion Theory – Journal of Dress Body and Culture, 12*(4), 427–446.

Croll, J. (2014). *Fashion That Changed the World*. New York: Prestel.

De Veirman, M., Cauberghe, V., & Hudders, L. (2016). Marketing Through Instagram Influencers: Impact of Number of Followers and Product Divergence on Brand Attitude. In *15th International Conference on Research in Advertising*. Luybliana, 2016.

Hill, J., & Lee, H.-H. (2015). Sustainable Brand Extensions of Fast Fashion Retailers. *Journal of Fashion Marketing and Management, 19*(2), 205–222.

Hines, T. (2001). Globalization: An Introduction to Fashion Markets and Fashion Marketing. In T. Hines & M. Bruce (Eds.), *Fashion Marketing: Contemporary Issues* (pp. 121–132). Oxford: Elsevier Butterworth-Heineman.

Hur, E., & Cassidy, T. (2019). Perceptions and Attitudes Towards Sustainable Fashion Design: Challenges and Opportunities for Implementing Sustainability in Fashion. *International Journal of Fashion Design, Technology and Education, 12*(2), 208–217.

Jain, S. (2019). Factors Affecting Sustainable Luxury Purchase Behavior: A Conceptual Framework. *Journal of International Consumer Marketing, 31*(2), 130–146.

Kawaf, F., & Tagg, S. (2012). Online Shopping Environments in Fashion Shopping: An SOR Based Review. *The Marketing Review, 12*(2), 161–180.

Ma, F., Shi, H., Chen, L., & Luo, Y. (2012). A Theory on Fashion Consumption. *Journal of Management and Strategy, 3*(4), 84–92.

Miller, K. (2013). Hedonic Customer Responses to Fast Fashion and Replicas. *Journal of Fashion Marketing and Management, 17*(2), 160–174.

Solomon, M. (2010). *Consumer Behavior*. Essex: Pearson Prentice Hall.

Solomon, M., & Rabolt, N. (2004). *Consumer Behavior in Fashion*. Upper Saddle River: Pearson Education.

Stepnov, I. M., Kovalchuk, J. A., Gorchakova, E. A., & Lukmanova, I. G. (2018). High Technology as a Driver of Changes in Industry (For Example Textile Industry). *Izvestiya Vysshikh Uchebnykh Zavedenii, Seriya Teknologiya Tekstil'noi Promyshlennosti, 3*, 268–272.

Wang, T. Y. (2010). *Consumer Behavior Characteristics in Fast Fashion*. Online at: http://bada.hb.se/bitstream/2320/7723/2/2010.13.16.pdf. Accessed 10 July 2016.

CHAPTER 19

National Innovation System: Formation and Development in the Post-industrial Economy

Maria Kozlova, Alexander Pavlov, and Dmitry Prozorov

Introduction

Nowadays when all countries compete against each other in the international market, much prominence is given to national innovation-driven development. A country can gain more benefits from innovation-driven development as compared to imitation and catching-up development. However, when examining the innovation process at the national scale, it is crucial to understand whether the state under consideration has a working national innovation system (NIS) or not and the distinct features of this system.

There are different definitions of the national innovation system. This concept was first mentioned in K. Freeman's book on technological development and economic growth in Japan, which was written in 1987. By the definition of K. Freeman, this is "a network of public and private sector

M. Kozlova (✉) • A. Pavlov
Moscow State Institute of International Relations (MGIMO University), Moscow, Russia

D. Prozorov
Moscow Aviation Institute (National Research University), Moscow, Russia

J. Kovalchuk (ed.), *Post-Industrial Society*,
https://doi.org/10.1007/978-3-030-59739-9_19

institutions whose activities and interaction give rise to the creation, acquisition, change and diffusion of new technologies" (Freeman 1988). Various countries' national innovation systems have been studied by M. Porter, C. Freeman, B.-A. Lundvall, R. Nelson, P. Pelikan, Ch. Edquist, B. Johnson, K. Smith, S. Radosevic, and so on.

Institutions in the science and technology sector are very important, and in Ch. Edquist and B. Johnson's opinion, (Edquist 1997), their functions are as follows:

1. lowering uncertainty by providing information;
2. managing conflicts and cooperation;
3. providing incentives to employees and enterprises.

Various researchers emphasized the importance of various institutions in the scientific and technical field. For instance, in Carlsson and Stankiewicz's opinion, the most important national innovation system institutions are "the political and educational system (including universities), patent law and labour regulations" (Carlsson 2002), and in R. Nelson's view, these are the innovative private firms, universities and government support of technological development (Nelson 1997).

Universities play a very important role in the national innovation system (Kolomytseva and Pavlovska 2020; Gokhberg et al. 2011; Torkunov 2017; Kasatkin et al. 2019). In 2013, M. Rangaa and H. Etzkwitz published an article titled "Triple Helix System: An Analytical Framework for Innovation Policy and Practice in the Knowledge Society", which states that there is a system that includes universities, industry and government (Rangaa and Etzkowitz 2013). Later, a fourth factor was added to them—civil society, and then a fifth indicator—the natural environment. Also, universities play a significant role in the model of the "knowledge triangle" (Unger and Polt 2017), which is the relationship between research, education and innovations (dissemination and use of knowledge).

Banks that provide money for innovation are also very important for the national innovation system. And we should especially mention innovative banks in developed countries, wherein a loan can be made for a new project or activity where the bank receives a share in the company's constituent capital (Prokopenko et al. 2019). In order to create a successful innovative company, it is also important to receive innovative business services from specialized consulting companies (Santos 2020).

K. Smith (1997) argues that the essential tasks of the national innovation system are as follows:

(a) production and diffusion of scientific and technological knowledge;
(b) education, training and skills;
(c) standardization and certification;
(d) creation of new firms;
(e) retention of scientific and technological data and provision of access to such data.

The interaction between various institutions and economic agents plays an important part in the development of new and enhancement of existing products and processes. This peculiarity of innovation activities has been noted by B.-A. Lundvall (1997), who developed a theory on the salience of interaction between consumers and manufacturers during the commercialization of a new product. He believes that to ensure success of an innovation, the manufacturer has to take potential customers' needs and requirements into account and interact with consumers. Otherwise, there are chances that the new products will not enjoy demand either in the domestic or in the international market, as would frequently be the case in the former socialist countries. P. Soderholm stresses the importance of network management in creating the NIS (Soderholm et al. 2019).

At the same time, T.X. Liu stresses that the motivation of interacting parties is also essential: if selfishness does not lead to a positive result, then cooperation, and especially altruism, leads to a long-term result rather than a short-term one (Liu 2019). Infrastructure is also of great importance, since the development of individual parts of the NIS does not ensure the success of the entire system (Delgado 2020).

When creating a national innovation system, the innovation- and diversification-based approach assumes that knowledge is at the core of this system. It is worth looking at the structure of the national innovation system in more detail. The national innovation system can be defined as a structured set of interconnected procedural and legal, social and economic, and institutional relations aimed at meeting the state's need in innovative commercializable ideas by means of multiple business entities and tools (Fig. 19.1).

The tools (incentives, financial and regulatory leverage) are implemented through funds (budgetary, private and personal funds), mediators and manufacturers.

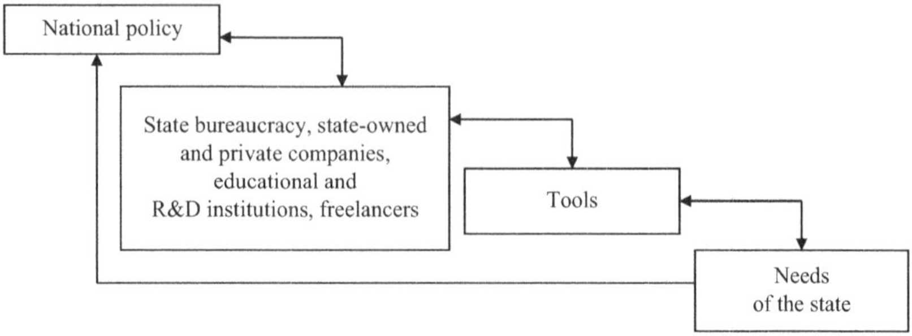

Fig. 19.1 Structure of the national innovation system. (*Source*: Created by the authors)

At the same time, some scientists criticized the national innovation system for the fuzziness of its definition and the blurring of concepts, since it was not clear what to include in it. It was also criticized for the fact that this approach does not take into account learning by doing, learning by using and learning by interaction (Caiyan et al. 2020). This has led to some new approaches that extend and complement the concept. An overview of these approaches is given in Sesay, Yulin and Wang (2018). The authors include a technological approach (when technology is taken as a basis, and then the institutions and participants that contribute to its development and dissemination are analysed—Karlsson and Stankiewicz approach), sectoral approach (innovation by sectors—Brescht and Malerba), regional approach (which also includes city-level innovation analysis—Okamuro and Nishimura 2020), and functions approach (Jacobson and Johnson proposed to distinguish the functions of a successfully functioning innovation system first, and then to think about the procedure for its application).

It should also be noted that national innovation systems have features that distinguish the institutional structure of the scientific and technological sphere in different countries. Thus, the innovation system of developed countries is characterized by the following features:

1. privatization of new technology deliverables, which encourages profit-seeking persons and companies;
2. multiple independent sources of new technology competing against each other;

3. heavy influence of market forces on the ultimate selection of viable innovations from the novelties brought up by various firms and selection of viable firms themselves.

At the same time, in some countries, the innovation system cannot be called truly national, since innovation systems operate only at the level of some states or regions of the country. For example, in the United States, only 5–6 states are actively engaged in innovation (Leydesdorff et al. 2019), it does not reduce the efficiency of the national innovation system.

To date, *the concept of national innovation systems* has already turned into a universally recognized tool for the analysis of developed countries; however, the research community lacks similar unanimity with respect to developing and post-socialist countries. Some researchers argue that only a mature and well-functioning structure turning innovations into the basis of the country's economic growth may be considered the national innovation system. Others, by contrast, construe the national innovation system as a set of institutions in the country's science and technology complex and their relations irrespective of their efficiency.

The question concerning the availability of the national innovation system or lack thereof first arose with respect to developing countries. R. Arocena and J. Sutz from Uruguay are among those scholars who claim that developing countries do not yet have a full-fledged national innovation system, and instead have certain disparate components thereof (Arocena 2000). They believe that out of the three components supposed to form the national innovation system (public sector, entrepreneurship and academic research), Uruguay had only two interacting components: the public sector and industrial enterprises, which at best can be referred to as the "national system of industrial growth" rather than as an innovation system. Eduardo da Motta e Albuquerque and Tristão Bernardes from Brazil claim that an immature national innovation system is typical for developing countries (Da Motta e Albuquerque 2001). The primary difference between developing and developed countries is the role of science, which is not a direct source of innovation in developing countries, but rather makes it possible to identify the most promising foreign technologies to be borrowed and to adapt domestic enterprises so as to enable them to embrace modern scientific developments.

But if there are problems with the formation of a national innovation system in developing countries, then developed countries may also face difficulties. For example, Kim, Bae and Byun note that the NIS actively developed in South Korea from 2003 to 2008, remained at the same level until 2012, and then there was even a decline in its development, so the national innovation system should not only be created, but should further develop, while continuity in its development should be observed (Kim et al. 2020). In addition, B. Jankowska, A. Matysek-Jedrych, and K. Mroczek-Dabrowska (2017) compared the innovation input and the innovation output in different countries and came to the conclusion that it is not enough to increase funding of the innovation system, since this does not always lead to the desired final result. The system is complex, so it is important to take into account the connections within the system and the diffusion of innovation.

It is noteworthy that Russia still lacks a legislative framework for the concept of the "national innovation system", and yet the acceleration of national innovation-driven development is among its national priorities. In 2014, the government drew up Russia's Innovative Development Strategy 2020, which includes the task of "ensuring the openness of the national innovation system and economy, and integrating Russia in global processes of the creation and use of innovations" (Strategy 2014). In 2018, the Analytical Centre for the Government of the Russian Federation prepared a report titled "Man and Innovations", and the Mechanism to Promote Development of Technology was created as part of Agenda 2030, supposed to contribute to the country's innovation-driven development. Thus, creation and further upgradation of the national innovation system is a priority for Russia.

Methodology

Research Method

The main methodology that was used in this chapter is a case study, which allowed us to answer the questions as to how the national innovation system should be organized and how it can become more effective. The main purpose was to analyse the most efficient examples from other countries in order to prepare the programme of reforms that was tested later in the Far Eastern region of Russia. The multiple-case research design integrates the data from different countries.

Case Selections

During the preparation of the programme of the national innovation system, the author Pavlov A.O. and the project team

(a) analysed the efficient international projects:
  - Korea Trade-Investment Promotion Agency (KOTRA);
  - The Republic of Turkey Prime Minister Investment Support and Promotion Agency (ISPAT);
  - Industrial Development Authority Ireland (IDA);
  - the service of "one window" from the city Iskandar, Malaysia;
  - the service of "one window" of the administration of the Shenzhen free economic zone;
  - the service of "one window" of the Jebel Ali Free Zone in the United Arab Emirates;
  - the procedure of granting services in the free economic zone in Palu, Indonesia;
  - the service of "one window" within the programme Make in India, India.

(b) analysed the work of public authorities regarding the provision of public services to legal entities (as one of the indicators of information and innovative development);
(c) conducted the survey of residents of territories of advanced development.

Results

After examining the international examples, the authors have made recommendations for the improvement of the Russian national innovation system and proposed a general framework to develop the NIS in Russia that includes five steps: creation of a virtual investment community, creation of advanced special economic zones (ASEZs), adaptation of the regional financial systems to NIS development goals, implementation of a new structural policy and fiscal optimization. These measures have been tested in the Russian Far East and proved their worth. Let us examine the proposed measures and their first deliverables in more detail.

Step 1 should involve development of public institutions necessary to implement an important principle of the new technological and economic paradigm providing for the virtualization of society, which requires a coordinating institutional policy. Therefore, Step 1 of NIS creation should involve establishment and modelling of virtual innovation-driven development institutions in a virtual environment embodying the institutional policy of the state.

This development will be directly enshrined in diverse web resources in the form of investment forums and websites attracting investors and providing them with a variety of consulting, online documentation processing, one-stop shop, request submission services, and so on, including information websites funded by government agencies.

A good example of virtual institutional environment development is the Far East Investor's Account designed by the Far East Investment and Export Agency and by the authors of this chapter themselves. This information system provides investors with such services as assistance with submitting documents and requests, document acceptance services, electronic reporting, direct line of communication with the officials of the Ministry for the Development of the Russian Far East and other services.

The system was created using international experience. Similar to Russia, foreign countries have dedicated development institutions created to improve the investment climate; furthermore, they serve as innovation-driven development institutions. For instance, "Make in India" is a programme geared towards the implementation of large-scale infrastructural projects through mobilization of external investors, who are offered the most favourable terms. The fundamental principle of the programme provides for an unprecedented opening of India's key economic sectors to foreign direct investments; access to India's 25 priority industries, including railways, military and insurance sectors; and medical technologies. The implementation of "Make in India" involved creation of a single online portal intended to register and licence companies in India and establishment of an agency intended to facilitate the investment process, encourage innovations, protect intellectual property and assist with the construction of infrastructure for investors, including by means of information technology and e-services.

Other countries have created similar virtual investment environment systems: BizPaL—a unified portal for permits and licences (Canada), and

GOV.UK—a unified portal of public services (United Kingdom). The key difference of the Far East Investor's Account from its foreign peers mentioned above consists in fostering a single mechanism of communication with investors by providing them with both public services based on the one-stop shop principle and all-out investor support on all matters of investment project implementation involving the provision of all necessary services.

Step 2 involves development of investment climate support mechanisms in the form of advanced special economic zones (ASEZs) and similar regional investment institutions. This area is being developed by means of proactive measures initiated by the government and implemented by the Ministry for the Development of the Russian Far East and regional administrations. To date, the Far Eastern Federal District has 18 ASEZs and 5 zones of the Free Port of Vladivostok with RUB 2.9 trillion worth of attracted investment.

Step 3 involves transformation of the region's financial architecture in line with the new technological and economic paradigm, to which end the regulator represented by the government should pursue a coordinating monetary policy.

The specific measures at this step should be geared towards further development of the region's financial infrastructure, including creation of the Bank of the Far Eastern Federal District and adoption of a subsidy policy to promote savings and lending in the innovation sector, specifically by attracting small investors through creating remote infrastructure for investment in ASEZ issuers' securities, creating large regional financial consortia, providing the process of corporatization with all-out support, and, in the longer run, through creating a regional stock exchange.

The following statistical diagram is based on the data from the Far East Investor's Account system and is a good example of the problems that investors encounter when implementing an investment project (Fig. 19.2).

The diagram shows that attracting financing and securing land resources are key problems. Financing problems should be addressed through direct coordination of the monetary policy and creation of new financial support mechanisms, while the problems of the second type should be addressed through a coordinating policy at all levels of the government.

Step 4 requires implementation of a structural policy by the government of the Russian Federation, specifically transformation of all public institutions so as to adapt them to the new technological and economic paradigm, with due regard to the implementation of preceding development

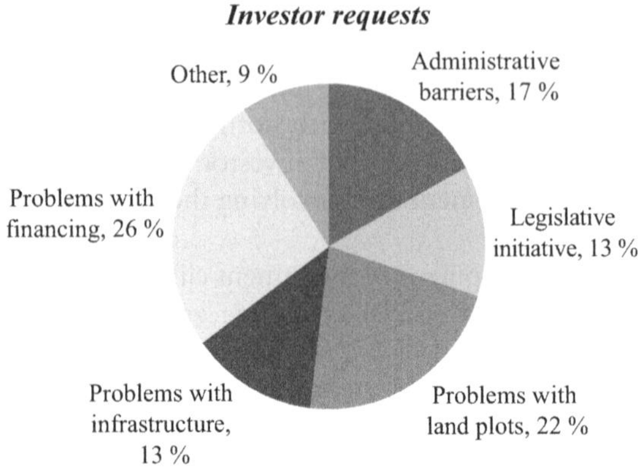

Fig. 19.2 Investor requests in the Far East Investor's Account system. (*Source:* Calculated by the authors on the basis of the study of 150 investor requests in the personal accounts in the Far East Investor's Account system, URL: ps.invest-vostok.ru)

steps, that is, creation of an efficient system of public investment and innovation institutions, ASEZs and financial environment. The transformation should primarily concern social public institutions, geared towards higher mobility and individualization, including virtualization and reformatting of the performance tracking system that is currently underway in the Russian Far East. Key performance indicators should be introduced everywhere (including government programmes) to make conclusions and relevant decisions. The management system created at Step 3 will make it possible to keep track of all relevant parameters and monitor the achievement of performance indicators in an automated mode, including such performance indicators as total private investment that was attracted, total private investment that actually took place and the amount of export transactions.

Step 5 involves transformation of the government's fiscal policy geared towards optimization of the tax and public expenditure system, which has been actually implemented on an ongoing basis since the 2000s. These measures have been modelled after Malaysia, which set a course for an innovation-driven economy. In order to attract hi-tech manufacturing companies that use state-of-the-art technologies in IT, medical equipment, pharmaceutical, polymer and other industries, such companies were

Table 19.1 Tax loads of residents and non-residents

Residents	*Non-residents*
0% income tax	20% income tax
7.6% total insurance contributions for 10 years	30% total insurance contributions for 10 years
0% land tax (first three years)	1.5% land tax (from 0.3% to 1.5%)
0% property tax	2.2% property tax

Source: This table was compiled by the authors on the basis of https://erdc.ru/about-spv/#anchor-lgoty

offered unprecedented benefits—income tax holidays for the first five years, exemption from investment tax, reimbursement of a portion of expenses by means of recalculating the tax rate after five years, free transfer of capital, duty-free importation of computer equipment and option to have 100% foreign staff (Parasyuk 2014). Malaysia offers dedicated support measures to the residents of the special economic zone (SEZ) Multimedia Super Corridor (a hi-tech space 15 km wide and 50 km long), which accommodates about 1000 electrical engineering companies (duty-free importation of multimedia equipment, guaranteed protection of intellectual property, provision of advanced IT infrastructure, preferential rates of excises and sales taxes for equipment and materials, etc.).

Obviously, a dedicated fiscal policy for depressed regions has already proved its worth. This is exemplified by the growing number of residents in ASEZs and the Free Port of Vladivostok. Different regimes for ASEZ residents and non-residents are stated in Table 19.1.

Furthermore, other laws and regulations are currently being developed that will establish state support principles and measures for investment projects implemented in the Far Eastern Federal District and amounts and types of tax benefits to reimburse costs of infrastructure facilities.

Conclusions

These measures were used in the Far Eastern Federal District and proved their worth. The Far East Investor's Account was presented during the 4th Eastern Economic Forum on 11–13 September 2018. As of 17 June 2020, the system was supporting 2435 investment projects and had over 1396 registered users. The total amount of planned investments exceeds RUB 4334 billion, whose realization will allow to create 168,384 jobs. As of now, many residents have already started their projects, having invested more than RUB 598 billion and having created 35,211 jobs (www.erdc.ru).

However, future research is needed; since this programme was organized only in one region, so it should be studied whether such methods would prove to be effective in other regions as well. However, the authors recommend to use the abovementioned suggestions in other regions of the country to make Russia's national innovation system more efficient. Implementation of this system will make it possible to return the country to the optimum development path of the technological and economic paradigm, boost labour productivity, raise the added value of the economy and restore its competitiveness in the global market.

References

Caiyan, J., Xiaoyun, T., & Zhehan, K. (2020). Does the Nation Innovation System in China Support the Sustainability of Small and Medium Enterprises (SMEs) Innovation. *Sustainability*, 12. https://www.mdpi.com/2071-1050/12/6/2562/htm

Carlsson, B. (2002). Methodological Issues in a Technological System Approach. In B. Carlsson (Ed.), *The Technological System of Bio Industries* (p. 71). London: Kluwer Press.

Corporation of Development of the Far East. www.erdc.ru

Da Motta e Albuquerque, E. (2001). *Cross-Over, Thresholds, and Interactions Between Science and Technology: A Tentative Simplified Model and Initial Notes About Statistics from 120 Countries.* https://papers.ssrn.com/sol3/papers.cfm?abstract_id=280649

Delgado, D. R. L. (2020). Vietnam: politicas publicas en ciencia, tecnologia e innovacion [Science, Technology and Innovation Policies of Vietnam]. *Estudios de Asia y Africa, 55*(2 (172)), 263–294. (In Spanish language).

Edquist, C. (1997). Institutions and Organizations in Systems of Innovation. In C. Edquist (Ed.), *Systems of Innovation: Technologies, Institutions, and Oraganizations* (p. 51). London: Pinter Publishers Ltd.

Freeman, C. (1988). Japan: A New National System of Innovation? In G. Dosi, C. Freeman, R. R. Nelson, G. Silverberg, & L. L. G. Soete (Eds.), *Technical Change and Economic Theory* (p. 65). London: Frances Pinter.

Gokhberg, L., Kuznetsova, T., & Zaichenko, S. (2011). Russia: Universities in the Context of Reforming the National Innovation System. In B. Göransson & C. Brundenius (Eds.), *Universities in Transition. Insight and Innovation in International Development* (pp. 247–260). New York: Springer.

Investment Support and Promotion Agency of Turkey ISPAT. http://www.invest.gov.tr/en-US/Pages/Home.aspx

Irish Development Agency IDA. https://www.idaireland.com/

Jankowska, B., Matysek-Jedrych, A., & Mroczek-Dabrowska, K. (2017). Efficiency of National Innovation Systems – Poland and Bulgaria in the Context of the Global Innovation Index. *Comparative Economic Research, 20*(3), 77–94.

Kasatkin, P. I., Kovalchuk, J. A., & Stepnov, I. M. (2019). The Modern Universities Role in the Formation of the Digital Wave of Kondratiev's Long Cycles. *Voprosy Ekonomiki, 12*, 123–140. (In Russ.). https://doi.org/10.32609/0042-8736-2019-12-123-140.

Kim, E. S., Bae, K. J., & Byun, J. (2020). The History and Evolution: A Big Data Analysis of the National Innovation Systems in South Korea. *Sustainability*, 12. https://www.mdpi.com/2071-1050/12/3/1266/htm

Kolomytseva, O., & Pavlovska, A. (2020). The Role of Universities in the National Innovation System. *Baltic Journal of Economic Studies, 6*(1), 51–58.

Korean Trade-Investment Promotion Agency KOTRA. http://www.kotra.or.kr/foreign/main/KHEMUI010M.html?LOCALE=en

Leydesdorff, L., Wagner, C. S., Porto-Gomez, I., Comins, J. A., & Phillips, F. (2019). Synergy in the Knowledge Base of U.S. Innovation Systems at National, State, and Regional Levels: The Contributions of High-Tech Manufacturing and Knowledge-Intensive Services. *Journal of the Association for Information Science and Technology, 70*(10), 1108–1123.

Liu, T.-H. (2019). The Philosophical Views of National Innovation System: The LED Industry in Taiwan. *Asia Pacific Management Review, 24*, 291–297.

Lundvall, B.-A. (1997). Innovation as an Interactive Process: From User-Producer Interaction to the National System of Innovation. In G. Dosi, C. Freeman, R. Nelson, G. Silverberg, & L. Soete (Eds.), *Technical Change and Economic Theory* (pp. 349–369). London: Pinter Publishers Ltd.

Make in India. http://www.makeinindia.com/home

Man and Innovations. The Report on Human Development in the Russian Federation. Russian Government Analytical Centre. (2018). http://ac.gov.ru/files/publication/a/19663.pdf (In Russ.).

Nelson, R. (1997). Institutions Supporting Technical Change in the United States. In G. Dosi, C. Freeman, R. Nelson, G. Silverberg, & L. Soete (Eds.), *Technical Change and Economic Theory* (p. 313). London: Pinter Publishers Ltd.

Okamuro, H., & Nishimura, J. (2020). What Shapes Local Innovative Policies? Empirical Evidence from Japanese Cities. *Administrative Sciences, 10*, 11. https://www.mdpi.com/2076-3387/10/1/11/htm

Parasyuk, I. (2014). Malaysia. Yesterday and Today. *Partner Journal, 11*(206). https://www.partner-inform.de/partner/detail/2014/11/247/7099/malajzija-vchera-i-segodnja?lang=ru (In Russ.).

Prokopenko, O. V., Biloshkurska, N. V., Biloshkurskyi, M. V., & Omelyanenko, V. A. (2019). The Role of Banks in National Innovation System: General Strategical Analytics. *Financial and Credit Activity: Problems of Theory and Practice, 3*(30), 26–35.

Rangaa, M., & Etzkowitz, H. (2013). Triple Helix Systems: An Analytical Framework for Innovation Policy and Practice in the Knowledge Society. *Industry and Higher Education, 27*(4), 237–262.

Santos, J. B. (2020). Knowledge-Intensive Business Services and Innovation Performance in Brazil. *Innovation & Management Review, 17*(1), 58–74.

Sesay, B., Yulin, Z., & Wang, F. (2018). Does the National Innovation System Spur Economic Growth in Brazil, Russia, India, China and South Africa Economies? Evidence from Panel Data. *South African Journal of Economic and Management Sciences, 21*(1). https://pdfs.semanticscholar.org/9324/fe9b1baa02eda51238ae845dca6ecd101ac6.pdf?_ga=2.85319578.28141339.1592375867-234582025.1592375867

Smith, K. (1997). Economic Infrastructures and Innovation Systems. In E. Ch (Ed.), *Systems of Innovation: Technologies, Institutions, and Organizations* (p. 96). London: Pinter Publishers Ltd.

Soderholm, P., Hellsmark, H., Frishammar, J., Hansson, J., Mossberg, J., & Sandstrom, A. (2019). Technological Development for Sustainability: The Role of Network Management in the Innovation Policy Mix. *Technological Forecasting and Social Change, 138*, 309–323.

Strategy of Innovative Development of the Russian Federation until 2020. (2014). http://ac.gov.ru/files/attachment/4843.pdf (In Russ.).

Torkunov, A. (2017). Internationalization of a University as a Challenge. *Mezhdunarodnye Protsessy, 15*(1), 6–12. https://doi.org/10.17994/IT.2017.15.1.48.2.

Unger, M., & Polt, W. (2017). The Knowledge Triangle Between Research, Education and Innovation – A Conceptual Discussion, Foresight and STI Governance. *Journal of the National Research University Higher School of Economics, 11*(2), 10–26.

Arocena, R. (2000). *Looking at National Systems of Innovation from the South.* https://www.researchgate.net/publication/227616191_Looking_at_National_System_of_Innovation_from_the_South

CHAPTER 20

Does a Solution Exist to the Paradox of Trust in Financial Institutions?

Irina Larionova, Elena Meshkova, and Galina Panova

Introduction

A theoretical examination of the nature and the sources of trust, alongside an analysis of its factors, may be witnessed in the works of both Russian and foreign researchers. According to one foreign author, 5148 potentially relevant articles have been published on this topic over the past 20 years (Altvater et al. 1999). Gradually, "trust" began to shift from the category

I. Larionova
Financial University under the Government of the Russian Federation, Moscow, Russia

Moscow State Institute of International Relations (MGIMO University), Moscow, Russia
e-mail: Ilarionova@fa.ru

E. Meshkova
Financial University under the Government of the Russian Federation, Moscow, Russia

G. Panova (✉)
Moscow State Institute of International Relations (MGIMO University), Moscow, Russia

J. Kovalchuk (ed.), *Post-Industrial Society*,
https://doi.org/10.1007/978-3-030-59739-9_20

of general perceptions and widely used terms to concepts of significant practical importance, including for the development of financial markets.

This issue has remained relevant throughout history, but recently it has received more attention across all levels: trust in countries, the state, companies, players on the financial market, and personal relationships. The issue of trust occupies a special place in relation to institutions working in sectors of the economy highly sensitive market fluctuation, in particular players of the financial market, as parties are to possess sufficient information on each other's activities to assess risks arising from fiduciary relations and others. In Russia the imposition of sanctions, which worsened the country's economic situation, provoked the downgrade of the sovereign credit rating by international rating agencies. In November 2014, rating agencies Fitch, Moody's and Standard and Poor's downgraded Russia's rating to BBB-, which led to a downgrade of the rating of National Banks in Russia. As a result, the level of confidence in them decreased, which, of course, negatively affected the investment attractiveness of domestic credit organizations in the eyes of foreign investors and depositors. Under these conditions, foreign banks began to reduce their activities in Russia (for example, UBS bank closed all its branches in early 2015). The number of Russian credit organizations also continued to decline. Improving the financial stability and reliability of banks has become one of the key tasks of the Central Bank of Russia—the regulator of financial markets. "Along with the economic losses for the Russian banking system, it is also important to take into account the socio-psychological effect. In these realities, banks had to solve problems of spontaneous behavior of depositors, adapt to low credit activity of customers and increased level of risks. Banks' reaction to the increase in funding has been a review of their policies. The requirements of banks for the reliability of borrowers have increased dramatically" (Panova et al. 2020, pp. 13–14).

The issue of trust in the financial services industry, and even at a higher level, has particular significance, as the results of the latest measurements indicate a decrease in the level of trust both in the players on the financial market (Fender et al. 2018) and in the country as a whole (Edelman Trust Barometer 2020). This is why the national regulator, the Bank of Russia, covered this issue in its "Main areas of development for the Russian financial market in 2019–2021" report, having identified the creation of a trust-based environment among the four areas of development for the financial market. Moreover, the Bank of Russia fairly defines trust as long-term social capital forming and accumulating over many years—a definition that is hard to disagree with. According to the regulator, trust is based on timely identification, notice, and prevention of improper behavior and financial problems in the activity of financial organizations that could potentially harm creditors (Central bank of Russia 2019).

At the same time, both Russia and foreign countries are known to be conducting measurements of the level of trust. The Edelman Trust Barometer, for example, evaluates the level of the population's trust in governing bodies, the media, businesses, and public organizations; experts from the Chicago Booth and Kellogg School have calculated the Financial Trust Index (Sapienza and Zingales 2009); the Eurozone has the commercial index of trust (European Monetary Union Industry Confidence) and consumer confidence index. In Russia, the evaluation and analysis of trust indexes is conducted by the National Agency for Financial Research, Levada-Center, the "Public Opinion" Foundation, and others. Generally, evaluation of trust is conducted on the basis of surveys serving as the main source of information. However, the authors of the chapter believe that in assessing the trust in players of the financial markets, it would be fair to measure the population's trust, but it is no less important to evaluate the level of companies' trust in their contractors. In this sense, the chapter attempts to conceptually describe the indicators and factors affecting trust in financial market players with the peculiarities of these institutions' activities in mind.

Methodology

The special nature of "trust" taking form in the financial market among its players is based on rather objective conditions described in the famous theory of information asymmetry. First studied in the works of Akerlof and Stiglitz, the theory implies that the often-controversial behavior among market players can, on the one hand, be explained through one of the market players possessing important and complete information as opposed to the other players; on the other hand, the theory has led to the appearance of the financial markets asymmetry escalation hypothesis, displayed by the rapid mastering of speculative financial technologies providing higher profit margins at the expense of reliability (Altvater et al. 1999; Binswanger 2004; Bozic 2017; Mundell 1963; Stiglitz 1989).

Taking into account that financial market institutions and players thereon function in conditions of uncertain development prospects, two groups of interconnected factors affecting trust should be identified: (1) information asymmetry, and (2) irrational behavior among financial market players, usually in the form of prompts for the making of investment decisions, which are often non-quantifiable.

The first factor group is fundamentally tied to loan-finance relations, as investment risks are always accompanied by market uncertainty adjusted for the comprehensiveness of information on the events transpiring in the market. At the same time, financial brokers, monitoring and accumulating large quantities of information on borrowers and financial markets, possess an indisputable informational advantage as opposed to other financial market players, putting them in a more powerful position (Feofanov 2014; Nagapetyan 2016).

The second factor group is linked to the irrational behavior of financial market players, usually in the form of prompts, for the making of investment decisions, often non-quantifiably. Such irrational behavior may, at the same time, be reflected in a multitude of motivations. Herein lies the increase in the risk of spontaneous actions, which leads to unpredictable behavior and is reflected in investment preferences and moods (Milovidov 2019).

These fundamentals of the financial market and the making of investment decisions by its players may, on the one hand, define a trust-based environment, but, on the other hand, may significantly hinder the identification of factors and the search for a quantitative evaluation of trust in order to identify the areas in which trust can be reinforced in conditions of digital transformation.

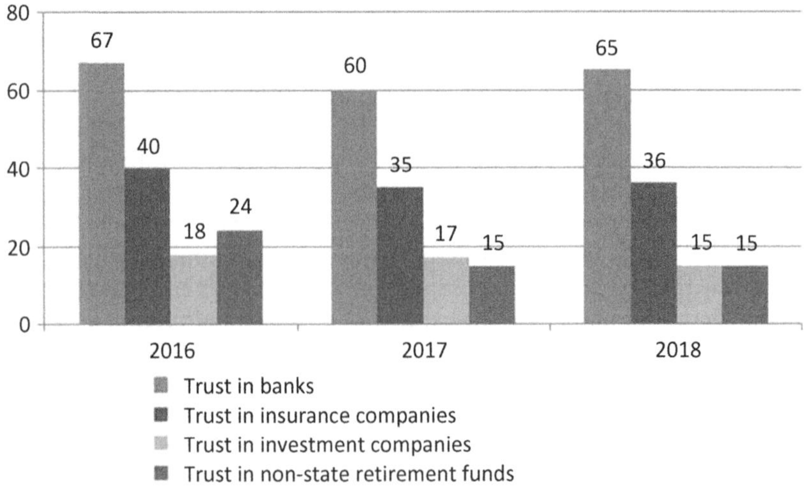

Fig. 20.1 Dynamics of trust in the main Russian financial market players. (*Source*: Bank of Russia. Medina E.V. Trust on the financial market 2019)

As noted above, data on the strength and trends of trust in the main players of the national financial market unfortunately fail to demonstrate its sustainable reinforcement.

The data in Fig. 20.1 showcase fluctuation of trust in monetary and loan institutions within the range of ±8–12 points. At the same time, the level of trust in the banking sector is 1.5–4 times higher than the level of trust in insurance companies (1.5 times), non-state retirement funds, and investment companies (4 times).

In contrast to global tendencies, the overall level of trust in Russian institutions generally takes last place, with a trust index of 29 out of 100, a leading position in decrease rates as of 2018. In order to form a trust-based environment in the financial market based on a substantial theoretical platform, as well as to reinforce trust between its players, it seems expedient to identify and to assess the factors both negatively and positively affecting trust in the financial market players.

Results

A Theoretical Basis of the Trust Factors Classification

Both expert and theoretical studies contain various groups of factors influencing the "trust" phenomena, including trust in the financial market in particular. For example, the Bank of Russia classification includes three factor groups: individual, institutional, and social (Fender et al. 2018). Foreign academics propose conceptual areas in which trust and a trust-based environment may be formed. Trust factors are differentiated depending on the nature of a particular financial market player and the existing standard of corporate culture in different countries, which allows them to use various tools for sustaining a comfortable trust-based environment.

In order to substantiate our scholarly opinion, we will present the following criteria for the classification of trust factors: sphere of influence, level of influence, and the boundaries of the influence. Based on the sphere of influence, factors may be divided into internal and external factors; based on the level of influence, they may be divided into macroeconomic and microeconomic; and based on trust boundaries, they may be divided into macro level, meso level, and the level of economic agents.

External factors are not directly linked to the activity of individual financial institutions. They are determined by political, macroeconomic, and social processes among others. The influence of external factors on trust features their incapability to provide direct influence; they may only be accounted for in an institution's activity. Internal factors, in turn, are determined by the activity of financial institutions and remain the object of management; therefore, their influence is direct.

Macroeconomic factors indirectly affecting the level of trust in financial market players include:

- the macroeconomic "state of the economy" (inflation, employment, key interest rate, dynamics of economic development, stability of the national currency, the defining features of the state's monetary policy, etc.);
- the state of the financial market, its stability, liquidity, transactional volumes, trends of financial assets prices—all of this concerns individual market segments as well;
- the stability of financial brokers' activity;
- the development of regulation and supervision;
- a guarantee system (deposit insurance, retirement savings insurance programs, etc.);
- others.

Microeconomic factors of trust in financial market players include:

- an institution's goodwill;
- financial reliability;
- quality and accessibility of goods and services;
- level of regulation and supervision;
- access to state support or support of the parent company;
- integration of online technology and its accessibility and security;
- level of financial literacy of consumers of financial services.

Grouping of trust factors based on the trust boundaries implies listing macro-level factors alongside with the microeconomic factors listed above. Meso-level factors reflect the specific nature of the financial broker industry; therefore, micro-level factors affect trust of financial market players in each other. The list of trust factors drafted based on the last criteria is presented in Table 20.1.

Non-detailed positive and negative factors have been identified in the scheme of external factors affecting trust in financial market players (macro- and meso-level factors) (Fig. 20.2).

The positive factors affecting trust in financial market players include:

Table 20.1 Trust factors classification based on the "trust horizon" criteria

Macroeconomic	The nature of the implemented monetary policy The state of the financial market (securities, capital, currency markets) The situation on the market GDP rates, deposits/GDP Inflation National currency rates Unemployment rates
Meso level (state of the segment)	An institution's financial reliability Regulation and supervision standards Accessibility of financial services (dynamics of the number of banks, insurance companies, non-state retirement funds, microfinance organizations) Online services, accessibility, security, regular service State support, state capital partnership, support from a group's parent company, etc. Members of the insurance and guarantee systems
Micro level (level of trust between market players)	Market experience Reputation, brand Accessibility of online services Duration of market activity Institution's reputation on the financial market (in the economy) Financial literacy

1. a moderately tough monetary and fiscal policy securing lower inflation rates, a budget surplus, lower national debt rates (14% of the GDP), a budget surplus, a significant rate of international reserves, and more;
2. legal protection for transactions and the operations of financial market players;
3. a classic model of banking activity due to a more rigorous approach to regulation;
4. guarantee and insurance systems;
5. socially oriented behavior by financial market players;
6. the convenience and security of digital technology providing easier access to financial broker services and similar.

Factors negatively impacting the level of trust in financial market players include:

1. an unstable macroeconomic environment;
2. lower savings among the population;

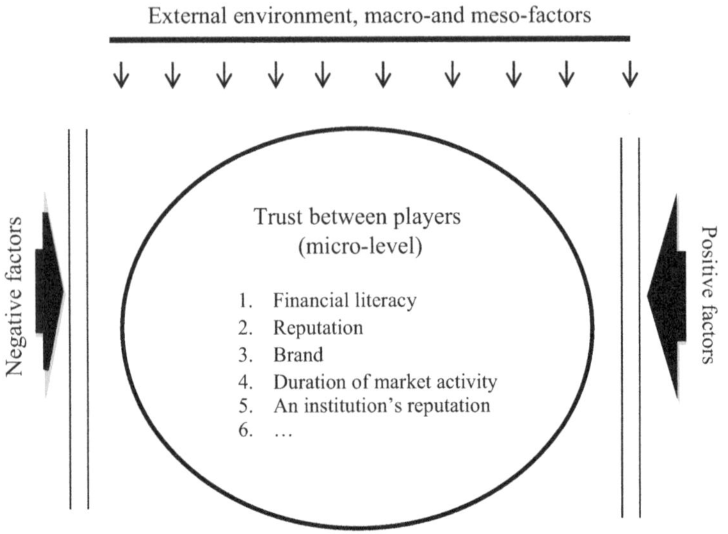

Fig. 20.2 Scheme of factors influencing trust in financial market players. (*Source*: Drafted by the authors)

3. unemployment growth;
4. mass revocation of financial brokers' licenses;
5. an increase in fraudulent activity;
6. a negative informational background.

The list of these factors may be subject to both expansion and narrowing. However, a number of inherent problems standing in the way of securing trust in financial market players may already be identified at this stage (see Fig. 20.3).

The issues depicted in Fig. 20.3 showcase the significance of sustainable macroeconomic indicators accompanying economic development, as well as the dangers hindering growth in trust levels: rapid technological development, especially in certain household age groups; an insufficient financial literacy across the population (despite efforts to change that); sometimes even socially irresponsible behavior from financial brokers in their relations between each other and with other market players.

Trust factors and indicators on the financial market. The following trust factors should be emphasized, as they form independent of the special

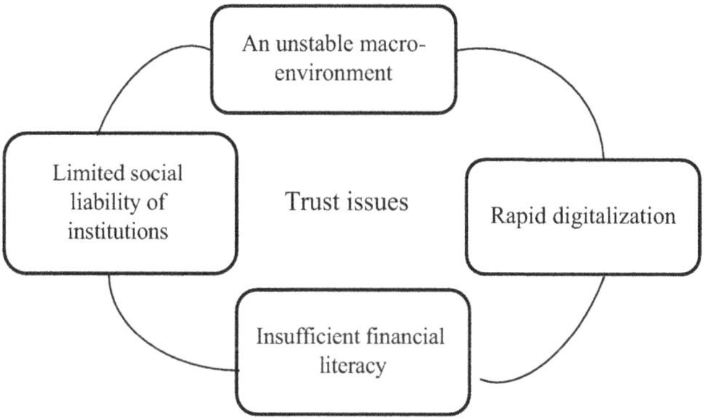

Fig. 20.3 Problematic areas in the way of increasing trust in financial market players. (*Source*: Drafted by the authors)

nature of the corresponding financial market players' industry. They can be categorized into the following areas: goodwill; reliability; quality of goods and services; regulation and supervision standards; level of trust in the state; the state of the macroeconomy and the financial market itself; financial literacy of consumers of financial services.

At the same time, some approaches to evaluating individual groups in the factor classification may remain common for all industries/financial market players, while other approaches will require the taking into account the specific nature of the industry.

Factors with common evaluation approaches and identical effects on the level of trust in financial institutions include goodwill (corporate reputation) most importantly, but some external factors as well: the state of the macroeconomy and the financial market, regulation and supervision standards, the level of trust in the state, and financial literacy of the market players.

Goodwill (corporate reputation). Over the last 15 years, a material increase in the significance of goodwill has been observed among Russian companies. Reputation has become a necessary condition for a company achieving sustainable and continuous growth, with the process of reputation management becoming a strategic competition tool.

An important issue in managing a company's goodwill is its qualitative and quantitative assessment. Despite special interest toward this issue on the part of the scientific and business communities, the issue remains unresolved and requires additional research. Along with a quantitative assessment of a company's goodwill, an otherwise important task is the determining of the practical values of goodwill (Kozlova 2014). Several attempts to assess and to publish companies' goodwill ratings have been made recently. However, a generally accepted rating has as of yet not been drafted. Generally, the rating is drafted based on: consumer opinions; brand awareness; the level of corporate culture and policy implementation in regard to stockholders; the quality of corporate social responsibility management and social investments.

The rating of the largest Russian companies, drafted by the Russian Regional Network on integrated reports in partnership with the "Da-Strategiya" Group, has been suggested as an option for the corporate transparency rating (Kasutin 2005; Fetisov 1999; Timofeyeva 2002). Expert assessment is possible in case of no rating.

Regulation and supervision standards have a significant effect on the forming of trust in financial market players and financial institutions. A significant breakthrough in standardization of regulation and supervision has been achieved since the Bank of Russia received the status of the financial markets' mega-regulator. However, the banking sector is currently extremely regulated, as opposed to microfinance institutions. Evaluating of the effect this factor has on the level of trust on the financial market is possible either on the basis of expert assessments or on the basis of quantitative data. For example, the Bank of Russia acts as a supervisory authority, and has data such as the number of revoked licenses and the number of insurance events with member banks of the deposit insurance system.

Level of trust in the state is the next factor affecting the level of trust on the financial market. A high level of trust in the government enables the forming of positive expectations, a stable socio-political situation in the country, and improvement in state-citizen interaction, and generally serves as a basis for the establishment of a trust-based environment in society and in the financial market. The published indexes of trust in the state (e.g., the Edelman rating) are proposed for use in assessment.

The state of the macroeconomy and the financial market determines the conditions under which financial institutions function. The instability of the financial market has a significant effect on investors (creditors) and borrowers' behaviors. Besides, there is a sustainable link between the financial market and the real economy. On the one hand, the price of assets on the stock market is influenced by consumption and investments, efficiency of production, and inflation rates. On the other hand, the events in the financial market have a strong effect on the real economy. The following indicators may be used to determine the state of financial market: the Moscow stock exchange index, the key interest rate of the Bank of Russia, the Mosprime Rate interest rate, national currency exchange rate, the rate of BRENT oil prices. The effect of other macroeconomic parameters may also be subject to evaluation. In order to assess the situation on the market we consider it possible to use the purchasing manager index (Table 20.2).

Financial literacy of the population and effective consumer rights protection in the financial field are important for providing financial security of the citizens and for setting their expectations from financial market transactions. Therefore, they significantly facilitate the formation and sustaining of trust in the financial market. Assessment of the population's financial literacy may be based on self-evaluation results (the percentage of satisfactory-perfect results) in accordance with research conducted by the NAFI analytical center (Milovidov 2019).

Unique factor groups, according to evaluation subjects, include a financial institution's reliability and the quality of the goods and services provided. The banking sector, as an example, is in possession of almost 90% of assets. Insurance companies, non-state retirements, and mutual funds possess less than 3% of controlled assets respectively.

Table 20.2 Macroeconomic factors with an effect on the level of trust among the financial market players along with the corresponding indicators

Factor	*Indicator*	*Source*
State of the stock market	Moscow stock exchange index, IMOEX	https://www.moex.com/ru/index/IMOEX
State of the monetary market	Key interest rate	https://cbr.ru/
	MosprimeRate	https://cbr.ru/
State of the currency market	Currency exchange rate, US dollars	https://cbr.ru/
Situation on the market	BRENT oil price rates	https://www.banki.ru/quotes/brent/
	Purchasing manager index (PMI)	https://nafi.ru/analytics/rossiya-na-9-meste-po-finansovoy-gramotnosti-sredi-stran-g20/

Source: Drafted by the authors

Reliability of financial institutions. According to sociological surveys, Russians' trust in financial institutions is directly linked to their reliability (Kozlova 2014). Russian economic research has various approaches to interpreting the terms "reliability" and its "financial sustainability" (NAFI 2017); for the purposes of this study, reliability presents itself as a qualitative characteristic of a financially sustainable financial institution with a positive reputation among its clientele.

It should be emphasized that institutions' sustainability should only be evaluated indirectly through financial sustainability ratings given to companies by rating agencies or directly through financial sustainability factors, which include:

- stable indicators of a company's financial activity;
- sufficient net worth as a basis for business activity and risk coverage;
- high-quality assets;
- quality risk management;
- fulfillment of the regulator's requirements in regard to legal compliance, including standards of capital adequacy, liquidity, borrowers' concentration, etc.

Table 20.3 includes typical financial sustainability indicators for institutions answering to the sustainability criteria listed above.

Quality of the financial institution's goods and services. The quality of banking goods and services, along with the costs thereof, is a key characteristic that determines demand arising on the market. It is qualitative characteristics that are of great significance for clients, due to restricted price competition between financial institutions. Quality is a complex, multifaceted phenomenon. Its characteristics are intrinsically linked between each other. The main elements of quality of services on the financial market include: accessibility, price policy compliance, clarity, security, and speed of service. However, taking into account assessment data, we propose analyzing such elements of quality as accessibility, price policy compliance, or company rating in mass media (based on one of the elements of credit capacity rating conducted by the REUTERS analytical agency, mobile apps rating, companies' internet apps rating [if available]).

Table 20.3 Institutions' reliability assessment as a trust factor

Institution	*Indicator—standard of the financial institution*	*Indicator—industry standards*
Banking institutions	Rating Capital adequacy, capital rates Return on equity (assets) Default levels State support/ parent company support	Sufficiency of capital, capital rates Return on equity (assets) Level of banking sector's assets concentration Default levels
Insurance companies	Rating State support/parent company support Insurance services market volumes Asset gain and insurance premiums rates Return on equity margins (assets) Capital adequacy (deviation of the actual solvency margin from the standard)	Insurance services market volumes Asset gain and insurance premiums rates Return on equity (assets) Capital adequacy (deviation of the actual solvency margin from the standard) Concentration levels
Non-state retirement funds	Rating Parent company support Assets and NPF retirement reserves rates	Asset and NPF retirement reserves rates Concentration levels
Microfinance organizations	Rating Asset rates Capital adequacy Return on equity	Asset rates Capital adequacy Return on equity

Source: Drafted by the authors

Conclusions/Recommendations

The development of a mutual trust system among financial market players requires a complex approach to solving new tasks, in light of the system's elements being interconnected and, at the same time, taking into account the special nature of the market players and the standard of the current trust-based environment in the country:

1. Factors of trust in financial market players are inherent to the trust-based environment at the macro- and micro levels of the financial market.
2. Micro-level factors make it possible to determine trust indicators between two parties in the same market segment and to calculate special trust indexes between them with all other factors in mind (e.g., index of trust of clients in a specific bank).
3. Factors and their respective trust indicators at the macro level of the financial market make it possible to determine the level of trust in a homogenous group of players (e.g., in all banks) or a special index of a players' group, and to calculate the effect that trust in all market players has on economic growth results based on an equation of regression.

References

Altvater, E., Krdtke, M., & Negt, O. (1999). *Turbo Kapitalismus: Geselschaft im Ubergangins 21. Jahrhundert.* Hamburg: VSA-Verlag.

Binswanger, M. (2004). Stock Returns and Real Activity in the F-7 Countries: Did the Relationship Change During the 1980s? *The Quarterly Review of Economics and Finance, 44*(2), 237–252.

Bozic, B. (2017). Consumer Trust Repair: A Critical Literature Review. *European Management Journal, 35*(4), 538–547.

Central Bank of Russia. (2019). *Основные направления единой государственной денежно-кредитной политики на 2019 год и период 2020 и 2021 годов* [Main Directions of the Unified State Monetary Policy for 2019 and the Period of 2020 and 2021]. Central Bank of Russia Official Site. Online at: https://www.cbr.ru/Content/Document/File/48125/on_2019

Edelman Trust Barometer. (2020). Edelman Trust Barometer Spring Update.pdf. Online at: https://www.edelman.com/sites/g/files/aatuss191/files/2020-05/2020

Fender, R., Stammers, R., & Urwin, R. (2018). *The Next Generation of Trust: A Global Survey on the State of Investor Trust. 2018 Report.* CFA Institute, Future of Finance. Online at: https://www.cfa_investor_trust_global_report.ashx (cfainstitute.org). Accessed 24 Nov 2020.

Feofanov, D. A. (2014). Асимметрия информации на финансовых рынках [Information Asymmetry in the Financial Markets]. *Стратегии бизнеса* [Business Strategies], *2*, 115–118.

Fetisov, G. G. (1999). *Устойчивость коммерческого банка и рейтинговые системы ее оценки* [Stability of a Commercial Bank and Its Rating Systems]. Moscow: Финансы и статистика [Finance and Statistics].

Kasutin, A. E. (2005). О понятиях надежности и устойчивости коммерческого банка [On Concepts of Reliability and Stability in Commercial Banking]. *Фундаментальные исследования* [Fundamental Studies], *4*, 32.

Kozlova, N. P. (2014). *Особенности формирования деловой репутации современной компании* [Features of Forming a Modern Company's Business Reputation]. Moscow: Дашков и К [Dashkov and Company].

Milovidov, V. D. (2019). *Факторы неопределенности мирового финансового рынка в условиях технологической революции* [Uncertainty Factors of the Global Financial Market in the Context of the Technological Revolution]. Moscow: MGIMO.

Mundell, R. (1963). Inflation and Real Interest. *Journal of Political Economy, 71*(3), 280–283.

Nafi Analytics Centre [Аналитический центр НАФИ]. (2017). *Доверие россиян к банкам. Социология. Статистика. Публикации* [Trust in Russian Banks: Sociology. Statistics. Publications]. Online at: https://nafi.ru/upload/thematic_review_dec.pdf

Nagapetyan, A. R. (2016). Асимметрия в динамике односторонних коэффициентов чувствительности активов к рыночным изменениям в контексте управления риском портфеля ценных бумаг [The Asymmetry in the Dynamics of Unilateral Coefficients of Assets' Sensitivity to Market Changes in the Context of Portfolio Risk Management]. *Общество: политика, экономика, право* [Society: Politics, Economics, Law], *5*, 97–102.

Panova, G. S., et al. (2020). *Банки и банковский бизнес в глобальной экономике* [Banks and Banking Business in Global Economics]. Moscow: MGIMO.

Russian Regional Network. (2020). *Портал исследования корпоративной прозрачности*. Online at: http://corptransparency.ru/rate. Accessed 14 Apr 2020.

Sapienza, P., & Zingales, L. (2009). *Financial Trust Index*. Chicago Booth/Kellogg School. Online at: http://www.financialtrustindex.org/resultswave1.htm. Accessed 8 May 2020.

Stieglitz, J. T. (1989). Using Tax Policy to Curb Speculative Short-Term Trading. *Journal of Financial Services Research, Columbia University, 3*, 101–115.

Timofeyeva, Z. A. (2002). Устойчивость коммерческого банка: содержание и специфика проявления на региональном уровне [Commercial Bank Stability: The Content and Stability of its Manifestation at a Regional Level]. *Экономические и социальные перемены в регионе* [Economic and Social Changes in the Regions], *18*, 43–50.

CHAPTER 21

Post-industrial Society: State Initiative and Social Conservatism

Julia Kovalchuk

In this book, we made an original attempt to analyze how to can change the competitiveness of countries, industries, and companies—using innovation, or, conversely, following traditional technologies and management methods. This topic we covered is certainly very broad and will require further research, especially since post-industrialization as a stage of social development is evolving, and this process will occur at an increasing pace, thanks to new digital technologies (innovations) and society's response to changes.

Each country is looking for ways to provide their own socio-economic development and achieve leadership, either on the global arena or at the regional level. The rate of economic growth can be increased in at least two ways: either a natural resource type of development or an innovative type of development.

History shows that most countries that have chosen the path of development based on the maximum use of raw materials have been caught by

J. Kovalchuk (✉)
Moscow State Institute of International Relations (MGIMO University), Moscow, Russia

Moscow Aviation Institute, Moscow, Russia

J. Kovalchuk (ed.), *Post-Industrial Society*,
https://doi.org/10.1007/978-3-030-59739-9_21

the "resource curse" and their global competitiveness reduces. If natural resources are extracted at low cost, it is profitable to develop their extraction, while other industries become unattractive from the investment perspective. Therefore, the resource development path is exhaustible, while an innovative trajectory requires adequate—and even advanced—institutional decisions and financial resources.

The global financial crisis of 2008 has significantly changed the priorities of economic growth in recent decades in almost all industrial powers around the world (Pianta et al. 2020). Most economists acknowledge that continued de-industrialization and lagging in the development of advanced technologies increases their dependence on other states (world leaders) and their economies, which upsets the balance of a market economy both globally and nationally (Belousov 2015; Bernard et al. 2017; Rodrik 2016; Felipea and Meht 2016; De Haas and Höflmayr 2019). Today, high-quality economic growth should be ensured by the transition to new technologies (resource-saving, digital) in the framework of the post-industrial development of society and its economy, the basis of which is the new industrialization (although, as we noted in the introduction, some authors tend to call this reindustrialization or neo-industrialization).

Of course, the design of future states and the development of economic systems are determined by many factors, which, taking into account the multidisciplinary character and the current stage of the cyclical economic development, can be grouped as follows:

1. technological trends: determined based on foresight research (Saritas and Nugroho 2011), and in turn determining the basis for a systematic analysis of the prospects for scientific and technological development, promising research topics, adjusting the composition of priority areas of scientific and technological development and new technologies, modernizing and creating new industries, and substantiating scientific and technical policies at both federal and sectoral levels;
2. competition that ensures market proportionality, dynamism, and efficiency and fair market exchange;
3. an institutional environment formed by renewing or creating new institutions, imitating and transferring them, and using other managed institutionalization methods;
4. resources (including key competencies) and their combinations defining competitive advantages in interaction and on the markets;

5. capital allocated for financing development, within the framework of financial decisions that lie in the plane of limited rationality, when investment decisions are aimed not at maximizing utility, but at satisfying it, as a search for alternatives that seem to satisfy the most important needs with limited perception and choice of information.

Each state is interested in its own prosperity, despite the differences between countries in terms of their stages and levels of industrialization, the values of their macroeconomic indicators, and their political regimes. Therefore, aspects of ensuring the interaction of the state and business in the development of the high-tech industry during the post-industrial period are significant for the development strategies. For this purpose, the practice of different countries (both developed and developing) needs to be taken into account; through this the benefits of state regulation, and the reaction of business and society to the proposed changes, can be assessed.

For example, industrial policy is important for ensuring the development of the country, increasing its economic independence, and optimizing the structure of export-import. We agree with the traditional understanding of industrial policy, provided by political scientist Wildavsky: "Industrial policy is economic policy; its purpose is prosperity" (Wildavsky 1986); in other words, industrial policy is not a bureaucratic intervention. However, the current understanding of industrial policy is filled with discussion, and even political debate (Chang and Andreoni 2020).

Indeed, industrial policy should be focused on developing the industry technological areas, diversifying the economy, and creating new sectors. This is extremely important in the post-industrial world, when countries stop de-industrialization and start new industrialization.

At the stage of forming the postindustrial process, according to the European approach, classical industrial policy is a combination of state measures to promote or prevent structural changes (Price 1981). American experts consider the industrial policy as a mechanism to facilitate the influx of resources into certain sectors, which the state considers important for future economic growth or effective for the economy as a whole (Krugman and Obstfeld 1991; Chang 1994). In developing countries, industrial policy there is more focused on deciding which products can be exported from a given country (Singh 1989), as well as in creating new industries that do not require significant investment when there is a budget deficit and the socio-economic situation is unstable. Consequently, industrial policy is a tool used by the state to promote the development of promising industries for ensuring national economic growth, which includes a set of economic regulators in innovation, tax, customs, monetary, and other sectors of the economy.

We sincerely recognize the valuable position of scientists and specialists who study the essence of industrial policy, which is important for manufacturing development in the modern post-industrial world. As Chang puts it, an industrial policy is “a policy aimed at particular industries (and firms as their components) to achieve the outcomes that are perceived by the state to be efficient for the economy as a whole” (Chang 2003). This notion of intentionality is important: as economist Mazzucato writes, it is up to the public sector to pick the direction of change (Mazzucato 2013). And far from being limited to developing countries, industrial policy and planning are highly relevant to efforts to transform developed economies into green ones, as noted by economists Altenburg and Rodrik (Altenburg and Rodrik 2017).

Turning to history, during the period of economic industrialization in developed countries (1950–1960), there was an industrial state support policy for emerging industries, which then led to the control of monopoly influence in the markets. During the de-industrialization period (the 1990s), the industrial policy included direct measures of influence (i.e. supporting the “champions” of global markets), while during the reindustrialization period (2000–2009), industrial policy was directed toward innovative development: selection and support of specific promising manufacturing technologies. This was typical of most countries, although some authors believe that industrial policy is a tool for developing countries only (Tucker 2019). This point of view is somewhat objective—the reason for this is East Asian industrial “miracle.”

At the same time, in practice this is not always seen. For example, despite large-scale government interventions to support Russian civil aviation as a traditional industry in a country with a rich history and legendary aircraft, the Brazilian government’s initiative included the aviation industry into a strategic national project. This is why Embraer has become the third leading aircraft manufacturer in the world, after Boeing and Airbus, in just a few decades. Also, Airbus was also originally a project of four European national corporations (Great Britain, France, Germany, and Spain), with the sole purpose of preserving the aircraft industry in these countries and implementing a technological breakthrough in the aircraft industry in competition with American and Russian passenger aircraft.

Nevertheless, getting back to the present, new industrialization is based on the priority of the manufacturing industry, with a focus on breakthrough technologies; different countries have relevant experience herein:

- The United States is focused on restoring localization: placing new industries near development and design centres or scientific and design divisions, which not only provides new workplaces but also improves national security; state support for new institutions (regional hubs) involved in developing and prototyping technologies has been strengthened; the Advanced Manufacturing Partnership, the National Additive Manufacturing Innovation Institute, and the National Network for Manufacturing Innovation have been created; state funding for R&D (digital production and design innovation, production of light and modern metals, a new generation of power electronics) is provided.
- The European Union has created the ARTEMIS technology platform to promote innovative projects, covering three important areas of industrial technology: embedded intelligence, Internet of Things, and digital platforms. It should be noted that during the period of economic recovery after the global financial crisis, a discussion document "The Future of Industrial Production 2.0 (Vision for Manufacturing 2.0)" was developed to determine investment priorities for the new comprehensive EU "Horizon 2020" program. Thus, large investments in R&D allowed made it possible to launch innovative projects in the European Union.
- Germany (the global leader in the production of industrial equipment) is separately implementing the "Industrie 4.0" program to maintain competitive advantages and create new markets in the face of the growing competitors of the United States, India, and China. Two global integration approaches were selected: the horizontal one (through networks, based on linking IT systems used at various stages of the manufacturing process and business planning, involving the exchange of materials, energy, and information both within one company and between several company networks) and the vertical one (through connected manufacturing systems, based on a combination of IT systems of various the hierarchy levels: process launch, control, management, production, implementation, corporate planning).

- China is focused on energy-efficient technologies and “new” energy, advanced means of production, and “new” materials. In general, China is changing its orientation from large-scale low-cost exports to stimulating high-tech manufacturing with a share of at least 50% of GDP. It should be noted that state-owned companies predominate in China, which is why its ongoing projects, such as high-speed railways, not only develop transport infrastructure but also solve many socio-economic problems ranging from industrial productivity to improving life quality.
- India, with an insufficiently developed industrial sector, which employs about 12% of the country’s population, is nevertheless aimed at innovations. For example, the Cyber-Physical Systems Innovation Centre was launched to conduct research in various fields, including humanoid robots, and research centers were created (by Bosch) to develop a working environment for IT professionals of the future. Internet of Things in India shows the best indicators in the world. One of the industry priorities for the development of the manufacturing sector is to increase the share of electrical equipment in the export structure.
- Asian industrial countries (Taiwan, Japan, South Korea, Hong Kong, and Singapore) have a long-term industrial and innovation-technological policy established; their development priorities are to enter into competition with both the traditional world leaders of the manufacturing sector—the United States and the EU—as well as with developing industrial giants—China and India. In Japan, industrial enterprises are more socialized, whereas in South Korea, they are aimed at making large industrial concerns cooperate with small and medium-sized businesses; in general, Asian leaders are interested in global value chains.

Thus, the analysis shows that industrial policy is in a state of adequate changes in accordance with the economic state of the country and its external environment. This reflects the important role the state plays in economic development and the use of innovations. The following key changes in approaches to industrial policy during the period of the active development of technologies of the Fourth Industrial Revolution can be distinguished:

- combination with the state's innovation policy, where industrial policy plays the role of a structural regulator, and innovation policy works in specific areas of technological development;
- possibilities of compliance between the state's industrial policy and the competitive strategy of industrial companies;
- finding a balance between the results of implementing industrial policy soon, while recognizing the risks in achieving long-term priorities.

In Russia, a law was adopted on a new industrial policy at the end of 2014 as a reaction to the changing geopolitical conditions and the sanctions. It was aimed at using the potential of reindustrialization and new industrialization of the economy. However, industrial policy instruments do not have a clear distinction, unlike innovation policy instruments. This implies a certain conservatism of state decisions, which is supported by society.

Technological platforms are widely known: they were developed in Europe and initiated by the real sector as a communication tool of industrial policy, which allows bringing together entrepreneurs and industrialists, government officials, and scientists on a single information platform to start a common trend of scientific and technological development, promote innovative development, and find approaches to the industrial development of appropriate technologies. Russia has also created similar technology platforms, but they have become an instrument of innovation policy and have contributed to fundamental scientific research. Technology platforms have created the potential to increase the competitiveness, productivity, and efficiency of industrial manufacturing.

It should be noted that opinions differ on what industrial policy should be in modern conditions, but it is undeniable that industrial policy should be harmonized, taking into account the trends of new industrialization and the need for developing a real economy—this is where its conservatism and its significance for society are manifested.

In Russia, there have been proposals to develop a comprehensive Program of State Incentives for Industrial Development within the framework of industrial policy, which, on the one hand, should facilitate the transition to a more balanced manufacturing structure, and, on the other hand, encourage enterprises to produce innovative and competitive products. At the same time, the Incentive Program should approve a list of criteria that must be met by enterprises who can receive state funding (Tsvetkov et al. 2016).

In general, innovative sectors, while still occupying a relatively low share in GDP, can provide a significant intersectoral effect for the entire economy as a whole, provided that technology is improved in the industries using innovative products. However, as the experience of several countries shows, attention to the development of *only* new high-tech economic sectors and the desire to make them a key factor in new industrialization did not lead to the desired result.

Nevertheless, we note that it has been theoretically proved and practically confirmed that the mechanisms created by the state allow for good strategic decisions, even though these decisions are not always equally effective in different sectors. In addition to government initiatives and promoting innovative development, there is also a need for consensus from both large corporations and small businesses; then, the goals of post-industrial development will have maximum value for society.

Finally, measuring economic development through GDP growth rate in the post-industrial economy now requires adjustment. History has shown that once, during the recovery period after World War II and large-scale national industrialization, the USSR was ahead of the United States in terms of GDP growth, while the situation with about productivity was quite opposite. This is a dilemma that is nipping at the heels of progress today, when digital technologies—especially robotics and artificial intelligence—are changing the determinants of the development of industrial manufacturing and the service sector. At the same time, developing countries show higher GDP growth rates than developed countries. Current GDP growth does not take leading non-economic indicators into account: quality of life (employment, housing, education, medicine affordability, life expectancy, social differentiation, etc.) or the environment (expenditure of non-reproducible and biosphere resources per unit of output, waste emission, recycling, etc.); nor does it acknowledge the global value creation chains. In general, resource-saving reduces GDP; it grows at the expense of digital services, which, despite their innovative character, are still insufficiently contributing to the increase of social wealth and human capital. We must realize this and solve this problem in the face of universal digitalization across the globe in our post-industrial world.

References

Altenburg, T., & Rodrik, D. (2017). Green Industrial Policy: Accelerating Structural Change towards Wealthy Green Economies. In T. Altenburg & C. Assmann (Eds.), *Green Industrial Policy. Concepts, Policies, Country Experiences.* Geneva: UN Environment/German Development Institute/ Deutsches Institut für Entwicklungspolitik (DIE).

Belousov, D. R. (2015). Long-Term Development: From a System of Challenges Towards Policy Determinants. *Journal of the New Economic Association, 2*, 201–204. (In Russian).

Bernard, A. B., Smeets, V., & Warzynski, F. (2017). Rethinking Deindustrialization. *Economic Policy, 32*, 89.

Chang, H. J. (1994). *The Political Economy of Industrial Policy.* New York: St. Martin's Press.

Chang, H. J. (2003). *Globalization, Economic Development, and the Role of the State.* London: Zed Books.

Chang, H. J., & Andreoni, A. (2020). Industrial Policy in the 21st Century. *Development and Change, 51*, 324–351.

De Haas, R., & Höflmayr, M. (2019). Deindustrialization, Job Polarization and Ageing in Emerging Europe (Chapter 11). In E. Nowotny, D. Ritzberger-Grönvald, & H. Schuberth (Eds.), *How to Finance Cohesion in Europe?* (pp. 123–134). Cheltenham: Edward Elgar Publishing. https://doi.org/10.4337/9781789902600.00020.

Felipea, J., & Meht, A. (2016). Deindustrialization? A Global Perspective. *Economics Letters, 149*, 148–151.

Krugman, P., & Obstfeld, M. (1991). *International Economics: Theory and Policy.* New York: HarperCollins Publishers.

Mazzucato, M. (2013). *The Entrepreneurial State: Debunking Public vs. Private Sector Myths.* London: Anthem Press.

Pianta, M., Lucchese, M., & Nascia, L. (2020). The Policy Space for a Novel Industrial Policy in Europe. *Industrial and Corporate Change, 29*(3), 779–795.

Price, C. V. (1981). *Industrial Policies in the European Community.* Basingstoke: Macmillan Trade Policy Research Center.

Rodrik, D. (2016). Premature Deindustrialization. *Journal of Economic Growth, 21*, 1–33.

Saritas, O., & Nugroho, Y. (2011). Seeing the Invisible and Making Sense of It. *Scanning, Networks and Scenario Analysis, Foresight-Russia, 5*(3), 58–69. (in Russian).

Singh, A. (1989). Third World Competition and De-Industrialization in Advanced Countries. *Cambridge Journal of Economics, 13*(1), 103–120.

Tsvetkov, V. A., Stepnov, I. M., & Kovalchuk, Y. A. (2016). Implementation of the New Industrialization Strategy in the Economy. *Finance: Theory and Practice, 20*(6), 19–30. (In Russian).

Tucker, T. N. (2019). *Industrial Policy and Planning: What It Is and How to Do It Better*. Roosevelt Institute. https://rooseveltinstitute.org/wp-content/uploads/2019/07/RI_Industrial-Policy-and-Planning-201707.pdf

Wildavsky, A. (1986). Industrial Policies in American Political Cultures. In C. Barfield & W. A. Schambra (Eds.), *The Politics of Industrial Policy* (pp. 15–32). Washington, DC: American Enterprise Institute Press.

Index

J. Kovalchuk (ed.), *Post-Industrial Society*,
https://doi.org/10.1007/978-3-030-59739-9

The manufacturer's authorised representative in the EU is Springer
Nature Customer Service Centre GmbH, Europaplatz 3, 69115 Heidelberg,
Germany. If you have any concerns regarding our products, please
contact ProductSafety@springernature.com

Printed and bound by CPI Group (UK) Ltd, Croydon, CR0 4YY
30/09/2026
02225457-0014